COLUMBIA UNIVERSITY ORIENTAL STUDIES
Vol. XXV

ANTHROPOS AND SON OF MAN

ANTHROPOS AND SON OF MAN

*A Study in the Religious Syncretism
of the Hellenistic Orient*

BY

CARL H. KRAELING

AMS PRESS, INC.
NEW YORK, N.Y. 10003
1966

Copyright 1927
Columbia University Press

Reprinted with the
permission of the original publisher

AMS PRESS, INC.
NEW YORK, N.Y. 10003
1966

Manufactured in the United States of America

**DEDICATED TO
MY FATHER AND MY MOTHER**

NOTE

Dr. Carl H. Kraeling has undertaken to discuss a subject that must always be of much interest to students of comparative religion. It is one that has taken him far afield, into Hellenistic and Gnostic systems, into Manichean and Mandean religious thought, into Jewish religious literature, and finally, to the New Testament. His book has been prepared with great thoroughness, and with a full knowledge of the difficulty of the subject that he was handling. I cordially recommend it to the many students who must be interested in this field of investigation.

RICHARD GOTTHEIL.

PREFACE

THE inquiry embodied in the following pages is the outgrowth of a paper presented by the author in a Seminar on the "New Testament Conception of the Person of Christ," conducted by Professor E. F. Scott at Union Theological Seminary in 1922-23. It represents the examination of a conclusion tentatively drawn by Professor R. Reitzenstein of Göttingen from his brilliant investigations into the development of religious ideas in the Hellenistic Orient, namely the conclusion that the Jewish-Christian Son of Man (literally "the man") is but one manifestation of an ubiquitous Oriental figure known in certain syncretistic circles as "the Anthropos."

Hypotheses such as this cannot be disposed of by *a priori* considerations. They require sympathetic appreciation and study of the materials with which they deal. As a consequence our inquiry has become a study in Oriental Syncretism, its roots and vagaries, rather than a discourse on Biblical Theology. In itself this constitutes no fault, for whatever conclusions one may reach regarding the merits of a specific hypothesis, it remains true that Oriental Syncretism is a territory the resources and strategic importance of which for the study of the development of religious thought deserve investigation.

The inquiry furnishes for the first time, we believe, a fairly complete account of the part played by the Anthropos in late Oriental thought. The fuller examination of the sources has made it possible to discover for the first time stratification in the tradition and thus to gain valuable criteria for the origin and antiquity of the figure and for the determination of its different associations, pagan, Jewish and Christian.

PREFACE

In entering upon a field of such diverse contacts and ramifications as the syncretistic, the writer has constantly felt the limitations of his own abilities. The counsel and assistance of his esteemed teachers and friends have therefore been of particular value. Sincere thanks are due to Prof. R. J. Gottheil, who supervised the labors involved, Prof. A. V. W. Jackson, whose intimate acquaintance with Manicheism and Iranian religion were constantly drawn upon, Prof. E. F. Scott, whose cautious scholarship assisted in preserving the perspective in dealing with New and Old Testament matters, Prof. J. A. Montgomery, whose hospitable home was the scene of many hours spent in the reading and interpretation of Mandaic texts, Prof. R. Reitzenstein, whose interest and criticism were very helpful, Profs. H. Offermann and M. Dibelius, to whom the author owes his interest in matters Hellenistic, and to my brother, Prof. E. G. H. Kraeling, whose sympathy and assistance in matters large and small were a constant source of inspiration.

This book is printed with funds coming in part from the legacy of Magdalena Schenk.

CARL H. KRAELING.

Krauth Memorial Library.
Lutheran Theological Seminary at Philadelphia.
May 31, 1927.

CONTENTS

CHAPTER I

	PAGE
THE PROBLEM OF THE ANTHROPOS	1–16

CHAPTER II

THE MANICHEAN PRIMAL MAN	17–37
1. The Manichean System	17
2. The Primal Man in Cosmogony	18
3. The Primal Man, the Soul and the Creation of Adam	21
4. The Primal Man and the Messengers	24
5. The Primal Man, Adam, Seth and Noah	28
6. The Primal Man, Buddha and Zarathushtra	28
7. The Primal Man and Jesus	31
8. The Primal Man and Mani	34
9. The Primal Man in Eschatology	36

CHAPTER III

THE ANTHROPOS IN HELLENISTIC AND WESTERN GNOSTIC SYSTEMS	38–54
1. The Provenience of the Anthropos in the Littoral Orient	38
2. The Anthropos in the Syncretism of Egypt	41
3. The Anthropos in Syrian Syncretism	47

CHAPTER IV

THE MANDEAN TRADITION CONCERNING THE ANTHROPOS	55–73
1. The Mandeans	55
2. Manda d'Haye and the Anthropos	56
3. Adam Rabba	59
4. Adakas	63
5. The Messengers and the Anthropos	64
6. Echoes of the Poimandres in Mandean Texts	70

CONTENTS

CHAPTER V

	PAGE
THE ORIGIN AND ANTIQUITY OF THE ANTHROPOS	74–127
1. Rival Hypotheses Concerning the Origin of the Anthropos	74
2. The Iranian Gayomart and the Anthropos	85
3. The Origin and Development of the Anthropos in the Role of Primordial Champion and Cosmogonal Agent	94
4. The Anthropos as the Soul and as the Creator of Man	109
5. The Anthropos in the Role of Savior	123
6. The Antiquity of the Anthropos Speculation	126

CHAPTER VI

THE ANTHROPOS IN JEWISH THOUGHT	128–165
1. Presuppositions	128
2. The Jewish Elements in the Figure of the Bar Nasha	130
3. The Non-Jewish Elements of the Bar Nasha and the Anthropos	141
4. The Anthropos, the Celestial Adam and the Adamites	151

CHAPTER VII

THE ANTHROPOS AND THE NEW TESTAMENT SON OF MAN	166–186
1. The Fourth Gospel and the Anthropos Speculation	167
2. Paul and the Anthropos	174
3. The Synoptic Son of Man and the Anthropos	180
SUMMARY AND CONCLUSION	187–190
ABBREVIATIONS	191

ANTHROPOS AND SON OF MAN

CHAPTER I

THE PROBLEM OF THE ANTHROPOS

In the history of the world's religious life, there is no period simultaneously quite as significant, fascinating and difficult as the Hellenistic. Significant it was, if for no other reason than that at this juncture the idea of a universal religion was firmly imbedded in the hopes and aspirations of the Western world. To us that may not seem a momentous achievement, for we lack the perspective. But if we look into the distant past when religion was but a family, a clan, a national and racial matter, and look ahead to a time when it may be truly an expression of the contact of humanity with the "one God and Father of us all," the appearance of this idea upon the world's religious horizon, is a moment of triumph.

New concepts such as that of a universal religion are not born in the human mind at will. They are the product of a "world pining in pain" and seeking "but to know His name." Wherever we look in the Hellenistic world we see the traces of its travail written large before us. Everything is turmoil and uproar. The ancient values are being subverted, national institutions and limitations are breaking down. There is a search for new forms of expression, and for that intangible something that looms darkly ahead. The religious world has become a vast melting-pot within which the currents of influence run hither and yon. The old order struggles for its preservation; human temperament employs its new freedom for higher and lower ends; religious anarchy overthrows all semblance of order and unity; the East pours the floods of myth and mysticism into the disintegrating forms of Western practise; old Gods and new, Jewish and Christian, Greek and Barbarian, all are drawn together under the common impulse of attraction, and are thrust apart by the common impulse of repulsion. These are among the signs of the times which produced religion's fairest flower.

Fascinating it is to gaze into a milieu charged with so many elemental powers, but difficult indeed to delve into its midst in search of knowledge, without being confused by the sight of how

> . . . the flaring atom-streams
> And torrents of her myriad universe,
> Ruining along the illimitable inane,
> Fly on to clash together again, and make
> Another and another frame of things
> Forever.

Yet the student of religion and particularly of Christianity cannot afford to shun the maze and the search for those guiding forces that produced in the midst of diversity a new and higher unity, the religion of salvation and of the one God.

It is not so long ago that scholars considered Christianity itself, as it spread from the narrow confines of Palestine to the "limits of the setting sun," the one potent and directive force in the midst of an impotent and bewildered world, the one ray of light in utter darkness. To-day that view is no longer tenable. True, no one will deny to Christianity an important place in the course of development, for Christianity was actually the form in which the new religious ideas were transmitted to posterity. Yet it is also true that from the moment when it spread beyond the limits of Judea and Galilea, it allied to itself forces already operative and at its disposal. To pass an intelligent verdict upon the course of affairs in the Hellenistic world we must need know those forces as well as the Christian. For a time scholars thought they had found them in the "Mystery Religions," the Hellenistic transformations of the fertility cults of the Near East. They too were teaching salvation in word and sacrament, and had a contribution to make to the progress of thought. As the ultimate origin of any far-reaching development they cannot serve, for they are themselves the product of forces that lie outside the sphere of the ancient fertility cults from which they have sprung.

To-day scholars, following the idea that the main channel of influence runs from East to West, are endeavoring to determine whether Syria, Mesopotamia and Iran were the source from which sprang the vivifying and transforming powers of Hellenistic religious life. Perhaps it is difficult to apprehend just how the test is to be made. Our knowledge of the religious history of these districts is but fragmentary. There is a great gap in the tradition that extends from the Persian conquest to the very end of the first Christian century and thus embraces that crucial period that lies behind the rise of the Mystery Religions and Christianity. The only Eastern religion the course of which we can follow during these centuries with some degree of continuity is Judaism, and Judaism, while it shows the effect of changes in regional sentiment, was on the whole too individualistic, too deeply rooted in the trend of its own development to make it a good source for the knowledge of that which stirred the soul of the greater Orient. The first development that we can trace in the Near East after the long eclipse is that form of religious anarchy known as Gnosticism, and defined by no less an authority than Harnack as the "acute Hellenization of Christianity."

What then may be the evidence upon the basis of which the contribution of the Near East to the religious life of the West is to be judged? Direct evidence there is none. Of indirect evidence, difficult to handle, there is a great deal. It lies imbedded in the "forgotten faiths" of which mention has just been made.

When Harnack produced his famous definition of Gnosticism, all that was known of the movement was contained in the polemical writings of the Christian heresiologists. To-day we have at our disposal in addition three great groups of first-hand sources, the corpus of Coptic Gnostic works, the large body of Mandean writings, and the great mass of Turfan texts on Manicheism.

The new sources have revealed that whatever be the origin of the Gnostic movement, the mass of phantasmagoria, ideas and practises in which it expresses itself embodies countless elements harking back to the religions of the ancient Orient. The analysis of the Gnostic sources and of Gnosticism as a whole will, therefore, eventually place scholars in a position to bridge the gap in our knowledge of the religious development in the East, and by the use of those ancient elements whose survival of the ravages of time is documented in Gnosticism, to reconstruct in part that Proto-Gnostic or Neo-Oriental sphere of thought within which may lie the key to the enigma of Hellenistic religious movements.

Gnosticism is not an easy task-mistress. Her world is not that of great minds and paramount personalities, but rather that of the many little folk. They were all men with a vision, these Gnostics. They made room in their minds for the whole world, so far as they knew it. Yet the product of their efforts was invariably a conglomeration rather than a creation. This characteristic of their work is responsible, of course, for the preservation of so many traditional religious elements. It is responsible, however, also for the difficulties inherent in the study of Gnosticism. Because they were conglomerations, the Gnostic systems disintegrated over night, to be replaced on the morrow by newer and more daring constructions. To look into the Gnostic world is thus to gaze into a kaleidoscope, and to behold a limited mass of material blending at each turn into new shapes and groups, with ever changing color and significance. Gnosticism is that part of the Hellenistic melting-pot most violently boiling.

To determine, in all the riot of Gnostic symbols, practises and ideas, those that are ancient and revert to a Proto-Gnostic period, is then by no means a simple matter. The associations of a figure or a practise, the form and temper of an idea vary continually. *Zoe*, "Life," for instance, is at times merely a concept expressing quality, or again the name of a divine emanation, or the name of Adam's spouse, or the designation of the supreme God, or the basic principle of divine existence. Which is ultimate, and where is the origin of the religious use of the term? Only a careful analysis of figure after figure, concept after concept, only the segregation of primary, secondary and tertiary associations on the basis of sound principles, and only a continual correction of results obtained at one point by the results of other inquiries will eventually give the desired information.

The following chapters represent an inquiry into the nature, origin and development of a Gnostic figure most conveniently referred to by the name it bore in Western Gnostic systems, namely "the Anthropos." We have chosen this figure as the subject of investigation for three reasons:

1. Because it is more widely known in Gnostic circles than many others and because its analysis, while proportionately more difficult, may therefore possibly lead to conclusions of greater import and validity in regard to the genesis and early character of Gnosticism.

2. Because the Anthropos has been the subject of extensive controversy within recent years in connection with Reitzenstein's work on syncretism.

3. Because numerous scholars have thought to see in the Anthropos the solution of the famous and long-standing "Son of Man" controversy.

To anyone interested in the development of later Jewish and early Christian thought, the last of these reasons will be of sufficient importance to merit further elucidation.

Twenty years ago Schweitzer, in surveying the course of Gospel criticism, declared that the Son of Man problem had been solved. For this contention he found support in three things, first, in the results achieved by the scholars of the nineteenth century in the historical and exegetical inquiry into the significance and use of the name, second, in the light thrown upon the name itself by the philological phase of the inquiry, third, in the eschatological interpretation of Jesus and the early Christian movement, an interpretation of which Schweitzer was a chief exponent.[1]

[1] The outstanding works on the history of the inquiry into the significance of the name Son of Man are the following, W. Scholten, *Specimen hermeneutico-theologicum de appellatione* ὁ υἱὸς τοῦ ἀνθρώπου *qua Jesus se Messiam professus est* (1809), pp. 142–208; L. T. Schulze, *Menschensohn u. Logos* (1868); A. Meyer, *Jesus Muttersprache* (1896); H. Lietzmann, *Der Menschensohn* (1896); P. W. Schmiedel, *Der Name Menschensohn*, Prot. Monatshefte (1898), pp. 252–267; W. Baldensperger, *Die neueste Forschung über den*

To the men of the nineteenth century New Testament scholarship in general and Schweitzer in particular owed most in this matter. Virtually, they were the discoverers of the Son of Man problem. The name about which so much was written by them, presented no difficulty at all to the scholars of the ancient and mediaeval Church. Almost without exception the Fathers agreed that its use by or of an individual designated him as a human being in a physical sense.[2] As employed by Jesus it was to be correlated with the name Son of God, as in the well-known hymn:

> Fairest Lord Jesus
> Lord of all creation,
> Son of God
> And Son of Man.

With the eve of the Reformation the artificiality of this interpretation began to dawn upon Christian writers. The contacts developing at this time between Jewish and Christian scholars were no doubt ultimately responsible for the suggestions that the designation was of Messianic significance, but might under certain circumstances be merely a circumlocution of a personal pronoun.[3] The suggestions advanced bore little fruit. The sense of the historical had not yet developed sufficiently. Three centuries later the Idealistic philosophers could still read the meaning "ideal man" into the words.[4]

Begriff Menschensohn, Theol. Rundschau (1900), pp. 201–10, 243–55; N. Schmidt, art. *Son of Man*, Encyclopedia Biblica (1903); P. Feine, *Theologie des Neuen Testaments* (1910), pp. 53–6; H. J. Holtzmann, *Neutestamenliche Theologie*, 2nd ed. (1911), vol. II, pp. 313–335; A. Schweitzer, *Geschichte der Leben Jesu Forschung*, 2nd ed., (1913), pp. 266–72.

[2] So already Ignatius, *Epistle to the Ephesians*, 20, 2, and thereafter, Barnabas, *Epistle*, 12, 9–10; Justin Martyr, *Dialogus*, 76, 100; Irenaeus, *adversus Haereses*, III, 3, 5, 7; Tertullian, *adversus Praxeas*, 33; Origen, *de Principiis*, II, 6, 3; Athanasius, *Epistula iv. ad Serapionem*, 20; Gregory Nazianzen, *Oratio*, xxxvi; Chrysostom, *Homilia in Iohannem*, 39, 3; Augustine, *contra Faustum*, II, 4; Jerome, *Commen. in Psalmos*, ad Ps. 8. The only one to depart from the orthodox conception was Irenaeus, cf. *adv. Haereses*, V, 21, 1.

[3] Cf. the list of authors in Scholten, *Specimen*, pp. 167–74, and N. Schmidt, art. *Son of Man*, § 15.

[4] So Herder, *Christliche Schriften*, II, 5, 6 (ed. Wiedemann, vol. 19), and Schleiermacher, *Der christliche Glaube* (first ed., 1821), 5th ed., II, p. 90 f.

As the nineteenth century wore on, matters changed with great rapidity. While the older school still considered it a crime against the originality of Jesus to suppose that he had adopted rather than coined the name, the majority pressed on in search of sources. A number of such sources were adduced, singly or in groups, to satisfy the demands of the three distinct connotations which the name bears in the New Testament, as the designation of one who is to come with the clouds of heaven, who is to suffer and die, and who lives as a man among men. It was particularly "the manlike one" of Daniel 7, 13 and of the apocalypse of Enoch, Ezekiel's use of *ben 'adam*, and the suffering servant of Isaiah 53 which were referred to. Soon it was no longer sufficient merely to point to a possible source. It became imperative to know whether the source was capable of bearing the testimony elicited from it. Scholars therefore inquired whether the "manlike one" of Daniel was a symbol of the nation or a concrete personality. They asked themselves whether the Apocalypse of Enoch was a pre-Christian product and Jewish in entirety, or whether it was Jewish with Christian interpolations or entirely Christian. They speculated whether *ben 'adam* had taken on the connotation "prophet" by being used of Ezekiel. Wide divergence of opinion upon these points did not materially increase the number of interpretations of the name. The majority considered it an intelligible or enigmatic messianic designation, others regarded it as a name connoting frail humanity, still others as a name indicative of prophetic character. But no two similar conclusions were reached upon an identical use of sources, and no one source furnished a satisfactory solution for the whole problem. Confidence was thereby shaken in all conclusions, and systematic scepticism, making itself felt in other spheres as well, added a further difficulty. It asked the question to what extent it is possible and psychologically intelligible that Jesus was actually conscious of his messianic calling. It was a question that had to be answered before further argument upon the Son of Man problem was possible.

After a temporary lull in the discussion of the name, opinion began to consolidate itself once more. That was in the nineties of the past century. Of course there were the usual extremes, a

Dutch school that denied the historicity of Jesus' use of Son of Man, and a group in England and France that endeavored to synthesize the manifold suggestions offered in explanation of its use, and make it a vehicle for the expression of many ideas. The opinion of the majority that stood between these two extremes was consolidated by two factors, first the conclusion that Jesus' messianic consciousness, though admittedly a development, had reached its climax and become an actual fact prior to or in connection with the episode at Caesarea Philippi, second, the conclusion that the Book of Enoch was essentially a Jewish product and not contaminated by Christian interpolations.

Studying the evidence in the light of these conclusions, scholarship achieved a number of definite results. It decided in the first place that the factor of greatest importance in the use and interpretation of the name was the connection with Daniel. The discrepancy between the Son of Man as a messianic personality with a proper name, and the "manlike one" of Daniel, a nameless symbol of the chosen people, was no longer troublesome. The Book of Enoch could now be used to prove that a transition in the direction of the New Testament conception had been in progress before Jesus' day. It determined also that since the designation in its messianic force is not found in the New Testament prior to the account of the Caesarea episode, therefore its use in this sense is unobjectionable and probably historical. Jesus, by the appropriation of the name Son of Man had, then, referred to himself as the Messiah of the apocalypses.

Significant as these conclusions were, they did not solve the problem entirely. Two difficulties remained, namely what to do with the passages where the designation lacked the messianic connotation, and, how to reconcile the reticence of Jesus and his presence among men with the brusque claim to transcendent messiahship registered by his use of the name Son of Man.

The philological phase of the controversy, covering the period between 1896 and 1901, permanently reopened an old way out of the first difficulty. It was due to the realization that Jesus and his disciples spoke an Aramaic dialect of Palestine, that the inquiry for a time entered different channels. Working with the new realization, Lietzmann set forth the fact that the New Testament form of the name Son of Man, namely ὁ υἱὸς τοῦ ἀνθρώπου, was a literal and inexact rendering of Aramaic *bar nasha*. This expression, he endeavored to show, signified merely "one" or "someone" and was too general to have been used as a proper name. Jesus had never identified himself with the "manlike one" of the apocalypses. Hellenistic Christians after Paul, half-ignorant of Semitic idiom, had read it into the record.[5]

When Wellhausen for a time accepted the conclusions of Lietzmann, the Son of Man problem seemed to have vanished into thin air together with the recently reaffirmed historicity of Jesus' use of the name. It was not long, however, before a closer examination of the Talmudic sources conveying a knowledge of the Palestinian dialects, showed that Lietzmann's conclusions had been hasty. After Dalman's unsuccessful attempt to uphold the individuality of the element *bar* in *bar nasha*, Fiebig finally clinched the argument by showing that the expression could and did signify either "a man" (i.e., "someone") or "the man."[6] In the latter sense at least, the words could serve as a name (even as in the name "the Anthropos" applied to our Gnostic figure) provided that there existed, when the name was coined, a set of associations which would make it intelligible. The Jewish apocalypses of course furnished these associations, and thus the problem was reopened.

The whole dispute had two visible results. It permanently established the original form and force of the name. In addition, however, it furnished scholars with a positive basis for erasing the name from those passages in which it lacked the fundamental messianic connotation. For while the fact that it pervaded all strata of New Testament tradition made it impossible to discount the use of the name entirely, its presence in individual passages could be the result of mistranslation.

The marks of the struggle in philological matters were rapidly obliterated by the rising tide of the movement in which Schweitzer played a prominent part, that of the Eschatological School.

[5] *Der Menschensohn* (1896).
[6] *Der Menschensohn* (1901).

Aiming to set aside the cold artificiality characterizing the Jesus of the rationalistic and psychological interpreters, and to resurrect the man of flesh and blood, the emotional child of the colorful Orient, it had ended in making him an enthusiast and dreamer whose outlook was determined entirely by the thought of the stupendous catastrophe impending upon the world. Only a carpenter's son, yet conscious of a mission to declare the coming of the Kingdom, he was torn between the hope and despair of its arrival and his success as its herald. In the face of public rejection and disbelief, he dared to grasp the hand of the Almighty and willingly sacrificed his life, believing that God in his inscrutable wisdom might have chosen to make him hereafter "the man" who was to usher in the consummation. By speaking of himself in those last days, as the Son of Man, he gave expression to what he dared hope to be, not that which he was, and to "refer in the only way possible to his messianic office as destined to be realized at his 'coming.'"[7] Thus interpreted the name was no longer in conflict with his humanity.

To hold this interpretation, and to reject the non-apocalyptic use of the name as secondary by the hypothesis of mistranslation, was to surmount the difficulties which the scholars of the previous century had faced but not conquered. Thus Schweitzer could claim that the Son of Man problem had been solved.[8]

If the discussions of the last twenty years have shown any one thing it is this that even the "eschatological" interpretation is not the last step in the long inquiry into the name Son of Man. There has been the usual reaction against the overaccentuation of a newly discovered principle. The words of Jesus have in this case furnished the strongest arguments against the views of the "consequential eschatologists." They are not merely sayings of one who expected the immediate and catastrophic end of the world. They are based upon a keen appreciation of ultimate and eternal verities, and look toward the positive transformation of society through the renovation of human character. Judging by his words Jesus was more than a dreamer and apocalypticist.

[7] Schweitzer, op. cit., p. 273.
[8] Ibid., p. 272.

Hence his adoption of the name Son of Man, particularly in the light of his reticence in employing other messianic designations, must have some further and broader foundation than the mere hope that he would some day play the role of apocalyptic Messiah. Its use must have roots that lie imbedded in the positive principles guiding his life and thought. In view of this fact, it is unwise to reject those New Testament passages in which the name lacks messianic connotation. They may yet have a service to render. Thus the question has once more been thrown open; indeed a new element has been added to the inquiry, namely, what is the ultimate origin of the Son of Man figure? Where did Daniel get it in the first place? Is it a creation or an importation as so much of the apocalyptic imagery? The question is not unimportant because its answer may shed light upon the particular nature of the ideas associated with the figure.

Recent discussion of the problem begins virtually where the scholars of the last nineties stopped. It begins with the fact that "Jesus is and is called Son of Man wherever forgiving and healing, teaching and suffering he heralds, spreads and witnesses to the Kingdom and especially where, coming with the clouds of heaven, he establishes it among men."[9] It endeavors to determine from this basis that interpretation of the name and its usage which will bring it somehow into relation with the controlling factors of Jesus' life and with his ethical and exemplary teaching regarding the Kingdom.

While the objective has never been more evident, and represents a goal correctly perceived, the actual progress toward it has proven slight. The majority seem to feel that in the non-apocalyptic usage of the name lies the key to the solution of the riddle. Not that they would make this the central factor in the significance and the choice of the nomenclature, but that they would use it as a bridge by which Jesus was led and could lead others to the higher messianic use of the name. What then may be the sense in which Jesus used "Son of Man" in the earlier period of his life? One of three suggestions is usually offered. He employed it to denote his ideal manhood, his frail manhood, or his prophetic

[9] H. J. Holtzmann, *Neutest. Theol.*, 2nd ed. (1911), II, p. 327.

calling.[10] These suggestions have a familiar ring. They were advanced early in the past century by Schleiermacher,[11] de Wette[12] and Weizsacker respectively,[13] and played no part in the consensus of opinion attained by scholars toward the end of that century. Their reënunciation shows that no actual progress has been made along the desired lines.

This peculiar state of affairs is evidence not of a lack of mental acumen on the part of recent investigators, but rather of the fact that the range of Biblical and Apocryphal sources for determining the desired force of the name is limited. Psalm 8, Isaiah 53 and Ezekiel's *ben 'adam* apparently exhaust the possibilities and have been reinvoked in spite of their insufficiency. Insufficient they are because no one of them will cover the range of associations

[10] IDEAL MANHOOD: S. R. Driver, art. *Son of Man*, Hastings Dictionary of the Bible, vol. IV (1902), § 21; G. Milligan, *The Messianic Consciousness of Jesus*, The Expositor, VI, 5 (1902), pp. 74–80; Grill, *Untersuchungen über die Entstehung des vierten Evangelium*, I (1902), p. 46–76; Zahn, Kommentar, *Evangelium des Matthäus* (1903), pp. 347–57; Shailer Matthews, *Messianic Hope in the New Testament* (1905), p. 102 ff.; C. H. Macfarland, *Jesus and the Prophets* (1905); J. A. Robinson, *The Study of the Gospels* (1906), p. 60 ff.; Sanday, *The Life of Christ in Recent Research* (1908), pp. 123–30; E. A. Abbott, Diatessarica, Pt. 8 (1910), *The Son of Man*; T. Stephenson, *The Title Son of Man*, Expository Times, May, 1918, pp. 377–8; Dougall and Emmet, *The Lord of Thought* (1922), chap. 23.

FRAIL MANHOOD: Milligan, op. cit.; M. Goguel, *L'Apôtre Paul et Jesus Christ* (1904), p. 222; G. G. Findlay, *The Theology of St. John*, Expository Times, vol. 16 (1904–5), pp. 76–8; Macfarland, op. cit.; Robinson, op. cit.; G. Peloux, *Le Fils de l'Homme* (1906); Sanday, op. cit.; Bard, *Sohn des Menschen* (1908); James Denney, *Jesus and the Gospel* (1909), pp. 255–65; D. Völter, Theol. Rundschau, 1909, p. 154 ff.; the same, *Jesus der Menschensohn* (1914); E. A. Abbott, op. cit.; E. C. Dewick, *Primitive Christian Eschatology* (1912); James Moffat, *The Theology of the Gospels* (1912), pp. 150–63; James Stalker, art. *Son of Man*, International Bible Encyclopedia (1915); A. Schlatter, *Geschichte des Christus* (1921), pp. 165–9; A. C. Headlam, *Life and Teaching of Jesus the Christ* (1923), pp. 305–7.

PROPHET: D. Völter, *Die Menschensohnfrage neu untersucht* (1916); Bornhäuser, *Das Wirken des Christus*, etc. (1921), pp. 30–1.

[11] Cf. above, n. 4.

[12] Kurzgefasstes exegetisches Handbuch, *Matthäus* (1st ed., 1836), 2nd ed., pp. 93–4.

[13] *Untersuchungen über die evangelische Geschichte* (1864), pp. 416–438.

born by the name in the non-apocalyptic passages, and because few would have been able to grasp in the use of the term the reference which would alone make the designation intelligible.

Must we then have recourse to the radical measures of Schweitzer in discounting the non-apocalyptic passages entirely, or must the question be left open? Recently a new hypothesis has been advanced which, it is claimed, obviates these extreme measures, operates with all the positive results achieved in the past and offers a vital basis for Jesus' adoption of the name and for its significance in both non-apocalyptic and apocalyptic passages. It endeavors to prove that the Son of Man, correctly "the man," whom we find in the Jewish and Christian documents, is but one particular phase of that figure to which our attention is to be directed in the ensuing pages and which appears in the Gnostic sources as "the man" or "the Anthropos." Reitzenstein, the author of this hypothesis, considers the ubiquitous Gnostic Anthropos to be a late but lucid manifestation of an ancient and ultimately Iranian figure which for centuries played an important part in the religious thought of the Orient. As such it was taken over into the Jewish apocalypses and became there the apocalyptic and messianic Bar Nasha. The Anthropos, however, is more than merely an eschatological figure. He is essentially a "messenger, . . . a stranger (in the world) faithfully executing the commands of his father and bringing (to the world) the word of life."[14] His activity involves him in trials and suffering, from which he is delivered by God's hand. In fulfilling his appointed task in spite of adversity, and receiving God's salvation himself, he becomes the agent and means and ensample of humanity's redemption, reappearing at the end of time as the head and pledge of the redeemed race. In these capacities he was known to Jewish sects in the days of Christ.

Jesus in adopting the name "the man" at the beginning of his ministry, identified himself with this expected "man," and designated himself thereby as "the bearer of a message who in humility sojourns upon the earth."[15] Its choice is but the expression of

[14] Reitzenstein, *Das iranische Erlösungsmysterium* (1921), p. 117.
[15] Ibid., p. 118.

his conviction that he has a mission to fulfill, and that an indissoluble bond connects him with the Father, both convictions arising from the innermost depths of his own personality. His statements that "the Son of Man must suffer" are entirely in accord with the current conception of "the man," though they have their basis in the historical circumstances of his life as well. From this view of himself as "messenger of God" he was led ultimately to messianic consciousness and to the use of "the man" in an apocalyptic sense, a transition that was intelligible to the people of his time, and was psychologically feasible so far as he himself was concerned.

There is one great objection to an hypothesis of this kind. It reinterprets Biblical and Apocryphal sources by the use of outside material and secondary evidence. A number of efforts have been made to solve the Son of Man problem in this way, and all have failed miserably. In the early years of this century when the individuality of Jewish and Israelitic thought was being sacrificed on the altar of Babylonian civilization, Jeremias,[16] Hommel,[17] Zimmern,[18] and Winckler[19] "proved" the Babylonian origin of the Bar Nasha and thought thus to decide the issue. Another group took recourse to Iranian prototypes for the Son of Man.

These efforts could be taken seriously only at a time when the novity of Oriental discovery destroyed the sense of distance and proportion.

The endeavor to link Son of Man and Anthropos goes back to the days of the earlier "religionsgeschichtliche Schule." It may be found in the earlier works of Bousset,[20] Gressmann,[21] and

---

[16] Art. *Oannes* in Röscher, Lexicon der Mythologie (1899), vol. III, col. 586 ff.
[17] Expository Times, vol. XI (1899–1900), pp. 341–5.
[18] Zimmern u. Winckler, *Die Keilschrift u. d. Alte Testament*, 3rd ed. (1903), p. 523.
[19] Altorientalische Forschungen, III, 4 (1904), pp. 296–301.
[20] Bousset, *Die Religion des Judentums im ntl. Zeitalter* (1st ed., 1903), 3rd ed. (1926), pp. 262–8.
[21] Gressmann, *Ursprung der israel.-jüd. Eschatologie* (1905), pp. 363–4.

THE PROBLEM OF THE ANTHROPOS

Clemen.[22] In its first form it was as objectionable as the theories of the Assyriologists, but to-day it has entered upon a new phase which may possibly remove from it the stigma attaching to it in the days gone by. It must now be considered in the light of the proto-Gnostic period of Oriental religious life, and in the light of the new sources at our disposal. Perhaps the Anthropos so universally familiar to the Orient at the end of the first Christian century, actually belongs to those survivals from ancient myth which bridge the gap between the early and the late East. His relation to the Jewish "manlike one" might then merit serious consideration.

There are additional observations which also commend the hypothesis in general. In the first place, the ultimate origin of the apocalyptic "manlike one" has not as yet been determined. In the second place, the exclusive consideration of primary sources has, as we have seen, produced no final solution of the Son of Man problem as a whole. A further factor might possibly be added. Ever since the days of the Apostolic Fathers orthodox Christianity has regarded Jesus' use of the name Son of Man as an indication that he claimed to possess a human nature. This interpretation was undoubtedly erroneous. The only ones to dissent from it were the Gnostics. They associated Jesus as Son of Man with the Anthropos current in their circles.[23] Did they, perchance, have the correct historical perspective?

The inquiry into the Gnostic Anthropos, made doubly important by these considerations, will therefore involve a number of elements:

1. The presentation of the source material relating to the Gnostic figure.

2. The analysis and interpretation of this material with a view toward determining as far as possible the origin and antiquity of the Anthropos.

3. The examination of the possible relations between the

[22] C. Clemen, *Die religionsgesch. Erklärung des N. T.* (1909), pp. 116–22.
[23] Cf. below, pp. 46–8, 51–3.

Anthropos, the Jewish Son of Man and other figures of later Jewish religious thought.

4. The discussion of the possible relations between the New Testament Son of Man and the Anthropos tradition.

Proceeding to the first of these topics we begin by presenting that part of the tradition in which the Anthropos appears in his most highly developed form, namely the Manichean, and shall follow this with the consideration of the earlier and more primitive forms as found in Syrian and Egyptian syncretism and among the Mandeans.

CHAPTER II

THE MANICHEAN PRIMAL MAN [1]

1. "KNOW ye then, Mazda worshippers of Zartusht, that the fundamental statement of Mani was about the endlessness of the first principles, the intermediate one about their mingling, and the final one about the separation of light from darkness." [2] With these words Mardan-farukh has ably epitomized the action of the great drama which Manichean doctrine unfolds before us on the stage of the universe. Its principals, "God and Matter, Light and Darkness, Good and Evil, in all things entirely contrary forces," [3] became engaged of yore in bitter conflict when Satan, a horrible creation of the powers of evil, invaded the upper spheres of Light with hostile intent. [4]

[1] Our reconstruction of the Manichean doctrine is based not only upon the traditional sources, the works of Christian and Mohammedan writers, but also upon the newly discovered Manichean texts, published in the Sitzungsberichte and Abhandlungen of the Berliner Akademie der Wissenschaften (quoted as SBA and ABA), as follows: F. W. K. Müller, *Handschriftenreste in Estrangeloschrift aus Turfan* I, SBA, 1904; II, ABA, 1904; *Ein Doppelblatt aus einem manichäischen Hymnenbuch*, ABA, 1912; A. von Le Coq, *Ein manichäisch-uigurisches Fragment*, SBA, 1908; *Koktürkisches aus Turfan*, SBA, 1909; *Türkische Manichaia aus Chotscho*, I, ABA, 1911; II, ABA, 1919; *Chuastuanift*, ABA, 1910. The new literature, embracing also "*Un traité manichéen retrouvé en Chine*" published in translation by Chavannes and Pelliot (Journal Asiatique (1911)), is brilliantly discussed in P. Alfaric, *Les Écritures Manichéenes*, 1920. New translation of the Chuastuanift (not accessible to me) made by W. Bang, *Der Manichaeische Laien-Beichtspiegel*, Museon, 36 (1923), pp. 137–242.

[2] *Shikand Gumanik Vijar*, xvi, 4–6. Sacred Books of the East (abbrev. SBE), vol. XII.

[3] Titus of Bostra, *Four books against the Manicheans*, I, 5 (ed. Migne, Patrologia Graeca, vol. 18).

[4] An-Nadim, *Fihrist*, ed. Flügel, Mani (1862), p. 86.

A champion of the powers of Light, evoked to oppose this invasion, succeeds in carrying the war to the lower realms, but is worsted there, a portion of the light being taken captive and commingled with the opposite element. There follow efforts on both sides to redeem or restrain the vanquished light, incidental to which is the creation of the present cosmic system and its living creatures. For it is in man, finally, that the divine and the material elements come into closest union, and by man's salvation that their separation is accomplished. But as salvation is never an automatic process, the higher self now dormant in the clutches of the material body, must first receive the knowledge of its former home and its destiny, before it is able to raise itself above the tyranny of the body and the world. Information of this sort comes to it directly or indirectly at the hand of some one of the messengers descending at intervals to the earth from above, namely, Adam, Seth, Noah, Buddha, Zarathushtra, Jesus and Mani.[5] When finally through the labors of these prophets, the saving knowledge shall have been brought to the last of the elect, and they have been saved, the cosmos, its role in the plan of salvation fulfilled, will be consumed by a tremendous conflagration in which the powers of darkness are subdued forever.

Our interest in this remarkable drama attaches itself to the person of the Primal Man, an actor who, contrary to what the name would suggest, is of great importance in the development of the plot.

2. When the King of the Realm of Light, so we are told, became cognizant of the efforts of Satan to invade his kingdom, he emanated from himself the Mother of Life, who in turn produced the Primal Man.[6] Summoned forth in the hour of peril, the latter proceeds on his way to engage the enemy in battle, though not without first gathering about himself his five celestial powers, as a means of protection. Referred to as his robes,[7] as pieces of

[5] Ibn al-Murtada, quoting the Manichean Jazdanbacht, Kessler, *Mani*, (1889), p. 354; cf. also Abu'lma'ali, ibid., pp. 370–2.

[6] Bar Khoni, cf. Cumont, *Recherches sur le Manichéisme*, I (1908), p. 14.

[7] T. II. K. 2a, recto, ABA, 1911, p. 21 (Of Azrua); T. II. D. 173b, verso, ibid., p. 14 (of Chormuzta).

armor,[8] as his sons,[9] sometimes condensed into one person: "the five-fold God,"[10] or again identified with the Primal Man,[11] these powers actually represent the five individual elements or genera of heavenly nature and being.[12] Between the champion of Light and the powers of evil a violent struggle then ensues. Its course is related in two distinct ways. According to the one version, the champion fares ill in the fulfillment of his mission. Only by continually altering his appearance can he elude the foe.[13] In spite of his mutability, his armor is cruelly penetrated.[14] The Primal Man becomes temporarily insensate, and loses control of his mental faculties.[15] Reawakening, he utters a prayer for release,[16] and but for the fact that his prayer was heard and he was succored by heavenly powers, he would have been detained permanently in the clutches of the adversary.[17] Even so a portion of his nature remains captive.[18]

The second version is in a different vein. According to the

---

[8] An-Nadim, Flügel, p. 87; Hegemonius, *Acta Archelai*, c. 7 (ed. Beeson, Die griech. christl. Schriftsteller, vol. 16, 1906). Epiphanius, *Panarion*, Heresy 66, c. 25 (Migne, Patr. Graeca, vol. 42).

[9] Bar Khoni, Cumont I, p. 16; Ephraem Syrus, *Prose Refutations*, lxix (ed. Mitchell, 1912).

[10] T. II. D. 178, IV, ABA, 1910, p. 8; M2, SBA, 1905, p. 1081; cf. Reitzenstein, *Das mandäische Buch des Herrn der Grösse*, Sitzungsberichte der Heidelberger Akademie der Wissenschaften, 1919, No. 12, pp. 26–8.

[11] According to Al-Murtada, the angel (Primal Man) is formed of the five genera of God, Kessler, p. 352. In the Acta c. 7 and Epiphanius, 66, 25, the text identifies and the context differentiates the elements and the Primal Man.

[12] An-Nadim, Flügel, p. 87, note 94.

[13] Ibid., p. 88; Augustine, *contra Faustum*, II, 4, (ed. Zycha, Corpus Script. Eccles. Lat., vol. 25, 6, 1).

[14] *Acta*, c. 7.

[15] Bar Khoni, Cumont, I. p. 20.

[16] Ibid., and Acta, c. 7. cf. also the Gods Chroshtag and Padwachtag of T. II. D. 173*b* recto, ABA, 1911, p. 13.

[17] *Acta*, c. 7.

[18] Al-Murtada, in spite of his leaning to the opposite interpretation, Kessler, p. 352; Acta, c. 7; An-Nadim, Flügel, pp. 88–9.

Acta Archelai,[19] Epiphanius,[20] and Titus of Bostra[21] the attack of the evil powers is offset by a clever strategem. The good God craftily and purposely exposes a portion of his power. By its absorption the powers of darkness are forced into submission.[22] There are two differences between this and the previous account, first the absence of the note of tragedy, second the use of abstract terms in place of proper names. The latter peculiarity might seem to stamp the second rendering as a pale and distant echo of the first. That is, however, scarcely the case. In the sources upon which we rely for our knowledge of the concrete and mythological form of the story, there are elements that are out of harmony with the tenor of the narrative as a whole. Bar Khoni (8.c.A.D.), for instance, relates that the champion on his way to defeat was accompanied by an angel Naḥash-shebet, who carried a crown of victory.[23] An-Nadim (10.c.A.D.) says that the Primal Man cut the roots of the powers of evil in the midst of the disastrous conflict.[24] Ephraem Syrus (4.c.A.D.) has him actually take the hostile archons captive at this time.[25] Bar Khoni and Augustine speak of a double of the Primal Man, namely Adamas Light, who is a warlike hero victorious in a struggle against demons.[26] These details must be elements of a second account of the primordial

[19] c. 28.
[20] 66, 44.
[21] Titus of Bostra, I. 12, cf. Baur, *Das manichäische Religionssystem* (1831), p. 56.
[22] Augustine, *de Moribus Manichaeorum*, II, 15, (ed. Migne, Patr. Lat., vol. 32), and Kessler, p. 352, n. 3.
[23] Cumont, I. p. 17, transcribes the name of the deity Naḥashbat and finds that its meaning is not clear. If, as we assume, the *shin* is doubled, the name becomes intelligible and the deity is the personification of the "snake-staff," the jagged representation of the lightning bolt, interpreted by the Manicheans as a lance, cf. below p. 101.
[24] Flügel, p. 89. In T. II. D. 173b, recto, ABA, 1912, pp. 13–14, the Primal Man and the elements are rescued together, and thereafter, only, is the fivefold God separated from the champion.
[25] Kessler, pp. 279–80. Does T. Ia, ABA, 1911, p. 19, Ormuzd defeating the demons belong into this connection?
[26] Bar Khoni, Cumont, I. pp. 22–3, p. 23, n. 2; Augustine, *contra Faustum*, xv, 6.

conflict, representing the Primal Man as a victorious champion. We have then to suppose that the story was told in two diverse forms, a supposition that finds adequate confirmation in the earlier strata of the Anthropos tradition.

3. The episode of the primordial struggle is followed by that embracing the creation of the world at the hands of powers of the second and third evocation. During this procedure the Primal Man himself is almost entirely lost sight of. He plays a role, none the less, in so far as the divine element lost by him in the conflict, is imbedded at this juncture in all forms of animated existence, from plants to man. Our knowledge of this fact is derived in part from the accounts of creation, and in part from the premises upon which the liturgies of the Manicheans are founded.

Creation, according to Mani, is the result of the efforts of divine and satanic powers to redeem or restrain the light-essence taken from the Primal Man. Particles of this essence repose in the bodies of a certain select few of the "archons," the commanders of the powers of evil, who are stated to have devoured them in the conflict. Subsequent to the release of the Primal Man the powers of light enter upon a struggle with the archons. Those having (presumably) no light-essence within them, are slaughtered, their pelts being used to fashion the canopy of heaven, their corpses serving to form the earths.[27] The others are fettered in the heavens where they appear as stars. Sensuously disturbed by the appearance of the powers of light, the fettered archons emit a portion of the captive element, which falls to the earth and there produces plant and animal life.[28] Another portion elicited from them is fashioned into the sun and moon, vehicles serving the redemptive work of the good powers.[29] Fearing lest they lose all of their choice possession, the archons conclude to pool the remaining elements and deposit them in the person and custody of a champion, Adam, the creature of Saklas their chief

---

[27] Bar Khoni, Cumont, I. pp. 25–9; Ephraem, Kessler, p. 279.
[28] Acta, c. 8 and Epiphanius, 66, 32; Augustine, c. *Faustum*, VI, 8.
[29] Bar Khoni, Cumont, I. p. 29; Alexander of Lycopolis, c. 3, (ed. Migne, Patr. Graeca, vol. 18).

and head.[30] Thus animate existence the world over is related to the primordial champion, since it contains a portion of his being, and vice versa, the Primal Man dwells in the world, macrocosmically as the "world soul" and microcosmically as the "individual soul."

To think of the Primal Man as dwelling simultaneously in heaven and on earth did not involve a contradiction for Mani. True to his Iranian heritage he divided the subjective or divine side of human existence into a number of distinct elements. What the Primal Man had lost, and what appears in man as the soul is but one of these elements, namely the "self" of the defeated champion.[31]

This fact of the relation of man and Primal Man is evident, we have said, from the liturgies as well. The Manichean service, so Reitzenstein has shown, was in the nature of a "mystery." In it the individual and the community rehearsed in word and thought, and by rehearsing assured their redemption. The hymns and liturgies therefore have but one burden. They speak of the human soul captive in the clutches of matter, of messengers that are sent to awaken it from lethal sleep, of the cry for release and the promise of aid and, finally, of the homeward journey of the soul in company of its mentors.[32]

The ultimate premises of redemption as described in the Manichean liturgies are to be found in the Soul Drama. Yet they have one particular and individual trait. Everything that is said about the fate of the individual soul is so stated that it holds true as well of the world soul and of the experience of the Primal Man in his initial conflict. This peculiarity is not an accident, it is a constitutive element. Its basis is to be found in the idea that the world soul and the individual soul are the lost portion of the being of the Primal Man, macrocosmically and microcosmically considered. And herein is a further guarantee

[30] Augustine, *de Natura Boni*, 46 (ed. Zycha, Cor. Scr. Eccl. Lat., vol. 25, 6. 2); Bar Khoni, Cumont, I. p. 42; *Acta*, 8; Alexander of Lycopolis, 4; Titus of Bostra, Preface to Bk. III; An-Nadim, Flugel, pp. 90–1.

[31] Cf. below, p. 30.

[32] Reitzenstein, *Das iranische Erlösungsmysterium* (1922), pp. 2–42.

of redemption, for just as the Primal Man was redeemed, so the souls of men, having their origin in him, will be redeemed.

Up to this point we have been dealing with the fate of the lost element of the Primal Man in the period of creation. According to some of the ancient authors, at least, the primordial champion appears himself at one point in the proceedings, namely in connection with the formation of Adam.

Man, all sources agree, is the product of the Archons, whether created by them collectively or by their leader Saklas acting for all. To them he owes both his physical and psychical nature, for his creation is due to the efforts of the archons to find a safe repository for the captured light-essence they still possess. In his outward form, however, he bears a dual likeness, for he is fashioned at once in their own image and in the likeness of a power of light that had recently manifested itself to them.[33] On the identity of the latter power the sources disagree. An extract from the Epistula Fundamenti of Mani, speaks only of a "great light that rises and causes the powers to tremble." Disturbed by its appearance, Saklas the archon urges his fellows to create a champion of darkness "in the image of that great one who appeared in his glory."[34] This "great light" is probably the sun. The sun, moreover, is the dwelling place of the "Messenger" whose first manifestation, so we are told in other accounts, had disastrous results for the archons.[35] Hence Bar Khoni may be quite right in maintaining that the divine power in the image of which man was made was the "Messenger."[36]

On the other hand, the Acta Archelai[37] and Alexander of Lycopolis expressly state that man was formed in the image of the divine Primal Man.[38] Nor will the statement of the Epistula Fundamenti be found to disagree with this contention, for An-

[33] *Acta*, 12; Epiphanius, 66, 76; Titus of Bostra, Preface to Bk. III.
[34] Augustine, *de Nat. Boni*, 46.
[35] Particularly since he is to be considered as Mithras, cf. M. 583, ABA, 1904, p. 20 and Reitzenstein, *Die Göttin Psyche*, Sitzungsberichte der Heidelberger Akademie, 1917, No. 10, pp. 3–4.
[36] Cumont, I. p. 46.
[37] *Acta*, 7 and 12.
[38] Alexander of Lycopolis, 4 and 23.

Nadim, at least, reports that after his release from the clutches of the archons, the Primal Man took up his residence in the sun.[39] We have then at this point a double tradition once more.

4. "Wisdom and deeds have always, from time to time been brought to mankind by the messengers of God. So in one age they were brought by the messenger called Buddha to India, in another by Zaradusht to Persia, in another by Jesus to the West. Thereupon this revelation has come down, this prophecy, in the last age, through me, Mani, the messenger of the God of truth to Babylonia."[40] Thus spake Mani in the all but vanished Shapurakan, indeed a beautiful expression of the universality of his religious conceptions, and simultaneously a statement that leads us to the heart of his soteriology.

The plurality of messengers is mentioned in other sources. Al-Murtada and Abu'lma'ali (A.D. 1092) report that the Manicheans speak of seven prophets, Adam, Seth, Noah, Buddha, Zarathushtra, Jesus and Mani.[41] The Chinese Manichean treatise fails to limit their number. They are here past, present and future.[42]

Yet the many messengers have the peculiarity of resolving themselves again into a single individual. The Shapurakan fragment just quoted speaks in its opening sentence of "the messenger." In the Chinese treatise, the messengers, past, present and future are but the representatives of a single type, the "Envoyé de la Lumière" whom the faithful adore with the words:

> Il n'y a que le Grand Saint, le Vénérable unique dans les trois mondes, qui soit universellement pour la multitude des êtres vivants un pére et une mère, doués de compassion; il est aussi le grand guide ... il est aussi le grand médecin ... l'espace merveileux ... le ciel supérieur ... la terre véritable ... la grande

---

[39] Alexander of Lycopolis, 4. cf. Baur, p. 140. The text reads merely "the man," but this approximates the terminology used to refer to the Primal Man in Syrian and Egyptian Gnosticism. Accepted as a reference to the Primal Man by Flügel, p. 342. At the end of time we again find the Primal Man in the sun, An-Nadim, Flügel, p. 100 and n. 292.

[40] Albiruni, *Chronology of Ancient Nations,* ed. Sachau (1879), p. 160.

[41] Cf. above, n. 5.

[42] Chavannes et Pelliot, p. 553.

mer... la montagne parfumée ... la colonne précieuse de diamant
... le pilote habile et sage sur la grande mer ... la main secourable
celui qui dans la mort donne la vie éternelle ....[43]

Finally there is the statement preserved in the Formula of Abjuration, acceptance of which was required of those entering the Church and leaving Manicheism, to wit, "I anathematize those who declare Zaradas (Zarathushtra), Buddha, Christ, Mani and the Sun to be one and the same person."[44]

On the basis of this testimony Mani's soteriology should be evident. The various prophets and messengers are diverse manifestations of a single power or person of the world of light. But who is the person into whom they resolve themselves? Reitzenstein finds an answer to this question in a difficult Turfan fragment. As translated by Andreas, the fragment conveys the following message:

> Thereupon God ... (created)? ... at first that human being, the primal one (and) primal Reason and Knowledge, and year by year and age by age he thereafter sent Reason and Knowledge into the (world). Even in that last age, close before the restitution (of the world) ... God ...."[45]

The translation of Andreas, itself a correction of an earlier rendering by F. W. K. Müller, has not solved the difficulties of the text in their entirety and is thus open to question.[46] Yet so much seems to be clear, namely that the God of the realm of Reason (the Primal Man) and the messengers are brought into intimate contact with one another. Reitzenstein considers this evidence of the fact that the coming and identity of the messengers is intimately bound up with the person of the Primal Man.[47] They might then be his manifestations.

[43] Ibid., p. 586.
[44] Kessler, p. 362.
[45] Fragment 473a, ABA, 1904, p. 22, given here in Andreas' translation, as found in Reitzenstein, MB, p. 50.
[46] Prof. A. V. W. Jackson considers the whole fragment eschatological and would supply "will appear" in the first lacuna.
[47] Reitzenstein, MB, p. 51.

A portion of the index of a Manichean hymnal throws additional light on the subject. Among the titles in the table of first-lines we find, in Müller's translation, the following:

400. Gekommen bist du mit Heil, der Geist . . . .
401. Gekommen bist du mit Heil der Geist des Lichtes . . . .
402. Gekommen ist dieser Geist der gefesselte . . . .
403. Gekommen is dieser Geist der erlöste . . . .
404. Gekommen bist du, edler Geist . . . .
405. Gesegnet bist du, grosser Geist, anfänglicher . . . .
406. Gesegnet bist du Geist des Lichtes . . . .
407. Gesegnet bist du Geist des Lichtes . . . .
408. Gesegnet bist du Geist, befreiter . . . .[48]

In view of the thematic arrangement of the index, there is no reason to argue for a variation in the person referred to in these hymns. There is only one divine being of which we know that it was pre-existent, once fettered, now freed and redeemed, namely the Primal Man. That he is called "spirit" should present no difficulty. The term, except in such cases where it is restricted by the use of a modifier, as in the case of "the Living Spirit," is a broad designation applicable to deity in general.[49] If then the fettered and released spirit is the Primal Man, the fact that he also comes to man bringing blessings and salvation from the world of Light, identifies him with the messengers, the saviors.

One of the Salemann fragments (S. 9, as noted below) necessitates a similar conclusion, in spite of the difficulties inherent in the text.

At the primordial revolt of the devils, we are told, Ormuzd descends to the lower spheres and there loses possession of the soul, an element of his body-guard. The powers of evil imprison her in the impurity of a material body. But Ormuzd takes pity on the souls (pl.?) and "causes (them?) to descend into the bodies (?), down to the earth." Thereupon he proceeds to instruct the soul opening her eyes revealing to her everything that was and shall be, and demonstrating the fact that Ormuzd

[48] ABA, 1912, p. 27.
[49] Reitzenstein, IE, p. 10.

had not created bodily pollution and had not himself fettered the soul. The trusting soul of the blessed, assured of the reward of resurrection, believed the wisdom of Ormuzd, and accepted the proferred instruction at his hand. This results in her final redemption.[50]

Clearly Ormuzd has here, as otherwheres, taken the place of the Primal Man.[51] What we hear of his "causing the soul to be lowered to the body" is entirely at variance with the statement made a few lines later, that Ormuzd is not responsible for bodily pollution. Reitzenstein has suggested that the text is corrupt and that it should be read "he lowered himself to the earth in the form of human beings," an emendation which, if correct, would clarify the sense of the passage, and directly identify the Primal Man (here Ormuzd) and the messengers.[52] Even without the emendation the fragment conveys the idea that the primordial

---

[50] Bulletin de l'Académie de St. Petersbourg, Ser. VI, vol. 6, no. 1, pp. 12–13. The text is replete with difficulties of no small caliber, particularly in the important phrase "He caused them? to descend." Bartholomae, *Zur Kenntniss d. mittelir. Mundarten, III* (SBA. 1920), p. 44 does not solve the problem, but inclines to a causative. Prof. Jackson would like to render "he allowed himself to descend." Waldschmidt and Lentz, *Die Stellung Jesu*, ABA (1926), p. 25, paraphrase "er selbst steigt herab."

[51] Le Coq (ABA, 1911, n. p. 40) and Chavannes et Pelliot (p. 513, n. 1) first showed that the Turfan texts identify Ormuzd (Ahura Mazda) and the Primal Man. This identification, accepted by Reitzenstein (*Psyche*, pp. 4–5) was questioned by Scheftelowitz (*Entstehung der manichäischen Religion, etc.*, 1922, pp. 63–4). The latter endeavored to show that the "five-fold God, the son of the God Chormuzta," i.e., the five elements, alone comprise the Primal Man. The position is untenable. The mere fact that the elements have been personified does not prove that they represent a subordinate emanation of Ormuzd. Baur had a better conception of the subtle relations between the members of the Manichean pleroma when he said: "The Manichean Christ, then, owes his existence to the person of the Primal Man, but we must guard against considering him an emanation of the Primal Man, to wit an aeon descended from him and subordinate to him" (pp. 208–9). Indeed, far from being inferior to the God Ormuzd, the Primal Man has a tendency to rise above him and to be identified with the supreme deity Zervan (cf. T. II. K. 2a, recto, ABA, 1911, p. 21).

[52] Reitzenstein IE, pp. 38–9 and 39, n. 1; so too Prof. Jackson, cf. above n. 50,

champion and the saviors of men are one and the same person.[53]

5. If the conclusions drawn from these texts are correct they should be confirmed by what the sources relate concerning the individual messengers.

In the case of Adam, Seth and Noah such confirmation is lacking. Apart from the statements of Al Murtada and Abu-'lma'ali, these persons are mentioned, Adam, only a few times,[54] Seth but once,[55] and Noah not at all. The reason for this is no doubt to be found in the fact that the antediluvians were too remote from the hopes of Mani's day to have deserved more than random attention. Consequently, the lack of further information concerning their relation to the Primal Man does not constitute disproof of the conclusion drawn above.

6. Buddha and Zarathushtra are one step nearer than the earlier messengers in the matter of interest. True their names are mentioned only rarely in the West, but in the Eastern documents, so far as they are intelligible to an uniniate, there is at least one trace of the kind of evidence required in the present discussion. It relates to the second of the two figures and is contained in the famous "Zarathushtra Fragment."[56]

Cast into the form of a hymn presenting to the believer instruction at the hand of the prophet of ancient Iran, the text relates how the "redeemer, the very Zarathushtra himself," in converse with his "self" (grēv) that is drunken with sleep, commingled with matter and held in the embrace of death, encourages it to look upon him, to be mindful of its divine origin, and, placing a

---

[53] Cf. also M2, recto, col. 1, SBA, 1905, p. 1081 and Reitzenstein MB, pp. 26–7 where Ormuzd promises to save the captive light elements.

[54] Augustine, *de Mor. Manichaeorum*, 19, cf. Baur, pp. 154–5; Bar Khoni, Cumont, I, pp. 46–7; An-Nadim, Flügel, pp. 91–3.

[55] Flügel, p. 92 and n. 184.

[56] Officially designated as M7 but not yet officially published. Quoted in full in the translation of Andreas by Reitzenstein, *Hellenistische Mysterienreligionen*, 2nd ed. (1920), pp. 126–7; IE., p. 3; Scheftelowitz, *Entstehung*, p. 72; Gressmann, *Das religionsgeschichtliche Problem*, etc., Zeitschrift, f. Kirchengeschichte, vol. XLI (1922), pp. 156–7.

crown upon its head, to follow him who brings salvation and life from above.[57]

The fragment has become the center of an extended controversy, partly because its importance was originally overemphasized, and partly because of the real difficulty of determining the identity of the imprisoned "self" and of the "Wahre Zarathushtra." Recent interpreters consider the latter the heavenly image or double of the prophet, his heavenly ego, after the analogy of the Iranian Fravashi and Daena.[58] If Gressmann be correct, the fragment means to say, that the prophet has died and that in death his heavenly image (daena) comes to meet him and assist him in the difficult task of ascending to his heavenly home. Of these difficulties of ascent, the soul, self or earthly ego (whichever translation we adopt) of Zarathushtra complains, only to be encouraged by the heavenly mentor.

The rendering of Gressmann is possible, but it fails to do justice to the instructive and devotional purposes which the text served[59] and to account for the nature of the embarrassment that has overtaken the captive self.[60] Scheftelowitz has been led by this difficulty, perhaps, to regard the moment pictured in the hymn as that in which the Fravashi of Zarathushtra comes to the soul

[57] The word "*grēv*" used in the text has been the source of difficulties First rendered "spirit" and thought of as being used in place of *giyān* "soul" in translating Aramaic *ruḥa* (covering both spirit and soul) it is now rendered "self" by both Reitzenstein and Gressmann the immortal portion of a human being, that portion which after death serves as the body of the Fravashi. ZKG, vol. XLI, p. 156. Waldschmidt and Lenz. *Die Stellung Jesu*, ABA, 1926, pp. 11 n. 1, 41, 70–77, etc., always translate *grēv* as "ich," which is not so good a rendering.

[58] Gressmann, ZKG, vol. XLI, pp. 156–8; Scheftelowitz, *Entstehung*, pp. 72–4.

[59] No exemplary or vicarious significance attaches to the death of Zarathushtra or Mani in Manicheism, as it does to the death of Christ in Christianity. As a general statement of the events following upon the death of an individual, the sentiments of the Z. fragment are not intelligible. Cf. the account of An-Nadim, Flügel, pp. 100–1.

[60] The difficulties attending the heavenward journey of the soul are those experienced in passing the hostile planetary powers. Cf. Wendland, *Die hellenistische-römische Kultur*, 2nd ed. (1912), pp. 170–6.

asleep in the body, intent on awakening it so that the prophet may enter upon his missionary and redemptive labors.[61] Of course the Fravashi is the mentor of the human soul[62] but its presence and operation is taken for granted from the time of birth like that of the conscience. It is difficult, therefore, to see why one particular moment of its action should deserve such extended attention, and why an account of such a moment should be cast into the form of a hymn. Surely those who sang the hymn in their devotions were not destined to be messengers of Zarathushtra's type. They could learn but little from an account of how he was awakened to his prophetic office.[63]

Reitzenstein, following a reverse method of procedure, begins by identifying the being captive in the clutches of death, born in a different world, yet mingled in matter and drunken with sleep. A comparison between the Manichean and Mandean texts reveals to him that the being usually referred to in this way is the soul, or in Manichean terminology the lost element of the Primal Man.[64] To the soul, then, Zarathushtra comes as the messenger of God, awakening and redeeming it. But if the soul is the "self" of Zarathushtra, then the latter is certainly the manifestation of the Primal Man, come to redeem his loss.[65]

[61] *Entstehung*, p. 74.

[62] Dhalla, *Zoroastrian Theology* (1914), p. 144.

[63] The text quoted by Scheftelowitz in substantiation of his interpretation, namely T. II. D. 178, may depict the moment of death as well as that of the religious awakening. Prophets are awakened to their calling by other means than those referred to in the Z. fragment, Adam, for instance, by the appearance of Jesus (Flügel, p. 91) and Mani by a revelation of the King of the World of Light (ibid., p. 84).

[64] IE, pp. 2–10, 99, 135.

[65] Reitzenstein (IE, p. 4) considers the Z. fragment a witness to a pre-Manichean form of the Anthropos theology in which Zarathushtra is the sole messenger to the "self" or world soul. This seems to be out of harmony with the opening lines of the text, which aim to give the "testimony of the fathers of old," i.e., to make the appropriation of salvation in the present (at the hands of Mani) more vivid by reference to the experience of previous generations. R. has been led to his interpretation by the consideration of the "crown of light" appearing in the text. The crown appears in Manicheism as one of the ornaments which the soul of the elect receives after the death of the body. (Flügel, p. 92; Müller, ABA, 1904, pp. 47, 98; Le Coq, cited by

Thus interpreted, the hymn may well be instructive and uplifting to the faithful, for the imprisoned soul is equally the world and the individual soul, and the salvation of former days is the guarantee of a present salvation. So interpreted, too, the Zarathushtra fragment confirms the statements already quoted that the messengers are the manifestations of the Primal Man.

7. The peculiar idea of the divided Zarathushtra to which the theology connected with the Primal Man gives rise, finds its counterpart in the Manichean conception of Jesus.

"How many Christs have you?" exclaims Augustine, our best authority on Mani's Christology. "Is there one whom you call the "mortal" (*patibilis*), whom the earth conceives and brings forth by the power of the Holy Spirit . . . and another crucified by the Jews under Pontius Pilate, and a third whom you divide between sun and moon? Or is it one and the same person, a part of whom is confined within the trees, to be released by the help of the other part which is not confined?"[66]

Even though there is a note of scorn in the passage from Augustine, it presents in admirable fashion the gist of the Manichean Christology. Like Zarathushtra, Jesus is to Mani a divided personality. He manifests himself in the first place, as the firstborn of the unspeakable and most holy majesty, as the "*omnium luminum rex*,"[67] and a form of the "*massa lucidissimae molis Dei.*"[68] As such he is the Son of God[69] and can be invoked together with Ormuzd.[70] His dwelling-place is the "visible light,"[71] characterized by power and wisdom,[72] namely the Sun

Reitzenstein, IE, p. 26, etc.) For the soul to place such a crown on its head does not necessarily signify that its earthly life has ended. In their ceremonial the Mandeans placed "crowns" on their heads, anticipatingly symbolizing their election. (Lidzbarski, *Mandäische Liturgien* (1920), pp. 4–5 for instances. Such ceremonial action may have played a part in Manicheism and find its reflection in our text.

[66] *c. Faustum*, XX, 11.
[67] Secundinus, *Epistula ad Augustinum*, c. 1 (ed. Migne, P.L., vol. XLII).
[68] *Confessiones*, V. 10 (ed. Migne, P.L., vol. XXXII, col. 716).
[69] M18, ABA, 1904, p. 34.
[70] TM327, SBA, 1909, p. 1053.
[71] *c. Faustum*, XX, 2.
[72] Ibid., cf. also Baur, pp. 206–8. The wisdom of the moon-god is mentioned also in T. II. D. 171, left col., ABA, 1911, p. 24.

and the Moon.[73] Hence he may be said to be *"per solem et lunam distentus."*[74]

It is this Christ who at the appointed time descends to earth, taking on, without incarnation, the guise of human form, and thus appearing as a man, though not polluting the purity of his divine nature.[75] Both the assumed likeness and the immutable personality behind it play a part in his work. The latter imparts to men a saving knowledge of the light,[76] while the former symbolically enacts the drama of life, from birth through suffering to death.[77] In that the Christ was able to play the part, in conjunction with his guise, quite without injury to himself, he has won a victory over Satan and has given man the surest guarantee of the validity of his message.[78]

In the second place, Christ manifests himself as the *Jesus Patibilis*. Augustine is again our best authority on the subject. Of Faustus, the Manichean, he says:

> You represent your fabulous Christ, the son of your fabulous Primal Man, as bound up in all the stars. For you say that he was mingled with the princes of darkness in that conflict in which your Primal Man himself contended with the race of darkness, as a result of which the world was built from the princes of darkness taken captive by means of this mingling . . . According to your profane fancies, Christ is not only mingled with heaven and all the stars, but conjoined and compounded with the earth and all its products.[79]

This Jesus who may be found in all plants, trees and fruit, *"omni suspensus ex ligno"*[80] as well as in human beings, was a novelty

[73] M176, ABA, 1904, p. 60 and *Acta*, 13. The moon-god and sun-god are mentioned as one person in T. II. D. 169, ii, ABA, 1919, p. 10, and T. II. Y. 60a, ABA, 1910, p. 16.
[74] *c. Faustum*, XX, 11.
[75] *Acta*, 54; *c. Faustum*, III, 1.
[76] *contra Fortunatum Disputatio*, 3. (ed. Zycha, Cor. Scr. Eccl. Lat., vol. XXV, 6, 1).
[77] *c. Faustum*, XXIX, 1 (of birth); ibid., XXIII, 3 (of baptism); ibid., XXX, 6; cf. Baur, pp. 390–404.
[78] Evodius, *de Fide*, 28 (ed. Zycha, Cor. Scr. Eccl. Lat., vol. XXV, 6, 2).
[79] *c. Faustum*, II, 4–5.
[80] Ibid., XX, 11.

even to the christologically developed minds of the Western Fathers. They lacked the clue that would lead to his identification. Yet from the above passage it should be clear to us that the *Jesus Patibilis* is the life principle indwelling in the world, the divine element imprisoned in material existence since the primordial conflict, in other words the lost "self" of the Primal Man.[81] This at once stamps the transcendent Christ as that portion of the champion which returned to heaven, an identification that is confirmed by his position as first-born, and his residence in the sun. Indeed the conception of the divided Primal Man is directly responsible for the partition of the divine Christ, a feat never attempted in other circles than the Manichean, so far as I know. Once more, then, a messenger proves to be but a remanifestation of the Primal Man. This was of course what Baur perceived when he pointed to the Primal Man as the concrete representation of the divine power which is mingled with matter,[82] to the *Jesus Patibilis* as the form in which that divine element presents itself to men[83] and to the Christ of the sun and moon as the light essence of the Primal Man which remained pure when he was overwhelmed by the powers of darkness.[84]

It is interesting to see how the identification of the Christ and the Primal Man has influenced the text of the Gospels as they were current among the Manicheans. The rendition of Mt. 25, 35–6 is a case in point.

Turfan Text	Current Text
I was hungered and ye gave me meat,	Vs. 35a.
I was thirsty and ye gave me drink,	Vs. 35b.
I was naked and ye clothed me,	Vs. 36a.
I was sick and ye visited me,	Vs. 36b.
I was fettered and by you I was freed,	Lacking.
I was in prison and by you was I redeemed,	I was in prison and ye came to me.
I was a stranger, a wanderer, by you was I taken in.[85]	I was a stranger and ye took me in.

[81] As we have already seen the lost "self" is frequently called the "son of" the Primal Man cf. above, p. 19.
[82] Baur, p. 69. [83] Ibid., p. 75. [84] Ibid., p. 209.
[85] M475, verso, ABA, 1904, pp. 12–13.

The Christ who is fettered, freed and redeemed, is the imprisoned "self" of the Primal Man to whom salvation comes through the piety of the individuals in whom he has his being.

8. The last of the messengers of whom the Formula of Abjuration says that they are the manifestations of one person, is none other than Mani himself. To prove that he too is to be considered a revelation of the Primal Man is more difficult, because of the fact that there is in every religion a discrepancy between that which its founder said of himself and that which his disciples claimed for him.

Certainly the prophet of Babylon laid no claim to that type of existence and divinity which he imputed to the transcendent Christ. His genealogy, frankly stated, shows no effort to connect his birth with divine intervention.[86] Spiritual insight came to him not as a matter of natural endowment, but by special revelation.[87] The name with which he generally introduced himself, in the West at least, was, "an apostle of Jesus Christ."[88] He thought of himself as the one divinely called and inspired to present in its unadulterated form the truth of Jesus' message, a message long since garbled and confused by self-appointed interpreters.[89] To this extent he may have been willing to call himself "the Paraclete,"[90] the guide into all truth.

A broad gulf divides that which Mani said of himself and what his followers made of him. By them he is spoken of as "Firstborn, mighty commander, my Lord Mani"[91] as "one born under a resplendent star in the family of sovereigns"[92] as a "son of the Gods,"[93] or directly as "Mari (Mani) God."[94] He is mentioned in one breath with "Jesus, the Virgin of Light and

---

[86] Flügel, p. 83, cf. Augustine, *contra Epistulam Fundamenti*, 8 (ed. Zycha, Cor. Scr. Eccl. Lat., vol. XXV.)
[87] Flügel, p. 84.
[88] *c. Faustum*, XIII, 4 ; *c. Epist. Fund.*, 5–6; 8.
[89] Cf. Baur, pp. 378–90.
[90] *c. Epist. Fund.*, 6; 8; 9 et al.; cf. Baur, pp. 370–2.
[91] T. II. D. 178, iv, ABA, 1910, p. 8, cf. Reitzenstein, MB, pp. 47–8.
[92] M7, ABA, 1904, p. 79; cf. Scheftelowitz, *Entstehung*, p. 15.
[93] M32, M311, ABA, 1904, pp. 62 and 66; cf. Scheftelowitz, p. 37.
[94] M64, ABA, 1904, p. 92.

Mithras"[95] and is said to perform the works of Ormuzd, the son of Zervan.[96] Manicheans put into his mouth the words "Come am I, the first-born, the intermediary"[97] or "I am the first stranger, the son of the God Zervan, the child of Kings."[98]

Clearly Mani has been elevated by his followers above the position to which he himself aspired. What else could they have considered him to be than the foremost and complete revelation of that power which he had taught them to see working in the person of the messengers, in other words the Primal Man. True, no one speaks of him as the Primal Man directly, but neither does anyone directly identify Zarathushtra or Jesus with that figure. As "First-born" in the sense of Monogenes,[99] as the son of Zervan, and as the "stranger" from the other world he certainly approximates the character and position of the primordial champion. As *"medius solis et lunae"* he even resides in the dwelling of the Primal Man.[100]

From the general statements presented at the beginning of this discussion, as well as from the data regarding the Manichean conception of Zarathushtra, Jesus and Mani, it should then be evident that Manichean soteriology regards the divine messengers as manifestations of the Primal Man. What the latter redeems, namely the macrocosmic or microcosmic soul, is thus actually himself, the lost element of the one divided divine personality.[101]

---

[95] M38, ABA, 1904, p. 77.
[96] M10, cf. Reitzenstein, MB, pp. 46–7.
[97] M3, ABA, 1904, p. 80.
[98] Mliturg, ABA, 1904, p. 29; cf. Reitzenstein, IE, p. 10.
[99] So Irenaeus, I, 1 et al.; cf. Bousset, HP, pp. 161; 171; 267, n. 2; not with Scheftelowitz recalling the title of the Babylonian kings, *Entstehung*, pp. 14–5.
[100] Secundinus, *Epistula ad Augustinum*, 3 (ed. Patr. Lat, vol. XLII, col. 574.).
[101] We are not ready to say whether the Primal Man plays any part in the deliverance of the individual soul above that of proclaiming its final liberation and of assisting in its purification and transfer from the moon and sun heavenward. At the moment of death, we are told, there appear to the departing soul the "wise conductor, the three other gods and the maiden in the likeness of the soul." Reitzenstein regards the last as the representative of the Primal Man, a representative that appears in female form because the soul is

Therein lies for the individual believer the assurance of salvation and for the divine world the guarantee of a final victory over the powers of darkness, their enemies since the beginning.

9. In the course of the events connected with the end of the world the Primal Man once more appears. What we actually know about those events is very little, considering the fact that in Manicheism as in Christianity, the final catastrophe is the climax of the drama of existence. The arrival of the end is determined by the completion of the process of liberating from matter those light elements that are worthy of salvation. As long as this process is under way the celestial portion of the Primal Man is located in the Sun where it is instrumental in cleansing and transmitting heavenward the redeemed souls (the earthly self). From this place, too, it issues forth into the world in the forms of saviors.[102] Once the process has been completed, the cosmos, itself nothing more than the machinery for the process of salvation, is consumed in a great conflagration and the powers of evil are isolated for ever. At this juncture the divine powers who have taken their stand within the cosmos during its existence, are relieved of their duties and gather before the throne of majesty. "The Primal Man" so An-Nadim reports, "comes from the world of Capricornus (the North), while the Spirit of Life comes from the West."[103] Under the name of Ormuzd, the same is recorded of him by a Turfan text.[104] Before the throne, then, he finally meets his lost "self," and, we may suppose, is united to it. Two

---

considered a female. We should be inclined to believe that the "maiden" is still merely the Iranian Daena of Yasht 22, 1-36, even as the "three other gods" are Mithra, Srosha and Rashnu and the "wise conductor" is probably *Naresap* or *Norisof*, the Iranian Neryosang. (Cf. Pavry, *The Zoroastrian Doctrine of a Future Life*, 1926, pp. 46-7, where A. V. W. Jackson is cited.) That An-Nadim has confused the "maiden" and the "wise conductor" (Flügel, p. 100) does not argue to the contrary. (Cf. on the discussion Reitzenstein, IE., pp. 28-42, and also below, p. 69.)

[102] Flügel, pp. 100-1.

[103] Ibid., pp. 101-2. From Flügel's translation it would appear as though the Primal Man comes from three directions at once, or via three points of the compass. Correct by reference to Kessler, p. 400.

[104] M470, ABA, 1904, pp. 19-20; cf. Alfaric, II, p. 52.

fragments give us at least a glimpse of this important meeting. The one speaks of the Mother of the Pious, the God Ormuzd and the five elements coming jointly to the throne from the north.[105] The other recounts the order in which the assembled stand before the presence and lists there, as the first, the God Ormuzd together with the last God, the Mother of the Pious, the Friend of Light, Norisof (Neryosang), Bam, the Living Spirit, Jesus Ziwa, the Maiden of Light, and the "Great Soul."[106]

This, then, is what the sources have to tell us concerning the Manichean Primal Man, the first link in our chain of evidence regarding the Gnostic Anthropos. It is a remarkable figure, undoubtedly, and one that is of central importance in cosmogony, anthropology, soteriology and eschatology. Indeed one might say without exaggeration, that the Manichean theology is an Anthropos Theology.

In its Manichean version, the Anthropos tradition is revealed to us in its most advanced form. It has been polished and adapted and blended into a beautifully coördinated unit. Having that finished product before us, we can endeavor to trace whatever signs of its growth and presence are visible in the data concerning the earlier Gnostic systems of the Orient.

[105] M583, ABA, 1904, p. 20; cf. Reitzenstein, *Psyche*, p. 4.
[106] M2, SBA, 1905, p. 1081; cf. Reitzenstein, *Psyche*, pp. 4-5 and his remark, p. 5, n. 1. It is possible that the Primal Man is the author of the great cry that is uttered over the world, the cry which is the sign that the consummation is at hand. (M473b, ABA, 1904, p. 22). Reitzenstein has maintained, in connection with another fragment (M4, ABA, 1904, pp. 49-52) that Mani is the one who utters the cry (IE. pp. 16-7). The cry referred to in M4 is probably a cry on earth, the annunciation of the message of salvation. The cry of M473b is one that reverberates through the universe, and should be uttered by a cosmic potency, the savior in his cosmic role, i.e., the divine self of the Primal Man. In M472, ABA, 1904, pp. 17-8, the "Sun-God" seems to be mentioned in this connection. That would be a confirmation of our contention, for the Primal Man resides in the sun.

CHAPTER III

THE ANTHROPOS IN HELLENISTIC AND WESTERN GNOSTIC SYSTEMS

THE Primal Man who played so important a role in the Manichean theology of the third century was known also to Gnostics outside the confines of Mesopotamia at least a century before Mani. To give an adequate account of the character of the figure as it appeared in the earlier days is by no means easy. In the first place we have to consider not one but at least ten individual interpretations of the one personage. In the second place our knowledge of these manifestations is derived, not from an extensive body of direct evidence and from quotations of Fathers intimately connected with the Gnostic movements, but from scanty first-hand material and from the writings of professional Heresiologists whose endeavor to refute at once all Gnostic "error" permitted neither detailed report nor study of any one or more of the forms of this movement.

1. Unsatisfactory as it is, the evidence shows that the Anthropos was a well-known figure in the two great centers of syncretistic thought, Egypt and Syria. According to the Fathers, he appeared in Egypt in the systems of Valentinus,[1] his pupils Ptolemaeus[2] and Marcus,[3] and the Barbelognostics of Irenaeus I. 29. What the heresiologists relate as evidence for the Valentinian system is borne out by quotations from Valentinus' writings preserved by

[1] Irenaeus, *adversus Haeres.*, I. 11, Hippolytus, *Philosophoumena*, VI, 21–37, Epiphanius, *Panarion*, 31, 32. Epiphanius uses the lost Greek original of Irenaeus.
[2] Irenaeus, op. cit., I. 1–10, Hippolytus, VI, 38. Epiphanius again uses Irenaeus, *Panarion*, 31, 9–32.
[3] Irenaeus, I. 13–21, Hippolytus, VI, 39–55.

Clement of Alexandria[4] and a source quoted by Epiphanius.[5] The account concerning the Barbelognostics is confirmed by the recently discovered Gospel of Mary[6] and by the great Coptic Gnostic documents.[7] Apart from this Gnostic evidence stands that of the first tract of the Corpus Hermeticum, commonly known as the Poimandres, and of the prophet Bitys, culled by Reitzenstein from the writings of an obscure alchemist Zosimus and from Jamblichus.[8] Arranging our witnesses chronologically, the Egyptian provenience of our figure is attested to by the Coptic Gnostic works, Bitys, the Valentinians, Valentinus, the Barbelognostics of Irenaeus, the Gospel of Mary and the Poimandres.[9] The evidence covers a period from the middle of the third to the first half of the second Christian century.

In Syria, according to the Fathers, the figure played a part in the systems of Monoimus,[10] the Christian and pagan Naasenes[11] and the pre-Valentinian Gnostics, probably Ophites, of Irenaeus I. 30. Direct evidence we have only for the conceptions of the Naasenes, from a document quoted in extenso by Hippolytus.[12]

[4] Collected and accessible conveniently in Hilgenfeld, *Ketzergeschichte des Urchristentums* (1884), pp. 293–301.
[5] Epiphanius, 31, 5–6.
[6] C. Schmidt, *Ein vorirenaeisches gnostisches Original-werk in koptischer Sprache*, Sitzb. Ber. Akad., 1896, pp. 839–47.
[7] Namely the Pistis Sophia, the Books of Jeu and the unnamed document of the Codex Brucianus, transl. C. Schmidt, Greichische christliche Schriftsteller, vol. 13 (1905), English translation of the "Pistis Sophia" by George Horner, 1924.
[8] All accessible in Reitzenstein; Poimandres (1904) pp. 102–8. The Hermetic tract now edited and translated in W. Scott, *Hermetica* (1924), vol. I.
[9] For the dating of the Poimandres cf. W. Scott, *Hermetica*, vol. II. p. 12, Ed. Meyer, *Ursprung u. Anfänge des Christentums*, vol. II (1921), p. 372. For the dating of the Gospel of Mary, cf. Schmidt in Sitzb. Berl. Akad. 1896, pp. 846–7, a note by Harnack.
[10] Hippolytus, VIII, 12–15.
[11] Ibid., V. 6–7, 2.
[12] Reitzenstein first proposed that Hippolytus in his treatment of the Naasenes (V. 6, 1–9, 9) excerpted and commented upon a pagan Naasene document in Christian redaction. (*Poimandres*, pp. 81–102). His analysis was accepted by Bousset (HP, pp. 184–5), P. Wendland (*Die hellenistisch-römische Kultur*, 2nd ed. (1912), pp. 172–3) and Leisegang (*Die Gnosis* (1924),

Our witnesses in this sphere present the following chronological sequence: Monoimus, Hippolytus' discussion of the Naasene system, the Christian Naasene theology as shown in the document of Hippolytus, the pre-Valentinian Ophites of Irenaeus and the pagan Naasene theology as shown by the document of Hippolytus. They cover a period from the middle of the third to the very beginning of the second century A.D.[13]

The figure to which our interest attaches in these diverse theologies appears under a great variety of names. Some of them recall the Manichean nomenclature, Primal Man. Such are the designations Protanthropos used by the Christian Naasenes of Syria,[14] and Archanthropos, employed by the Barbelognostics of Egypt.[15] If there were any doubt of the identity of the Manichean Primal Man and his west-gnostic counterpart, these designations would serve to remove it. Other designations like "Adam" or "Adamas"[16] give a Judaizing touch. The one most frequently employed, however, is "the Man" ($\dot{o}$ $\ddot{a}\nu\theta\rho\omega\pi os$).[17] Its form is modified by the addition of descriptive adjectives, such as "the preëxistent,"[18] "the perfect"[19] "the great, beautiful and perfect,"[20] the "upper,"[21] or finally by the omission of the article,

p. 115). For further discussion of the distinction between pagan and Christian strata in the document cf. Reitzenstein u. Schaeder, *Studien zum antiken Synkretismus*, (1926), pp. 104–21, 161–73.

[13] The date of Monoimus is difficult to establish. Hippolytus, writing before A.D. 250, first mentions him, and places him in his treatment between the Docetics (early 2. c. A.D.) and Tatian (late 2. c. A.D.). The Ophites of Irenaeus I. 30, are said to be pre-Valentinian (ibid., I. 30, 15). The pagan Naasene document of Hippolytus is dated by the Attis hymn underlying its structure. This hymn is placed by Willamowitz-Moellendorf in the time of Hadrian, Hermes, vol. XXXVII, p. 329.

[14] Cf. Hippolytus, V. 7, 30.

[15] Irenaeus, I. 30, 1, Latin translation, and Gospel of Mary, Sitzb. Berl. Akad., 1896, p. 843.

[16] Ibid. V. 7, 2, 6, 35; V. 6, 5; Irenaeus I, 29, 3; Griech. christl. Schriftst. vol. XIII, p. 15, 9, passim.

[17] For instance Hipp. V, 6, 4; Irenaeus, I, 11, 1.

[18] Clem. Alex. *Stromata*, II, 8, 36.

[19] Hipp. VIII, 13, 3; Irenaeus I, 29, 3.

[20] Ibid. V, 7, 7.

[21] Ibid. V, 7, 30

Anthropos thus becoming the equivalent of proper name.[22] Of these designations "the Anthropos" is thus probably a later abbreviation of the more original name "Primal Man." Yet it was this name that was attached to the figure in the sources to which scholars first directed their attention, and it is this name by which the figure is commonly referred to.

2. As we find him in Egyptian syncretism, the Anthropos is a shadowy but apparently not completely abstract figure. He belongs to the preëxistent powers that comprise the pleroma. In the Coptic-Gnostic works, as "Jeu" the "first man" he dwells in a Topos immediately outside and to the right of the Treasury of Light, the source from which sprang those elements of deity which the diverse gradations of material existence reveal.[23] The disciples of Valentinus give him a place in the primal Ogdoad of divine emanations, moving him slightly up and down the scale, from first,[24] to second[25] and even third place.[26] Valentinus himself placed the Anthropos and the consort Ecclesia invariably attached to him in the Valentinian systems, in the fourth and final position in the Ogdoad, that is after the Ineffable, Pater and Logos.[27] In the Poimandres, he is again the fourth in the order of emanation, that is, he comes into being, after Nous, Logos and Nous Demiourgos, but actually he is the offspring of the Nous, and thus coequal with the Logos.[28] On the other hand, the Barbelognostics of the Gospel of Mary, had no scruples in making the Protanthropos the fountainhead of all existence.[29] The phenomenon evinced by this fluctuation in position, has its counter-

[22] *Poimandres*, 12; Scott, *Hermetica*, I, p. 120, 5; Irenaeus, I, 11, 1; 15, 1–3; 14, 5.
[23] C. Schmidt, *Gnostische Schriften in koptischer Sprache*, Texte u. Untersuchungen, vol. VIII (1892), p. 372, Griech. christl. Schriftst. vol. XIII pp. 126–6; 184–5; 237.
[24] Irenaeus, I, 12, 4.
[25] Epiphanius, 31. 5, 5.
[26] Irenaeus, I, 12, 3.
[27] Irenaeus, I, 11; Hippolytus, VI, 29, 7; cf. Epiphanius, 31, 2, 10.
[28] *Hermetica*, I, pp. 116–20.
[29] Sitzb. Berl. Akad. 1896, pp. 843–4.

part in the Manichean texts, where, it will be recalled, the Primal Man usurps the role of Ormuzd and even Zrvan.

All this affords us little insight into the nature of the Anthropos' being, and his character. The Poimandres alone adds a bit of flesh to the dry bones. It relates that:

> "Mind, the Father of all, he who is Life and Light, gave birth to Man, a being like to himself. And he took delight in Man, as being his own offspring; for Man was very goodly to look on, bearing the likeness of his Father. With good reason then did God take delight in Man; for it was God's own form that God took delight in." [30]

Evidently the author of the Poimandres is drawing in some way upon the Old Testament account of the creation of man to enliven the picture.

Of primordial activity on the part of this pallid Anthropos, only the Poimandres gives us evidence. We are told that "God delivered over to Man all things that had been made" and that Man,

> "having considered the creation of the Demiurge, in the Father, willed to make things for his own part also, and was permitted by his father to do so. Taking his place in the sphere of the Demiurge, and having all power, he considered the creations of his brother. But they (the Administrators) took delight in him and each of them gave him a share of his own nature.
>
> And having learnt to know the being and having received a share of their nature, he willed to break through the bounding circle of their orbits and to subdue the power of the one who was set over the region of fire." [31]

---

[30] Translation and text of Scott. *Hermetica*, I, p. 120, 4–8. *Poimandres*, § 12.

[31] *Poimandres*, §§12–3, text of Reitzenstein (*Poimandres*, p. 331 and *Studien*, p. 156) translation after Scott. At this point Scott seems rather free in his restoration of the text. The reallocation of § 13b (W. Scott, p. 120), where the Anthropos threatens to subdue the Adminstrator of Fire, is unnecessary because the warlike activity is a constant element in the Anthropos tradition, cf. above p. 19f., and below, p. 97ff. The situation in which the Anthropos here finds himself was familiar also to the Barbelognostics of whom Irenaeus relates that in their opinion Adamas, the unconquerable heavenly man, leaves Harmozel (correct form of the place name supplied by the Gospel of Mary,

The passage distinctly recalls the Manichean conception to the effect that the Primal Man is sent forth into a primordial conflict, endowed with the powerful elements of divine existence. Of the conflict itself nothing is said in the Poimandres.

In some form or other almost all of the Egyptian sources connect the Anthropos with extra-pleromatic existence, and more specifically with a divine principle indwelling in mankind. The Coptic-Gnostic works establish only an indirect relation. Jeu, the first man, is the overseer over the light-essence that has been estranged from the Treasury of Light in the course of time.[32] The writings of Zosimus have yielded to Reitzenstein a more direct connection. The Alchemist at one place speaks of the liberation of man from Heimarmene, and vouchsafes the opinion that the man of spirituality does not need to use magic to overcome Fate. Knowing himself as he does, this man will soon discern within himself a universal power, the Son of God, who becomes all things for all men, particularly for the sake of the pious souls and their release. The idea is that the one who is spiritually minded will discover that his spiritual self is a part of an individual transcendent being which furnishes him who listens to its message the necessary help against the power of Fate. This transcendent being Zosimus, on the authority of Bitys, Plato and Hermes, considers as the Primal Man, called Thot by the Egyptians, and Adam by the Chaldeans, Medes and Hebrews.[33]

The school of Valentinus shared such an opinion at least as far as Adam the protoplast was concerned. Clement of Alexandria quotes from an epistle of Valentinus words to the effect that "Adam

SBA, 1896, pp. 839–47) equipped with *agnitionem perfectam* and a *virtutem invictam*. (Iren. I, 29, 3.) This again recalls very distinctly the ideas recorded in the new Hermetic text discovered by Reitzenstein where Horus (who replaces the Anthropos) goes forth from heaven equipped with many powers, and particularly with one which like the Barbelognostic Adamas he receives from *virgo*. (Cf. Irenaeus, I, 29, 3 *virginalis spiritus*); see Reitzenstein u. Schaeder, *Studien*, pp. 113–4.

[32] TU, vol. VIII, p. 372; Griech. christl. Schriftst., vol. XIII, pp. 125–6; 184–5; 237.

[33] Reitzenstein, *Poimandres*, pp. 102–8.

was formed in the name of Man"[34] and inspired fear of the pre-existent Man into the angels, his creators, by reason of that Man's having his being in him, and having communicated to him a germ of the supernal essence, so that he "uttered greater things than proceeded from his formation."[35] The Valentinian Marcus apparently shared this conception.[36]

Of the nature of the divine element in man, its origin and how it came into the human body, the Poimandres furnishes another account. The Anthropos, we are told, though he planned to subdue the powers of fire,

> "looked down through the structure of the heavenly harmony, having broken through the (lowest) sphere, and showed to downward-tending Nature the beautiful form of God. And nature, beholding his beauty insatiate, as one who had in himself all the power of the Administrators, as well as the image of God, smiled with love as she saw the reflection of that most beautiful form in the water and its shadow on the earth. And he, seeing this form, a form like his own, in her, in the water, loved it and willed to dwell there . . . .

[34] εἰς τὸ ὄνομα really denotes "in his image," the name being, for Valentinus, attached to the image by the painter (the demiurge) to complete the similarity between original and copy. Clem. Alex., *Stromata*, IV, 13. Cf. Hilgenfeld, p. 299.

[35] Clem. Alex., *Stromata*, II, 8, 36; Hilgenfeld, p. 293. Leisegang, in defending his conception that the origin of the Anthropos is to be sought in the Hellenistic macrocosm speculation, identifies the ὁ ζῶν αἰων (Clem. Alex. *Stromata*. IV, 13; Hilgenfeld, p. 299) with the Anthropos. This αἰων need not be the Anthropos at all. It might be considered the Pleroma as a whole, or the primal Ogdoad; cf. the ὁ ἄφθαρτος αἰων of Irenaeus I, 30, 2, and the ἄνω αἰων of Epiphanius, 37, 1. The only evidence for cosmogonal associations on the part of the Anthropos, to be found in Egypt, appears in the Coptic Gnostic works. (TU, vol. VIII, pp. 227; 278–9; 384.) Here, however, the Anthropos, as the Man Adamas has already been fused with the revolting demiurge Sabaoth, and thus appears as Sabaoth-Adamas. The cosmogonal associations may thus have been introduced in connection with the figure of Saboath. Irenaeus, I, 11, 1 distinctly says that it was one of the twelve aeons produced by the Anthropos, who created all the "rest of the universe" according to Valentinus. Cf. also Irenaeus, I, 17, 1.

[36] Irenaeus I, 14, 6; 15, 3. The spiritual man of Marcus like the Anthropos of the Poimandres is bisexual, Iren., I, 18, 2.

"Nature, receiving him with whom she was enamoured, wrapped him in her clasp, and they were mingled in one; for they were lovers.

"For this reason man, unlike all other living creatures upon earth, is twofold, being mortal by reason of the body and immortal by reason of the man of eternal substance . . . .

"Nature, mingled in marriage with Man, brought forth a marvel most marvellous. Inasmuch as Man had got from the structure of the heavens the character of the seven Administrators, who were made . . . of fire and air, Nature tarried not, but forthwith gave birth to seven Men, according to the characters of the seven Administrators; and these seven men were bisexual . . . .

"These seven men then . . . were generated in this wise. Nature brought forth their bodies; the earth was the female element and water the male element; and from fire she received the maturity (the seed) and from aether the spirit, and according to the form of Man she produced the bodies. But the Man in them changed from Life and Light into soul and mind, soul from Life and mind from Light."[37]

The account of the Poimandres testifies, together with the evidence quoted from Valentinus, that a divine element indwelling in humanity is derived from and related to the transcendent Anthropos. Yet it has a number of peculiarities. In the first place it makes the Anthropos himself the agent in bringing about the union of divine element and Physis, a thing which his metaphysic did not permit Valentinus to do. Secondly, it describes the manner in which the union was achieved in a graphic way, placing the Anthropos into an amorous situation which we have not previously encountered.[38]

Of our Egyptian sources only the Gospel of Mary echoes this

[37] *Poimandres*, §§ 14-17; text according to Reitzenstein, translation according to Scott.

[38] A distinct echo of the descent of the Anthropos armed with many powers and his creation of the first man is preserved in a Hermetic text which Reitzenstein has recently culled from an Arabic MS. of the eighth century. The Anthropos here appears as Harus (Horus). The amorous motif is missing, Horus fashioning the first man, Adamanus after the fashion of Jahve and supplying him with powers taken from the stars; cf. Reitzenstein u. Schaeder, *Studien*, pp. 112-8.

situation, and that in a different connection. It relates that at the very beginning of things the Father, the Protanthropos, conjured up for himself his image and beheld it in the waters of pure light surrounding him, thereby giving birth to Ennoia, who since she is his image can also be called Protanthropos.[39]

The Egyptian Anthropos is connected not only with the divine element in man, but with the soteriological powers as well.

Jeu in the Coptic-Gnostic works gathers from a group of fettered aeons the light-elements which their revolt has temporarily estranged from the Treasury of Light. Other elements, such as reside in men and are released from the clutches of matter at the death of the body come before him as well. If they are pure, Jeu returns them to the Treasury, if not, he hands them to the Maiden of Light to be sent back for further incarnation.[40] Jeu bears here a remarkable resemblance to the Primal Man and the Third Messenger of the Manichees, who, as we recall are located in the sun and there perform the tasks ascribed here to Jeu. How the resemblance is to be explained has not yet been determined by scholars.[41]

In the Manichean system, the Primal Man functions as savior not only in transmitting the heavenly souls homeward; he appears in human guise among men on earth. The same is true of the Anthropos in the systems of the Valentinian school. Irenaeus heard it said that, according to Valentinus, Jesus was emanated from the Anthropos and his partner Ecclesia.[42] He later reports that certain Valentinians believed the savior as Son of Man to be a descendent of the Anthropos, that is one of the aeons produced by the Anthropos[43] while still others made him the offspring of the Pleroma as a whole, that is of the ultimate Propator (the

---

[39] SBA, 1896, p. 843. For parallels in Syria cf. below, pp. 70-2.
[40] TU, VIII, p. 372.
[41] Cyril of Jerusalem makes Mani dependent upon Egyptian speculation such as came to him at the hands of Scythianus and Terebinthus (Cat. 6, 20 ff.) It is more probable that Mani and the Coptic works draw upon a common (Syrian?) source.
[42] Iren., I, 11, 1
[43] Ibid., I, 12, 4.

Anthropos) in whom the whole pleroma is contained.[44] A longer and more complex account he gives of what is said to be Marcus' view in the matter. Here, we are told, the Jesus who appeared on the earth was generated by four powers who were the representatives of the first Tetrad of emanations. In this group of four the Anthropos was represented by the "power of the Highest" (Lc. 1, 33.) Thus Jesus can call himself the Son of Man.[45]

Manicheans and Valentinians agree in the belief that the Anthropos is active in the work of salvation. They disagree in so far as the Valentinians' savior is an emanation and son of the Anthropos, rather than the latter's personal manifestation.[46] Whether this phenomenon itself represents an earlier or a later stage in the development of the soteriological role of the Anthropos remains to be seen.

There is no evidence to show that in Egypt the Anthropos played an eschatological role, except it be found in the statement that Jeu, after he has gathered the estranged light-essence, is himself elevated to a position within the Treasury of Light.[47]

3. Turning from the pallid Anthropos of our Egyptian Gnostics to his Syrian counterpart, we find the latter more liberally attested to but often shrouded in a persiflage of philosophic terminology that veils his inner being. What is more, the use of philosophic terminology brings with it a realinement of those central concepts in which the Anthropos Theology expresses itself. In both Mesopotamia and Egypt, for instance, the divine element indwelling in man was considered a portion or manifestation of the one person known as Anthropos or Primal Man. In the systems of the later Syrian Gnostics it sometimes appears as the immanent counterpart of the transcendent personality. The two manifesta-

[44] Ibid.
[45] Ibid., I, 15, 3.
[46] Of course Augustine speaks of the Manichean Christ as the son of the Primal Man (cf. above, p. 32), but, as we have seen, the use of "son" does not imply emanation from the Anthropos. Cf. Baur, pp. 208–9 and above, p. 27, n. 51.
[47] TU, VIII, p. 372.

tions are determined in their nature by the metaphysical postulates of the Greek philosophers, which attribute to existence absolute and relative forms. Thus we have frequently in Syria two Anthropoi, designated by the names Anthropos and Son of Man respectively.[48]

Of the first of these, Monoimus the Arabian speaks as the All[49] whose symbol is the iota, the numeral letter in which all the numerals are potentially but not expressly contained.[50] To the Christian Naasene redactor of the pagan Naasene Document, he, the Anthropos Adamas,[51] a blessed being of blessed nature[52] is the "pure mind," the unshapen brain,[53] the unshapen Logos (Mind).[54] He stands beyond the pale of both the physical and the intelligible world, yet contains within himself in potential form the elements of these worlds. Thus he may be called an hermaphrodite.[55] The Ophites of Irenaeus I. 30, echo the same conception when they speak of the First Man as Bythos, the Father of All.

The second Anthropos, the Son of Man, Monoimus considers the objectivation of the transcendent monad. If the Anthropos proper is the iota, the latter is the one iota.[56] He is a being generated by the Anthropos independently of time but subject to passion. All this cosmos is actually produced from some part of him and has its unity in him, but no one of its elements manifests him completely.

While Hippolytus and Irenaeus in their descriptions of the Naasenes and Ophites mention but do not characterize the Son of Man, the Christian Naasene redactor is quite discursive on the subject. The second Man, whom he prefers to call the "Perfect

[48] Hippolytus, V, 6, 4–5.
[49] Ibid., VIII, 12, 2.
[50] Ibid., VIII, 12, 6.
[51] Ibid., V, 7, 2 and 30.
[52] Ibid., V, 8, 2.
[53] Ibid., V, 8, 13.
[54] Ibid., V, 7, 33.
[55] Ibid., V, 6, 6; 7, 14.
[56] Ibid., VIII, 13, 4.

Man"[57] is the shapen or moulded Mind from which the entire family of things is fashioned,[58] in short the "moulded Son of Man."[59] Mind, however, not only contains within itself the cosmos, it is in turn contained within the world as an active agent and an indwelling principle. Thus the Son of Man may be likened to Oceanus, the great stream flowing downward from above and upward again from below.[60] This stream is Reason, the ineffable and mystical Logos, the seed of things, to be found in men after their seventh year.[61] While his voice is heard within men, the actual shape in which this Son of Man descends from above is quite unknown.[62] He passes into the body as the Perfect Man Within, is overwhelmed by passion and must needs be reborn to return upward and become a God once more.[63]

For this indwelling Son of Man, the Ophites of Irenaeus have an indwelling Sophia. Whether she has replaced the Son of Man or is indigenous in her role here is difficult to determine. This much is clear, that Adam, when endowed by her with the divine element from above, begins to revere the Anthropos,[64] and that at her hands, humanity is the recipient of a message the burden of which is the same Anthropos.[65]

The earliest of our Syrian sources, the pagan Naasene Document quoted by Hippolytus, presents a different picture. Its author is not a philosopher but a religious mystic and syncretist. He thinks in terms of God, the intermediary sphere and the world, and searches among the traditions of mankind to find evidence and confirmation of his belief that in man there dwell elements of divinity. Among the many traditions that have come to his knowledge there is one that connects itself with the Anthropos. The Anthropos as our pagan author knew him is not an abstrac-

[57] Ibid., V, 8, 5, 20, 21, 38, 39; 9, 18.
[58] Ibid., V, 7, 35; cf. V, 8, 5.
[59] Ibid., V, 7, 33.
[60] Ibid., V, 8, 19–20; cf. V, 9, 15–19.
[61] Ibid., V, 7, 20–22.
[62] Ibid., V, 8, 14.
[63] Ibid., V, 7, 39–40; 8, 18–21.
[64] Irenaeus, I, 30, 6.
[65] Ibid., I, 30, 11.

tion, he is a celebrity, "the Great, Most Glorious and Perfect Man" as he calls him.⁶⁶ What interested him in this celebrity is that fact the from him is said to be derived the "inner man" who has "fallen into man from Adam the Primal Man above,"⁶⁷ in other words "the spiritual man who is born again, being in every respect of the same substance with that (heavenly) man."⁶⁸

The author of the pagan Naasene Document found in the Anthropos tradition more than mere confirmation of his belief that humanity is somehow related to the Gods. He discovered there as well an interesting account of how this relationship had been established. It is contained in a story of the creation of the protoplast, a story which the author takes pains to quote in detail and to which he ascribes Chaldean provenience. The account, edited to be intelligible apart from the context and to discount those elements accruing to it at the hand of the writer and his over-writer, reads as follows:

> The Chaldeans [say that the first man to come into being was] Adam. And he (they say) is the man whom the earth brought forth as the only one.⁶⁹ And (that) he lay inanimate, unmoved, motionless as an effigy, being an image of the man above [namely] (the celebrated Adamas), [having been] produced by the agency of many powers (concerning whom there is individually much discussion). In order, therefore, that finally the great man above ⁷⁰ may be overpowered (by whom, as they say, the whole family named on earth and in the heavens has been formed), to him [the earthly man] was given also a soul,⁷¹ that through the soul, the enslaved creation ⁷² of the great and most

---

⁶⁶ Hipp. V, 7, 8.
⁶⁷ Ibid., V, 7, 36.
⁶⁸ Ibid., V, 8, 10. The author sometimes identifies and sometimes distinguishes between the soul and the inner man.
⁶⁹ Reitzenstein reads "body alone," *Studien*, p. 161. Quite probable.
⁷⁰ Reitzenstein construes ἄνωθεν with ἐδόθη and reads "from above there was given" (ibid., p. 162). Possible but not necessary, since ἄνωθεν can be used interchangeably with ἄνω; so Hipp., IV, 14, 14, and particularly V, 7, 36.
⁷¹ Reitzenstein considers the "upper man" to be given, in the story, as a soul to the earthly man (*Poimandres*, p. 84, n. 7).
⁷² πλάσμα.

glorious and perfect man (for even so they call him), might suffer and be restrained.[73]

The "Chaldean Tale," as we shall call it, is of importance for the analysis of the Anthropos tradition in a number of ways. It is, in all probability, the oldest of the datable elements of this tradition. It takes us out of the littoral Orient and back to Mesopotamia. It shows us that in Mesopotamia there existed long before Manicheism and the systems of the Syrian Gnostics a mythological celebrity, known as the Great or Upper Man, and said to have been embroiled in a primordial conflict of disastrous results. To the author of the pagan Naasene Document the tale was significant because it gave further proof of the presence of a divine element in man, the spirit, the "inner man" of whom we have heard him speak, and to whom he no doubt found reference in the "image" which the earthly man possesses.[74]

The pagan Naasene Document, we therefore conclude, knows but one Anthropos, a heavenly celebrity whose image is found in man and represents there a spiritual power, the "inner man." This Anthropos is not a metaphysical postulate, he is a mythological character.

The Manicheans connected the Primal Man not only with a divine element indwelling in man, but also with the saviors who come to redeem that element. Is there evidence that this conception was shared by the Syrian Gnostics?

In the case of Monoimus it is difficult to arrive at any conclusion in the matter. We have only one statement upon which to base an opinion. Hippolytus has the Arabian say that "every creature ignorant of the Son (of Man) considers him the offspring

---

[73] Hipp., V, 7, 6–8. As the last sentence indicates the names applied to the Anthropos in the Chaldean Tale proper were descriptive. Adamas is the designation added by the author of the pagan Naasene Document in relating the story. It is therefore placed in parentheses. Originally the Chaldean Tale may well have been told in an Aramaic dialect.

[74] The "image of God" is a divine entity according to Philo (*de Somniis*, ed. Cohn-Wendland, I, 239; *de Opificio Mundi*, 25), Paul (Col. 1, 15) and the Simonians (Hipp., VI, 3–6). For Philo it is the Logos, for Paul the Christ, and for the Simonians the Spirit of God.

of a woman."[75] That may signify either that Christ, "incarnate of the virgin" is not the true Son of Man, or that Christ is the Son of Man but that his nature must be docetically interpreted. The statement is therefore valueless as evidence.

According to Hippolytus the Christian Naasenes shared the Manichean opinion. In his account of their theology he tells us that "they derive, partly from the gentiles the generation of the man Adam (the upper man) . . . and ficticiously apply it to Christ."[76] They are said to cherish a direct literary tradition that connects them with Christ through James and Mariamme.[77] "They believe that the three elements, rational, psychic and earthly, which compose the Anthropos Adamas, have descended simultaneously into Christ and speak through him."[78]

The Christian Naasene redactor of the pagan Naasene Document partly substantiates the Heresiarch's statements. The views of the former are most lucidly presented in his interpretation of the words "I am the true gate." These words, he tells us, signify that Jesus is the sole way toward the rebirth of the spiritual man,[79] and the agency that turned the flow of the Jordan (i.e., the stream of spiritual life flowing from the Perfect Man), the transcendent Adamas. Jesus is himself the manifestation of the "moulded mind," the "perfect man who is imaged from the unportrayable one above."[80] We have in this instance, then a closer parallel to the Manichean conception of the redeemer redeeming himself than was furnished in the Egyptian systems, for the redeemer is here the full revelation of the Logos or Reason which dwells in mankind.

Exactly what the views of the Christian Ophites of Irenaeus may have been on this subject is again difficult to determine. Whether this is due to a crossing of two streams of influence in the growth of their theology, or whether our accounts are at fault is

[75] Hipp., VIII, 11, 3.
[76] Ibid., V, 7, 2.
[77] Ibid., V, 7, 1.
[78] Ibid., V, 6, 5–7.
[79] Ibid., V, 8, 21.
[80] Ibid.

not apparent. On the one hand we are told that Christ (the divine element that dwells in Jesus) is the son of both the First Man, the Second Man (Son of Man) and the Mother of Life.[81] On the other hand it is said that he uses the name Son of Man to designate himself as the son of the First Man,[82] a statement that probably presupposes his identity with the Second Man from whom he is otherwise differentiated. In view of the fact that the life principle indwelling in man comes to him ultimately also from the First Man, the latter statement would place the Ophite Christology on a level with the Christian Naasene and the Manichean, while the former would bring it into line with the Egyptian Anthropos theology. There is little choice between the two possibilities.

The author of the pagan document which the Christian Naasenes interpolated does not, if we construe the sense of his words correctly, know of a soteriological manifestation of the Anthropos. True, he attributes objective reality to none of the saviors in whose names salvation was being proclaimed throughout the Hellenistic world. Most of them are to him symbols of the soul. Hermes, who as Psychopomp aspires to a higher role, is not to be distinguished from "reason" as a natural part of man's endowment.[83] Even a soteriological form of the Anthropos he would have been prone to transfer from the sphere of the objective to that of the subjective. But no such transfer is made. Anthropos and man are related because of the creative activity of the former. Perceiving the avidity with which our pagan author syncretized verything that came under his observation we can draw from his use of the Anthropos tradition but one conclusion. The Anthropos as he knew him did not manifest himself in the form of a savior.

The eschatological role of the Anthropos has at best only one echo in Syrian Gnosticism and that is seriously open to question. It is preserved in a statement concerning the Christ of the Ophites of Irenaeus, who, as we recall, is either a son or a manifestation of the lower or second heavenly man. Of him we are told that he

[81] Iren., I, 30, 1.
[82] Ibid., I, 30, 13.
[83] Hipp., V, 7, 35–7.

is seated by the side of the demiurge receiving to himself the souls of those who have in life known him, and that having gathered the light-essence that is embraced in the world in the form of souls, carries it off to form an incorruptible aeon.[84] The idea of the session with the demiurge, recalls the Jewish and Christian view of the execution of judgment by the Son of Man. Hence the uncertainty of the testimony. The carrying off of the light-essence and the formation of an incorruptible aeon, on the other hand recall the reunion of the Primal Man and his lost self, and their return to the home in which they existed at the beginning.

The Anthropos as we have met him in Egypt and Syria is in many respects similar to the Manichean Primal Man, even though in some of his manifestations he is a century older than his Mesopotamian counterpart. We have here the same transcendent and pre-existent figure, similarly connected with the creation of man and with a divine element indwelling in man. The basic identity of the two cannot be questioned; yet each has his individuality. The latter lacks the plasticity and the dramatic vicissitudes of the former. Abstractions and shadowy existence characterize his being. The relations between him and his psychic and soteriological manifestations are often altered, so that reason is his immanent counterpart and the savior his son or emanation. Indeed the soteriological and eschatological elements of his role have a tendency to disappear entirely. Even so, the earliest elements of the Western tradition show a tendency to revert to the Manichean type, for they record some traces of the primordial conflict and lead us back to Chaldea. How these similarities and differences are to be reconciled is a matter to be considered after we have followed the fourth strand in the Anthropos tradition, the Mandean.

[84] Iren., I, 30, 14.

CHAPTER IV

THE MANDEAN ANTHROPOS

In the reconstruction of later oriental syncretism as a whole, and the analysis of the Anthropos speculation in particular, the Mandeans have latterly come to play an important part.
1. Comprising a baptist communion still surviving in the swampy lowlands of Mesopotamia, the Mandeans are known to us from their voluminous sacred books brought to Europe in the latter half of the last century by prominent orientalists, and since made readily accessible in the editions and translations of Lidzbarski.[1] Historical and philological inquiry soon revealed that the Mandeans represent one of the sects classed in Mohammedan times as Sabean and that their language is an Aramaic dialect akin to Syriac and to the idiom of the Talmud Babli. But the theology and religious lore of the Mandeans remained an enigma until approached by students of Hellenistic antiquities like Bousset.[2] This, it has now developed, bears the unmistakable stamp of the great syncretistic era of ancient times, a fact that is corroborated by the name Mandean, i.e., Gnostic, as well as by the close relation between many of the Mandean conceptions and those of the Manichean Turfan texts. Manichean and Mandean religions are contemporary elements of Mesopotamian Gnosis.

Now Mandean tradition records that the sect migrated to its Mesopotamian center from some other place.[3] Lidzbarski, in working on the texts, collected a goodly amount of evidence to show that the original home of the sect was the Hauran district

[1] Cf. my "*Mandaic Bibliography*" JAOS, vol 46, No. 1 (1926), pp. 49 55.
[2] Bousset, HP, pp. 176-7.
[3] *Das Johannesbuch der Mandäer*, ed. Lidzbarski, vol. 2 (1915), pp. 123-38 (abbrev. JB.), *Mandäische Liturgien*, ed. Lidzbarski (1920), pp. 209-212 (abbrev. ML.).

between Palestine and Arabia. In the Palestinian stage of their development they represented a syncretizing type of Judaism, of the kind known from the Christian heresiologists and from Philo.[4]

These observations at once raise the question as to how much the Mandeans antedate the days of Mani, a question more readily put than answered. Reitzenstein endeavored to prove that the apocalypse found at the beginning of the Ginza is more ancient than the Logia source of the Synoptic Gospels, but without success.[5] Yet extensive similarities in form and thought between the Mandaic Liturgies and the Odes of Solomon, show that they flourished in an atmosphere that existed as early as the first Christian century.[6] That being the case, the strong tradition by which they declare themselves to be the disciples of John the Baptist may contain at least this grain of truth, that the formation of their sect was due in part to the influence of men perpetuating in one form or another the movement begun by the Baptist.[7]

The Mandean evidence for the Anthropos may for this reason be highly important and lead us into the proximity of Judaism. But two facts must be constantly kept in mind. Since our texts present the Mandean theology in a reconciled form of at least the third or fourth century A.D., specific reasons must be given to prove greater antiquity for individual elements thereof. Moreover, since the Anthropos' role has, as we shall see, been divided among a number of figures, not everything said about them relates to the Anthropos.

2. One of the Mandean figures recently associated by scholars with the Anthropos, is Manda d'Haye, the "Knowledge of Life."[8]

[4] Cf. the introductions to JB, and ML, and to *"Ginza, das grosse Buch der Mandäer,"* ed. Lidzbarski, in "Quellen der Religionsgeschichte," vol. 13 (1926). (The Ginza is quoted as "right" and "left" and abbreviated RG, and LG.)

[5] This is the thesis of Reitzenstein, MB.

[6] Cf. IE, pp. 84–92 and the summary of my paper, *"The Odes of Solomon and the Protognostic Hymns of the Manichean and Mandean Liturgies,"* Proceedings of the American Oriental Society (1926), No. 33.

[7] Paul met such men in Greece. Cf. Acts 19, 1–3. Simon Magus was considered by some to be a disciple of the Baptist, Clem. Hom. II, 23.

[8] Brandt, *Mandäische Religion* (1889), p. 189 (abbrev. MR,) and IE, p. 54.

THE MANDEAN ANTHROPOS

A son of the Great First Life, and the ultimate progenitor of many heavenly beings, Manda d'Haye appears in a number of capacities, first as the champion of Light in the primordial conflict of Light and Darkness, then as the guardian of the soul in its descent to the body. Having implanted the heavenly Mana in its corporeal frame, he ordains guardians and messengers who shall comfort and instruct it. Indeed throughout all the ages and generations he himself appears in the world, a messenger baptized by John, teaching the way of life, leading the souls upward at death, establishing them in the Treasure-House of Life and functioning at the end of the world as the judge of the holy and the wicked.

In the general range of his activities Manda d'Haye potently recalls the Manichean Primal Man, yet it is a question whether and to what extent he may, even as the latter, be a manifestation of the Anthropos. A careful consideration of a few of his functions may serve to justify our hesitancy in the matter. Let us take, for example his role in the primordial conflict. It develops along lines familiar to us from the Manichean texts, but entails a subtle difference. The Primal Man, as we shall see, is essentially a defeated champion. Only rarely is the note of tragedy dispelled from the story, when we hear that the loss of his "self" was dictated to the First Man by a strategy looking toward an eventual victory.[9] Manda d'Haye, on the other hand, is predominantly victorious.[10] No one ever really questions the fact. The best that the author of the third book of the right Ginza can do is to consider the dire possibilities attendant upon the mission of the champion. Thus Manda d'Haye, when appointed to subdue the rebellious powers of darkness, plies the First Life with a series of questions:

> When I search for you where shall I look?
> When I am in trouble, upon whom shall I rely?

But even here, we are told:

> The Mana answered in majesty and said to Manda d'Haye:
> Thou shalt not be separated from us.[11]

[9] Cf. above, pp. 18–21, and below, pp. 99–101.
[10] So for instance in the great third book RG.
[11] RG, p. 68, 14–18.

A passage in the Book of John is practically the only echo of the Manichean conception. Here the First Son of the Great Life, under conditions similar to those obtaining in the portion of Book 3 of the Ginza, already alluded to, asks:

> If I descend, who will bring me up again?
> If I fall who will hold me?
> Who will enfold for me my soul, lest we fall into the burning water?
> Who will produce a solidification (on the surface of the water) lest we fall into the murky deep?
> Who will set my crown upon my head and arrange the forelocks of brilliance?
> When the Evil Ones hold me a prisoner in their castle, who will be my liberator? [12]

The last verse of the passage is especially suggestive. The fate which Manda d'Haye anticipates is that of the Manichean Primal Man. But even in this instance he returns unscathed.

In the Manichean texts, as we have seen, the champion loses a portion of his self, which remains in the world as the soul. The struggle of Manda d'Haye, on the other hand, is almost entirely disassociated from the animation of material existence. The only evidence to the contrary is again a section of the Book of John, where we read:

> ... the messenger was sent to overthrow the power of the rebels. Lo, they brought living water and poured it into the murky water; they brought shining light and threw it into dismal darkness; they brought the pleasing wind and cast it into the raging wind; they brought the living fire and cast it into the devouring fire; they brought the soul, the pure Mana and cast her into the worthless body.[13]

The mingling of two groups of five elements each, and the connection of this act with the coming of the champion, again recall the Anthropos theology of the Manichees, but are by no means integral part of the Mandean system that lies before us in the bulk of the texts. True, Manda d'Haye, in an entirely different

[12] JB, p. 223.
[13] Ibid., p. 56.

connection shares with others the honor of placing the soul in the body of Adam, but the soul is never represented as a portion of his being or person under those circumstances.[14]

In what the sources tell of him as savior, there is nothing that would be intelligible only in the light of the Anthropos speculation. In this capacity he may with equal justice be considered a type of the Gnostic Soter, or of the person of "Wisdom" as she was known in the more westerly Gnostic circles.[15] What is over and above the universal Gnostic substratum in his role as savior, namely his baptism by John and his *descensus ad inferos*, merely indicate that it is a Christian-Gnostic type of Soter whom he approximates.

From what has already been said it will be evident that while Manda d'Haye and the Anthropos are in many respects similar, the two figures are fundamentally unrelated. With this conclusion the majority of those who have busied themselves with the Mandean texts are in agreement. Most scholars consider Manda d'Haye a form of the ancient Babylonian Marduk.[16] Yet, it must also be evident that at one time people did regard Manda d'Haye and the Anthropos as identical. That is shown by the injection of incongruous elements into the Mandean tradition, such as those which anticipate for Manda d'Haye the fate of the Anthropos, or connect the mingling of the five elements with his activity. It is apparent also from the name "*gabra qadmaya*," Primal Man, sometimes applied to Manda d'Haye in the Mandean sources.[17] This fact of the interrelation of the two figures is of no significance so far as the origin of the Mandean figure is concerned. For the origin of the Anthropos it may yet be of importance.

3. In searching for genuine and more readily intelligible evidence of the Anthropos in the Mandean sources it is best to

[14] In the LG the soul and the messenger are related, as Reitzenstein contends, IE, pp. 53–5. But cf. below, pp. 68–70.
[15] HP, pp. 242–51.
[16] HP, loc. cit., and Kessler, art. "*Mandäer*," Prot. Realenzyk. (3rd ed.), vol. XII, p. 182.
[17] MR, p. 189; MB., p. 46; ML, p. 3.

begin with an analysis of the conceptions associated with the name Adam. The name is employed in a number of different ways. It designates the protoplast as an individual,[18] the earthly element of his physical structure,[19] the corresponding divine element,[20] and a heavenly being independent, in part, of the whole of material existence.[21] In order to distinguish them one from another, descriptive adjectives are liberally employed, thus giving rise to the names "corporeal Adam," "hidden Adam" or "Adakas," and "Adam the Great." Our interest naturally attaches to the figures denoted by the last two names.

Adam the Great, is little more than a shadow flitting across the many pages of Mandean texts. He is mentioned by name as the progenitor of the Hibil-Sitil-Anosh group of messengers in the introductory words of Books 11 and 12 of the right Ginza.[22] His name is said to be the property of the Great Life, the supreme being, and was at one time willfully adopted by Bhaq-Uthra, that is Abatur.[23] He is thought of as identical with Shaq-Uthra because the latter is called the "Great and First."[24]

The passages in which the Great Adam is thus explicitly mentioned are all later than the main body of the Mandean writings. The captions of Books 11 and 12 of the right Ginza do not correspond to the material of the books to which they are prefaced. The mention of Bhaq-Uthra's adopted name interrupts the continuity of thought in the context where it appears, while Shaq-Uthra is identified with Adam Rabba only in very late texts that are virtually extra-canonical. These facts have led Brandt to believe that the figure of the Great Adam is the product of modern Mandaic theology which regards the divine world as an ideal copy of the earthly world.[25] While modern speculation may have

[18] RG, p. 15, 9.
[19] LG, p. 456, 29–30.
[20] RG, p. 243, 4.
[21] ML, p. 110, 3–4.
[22] RG, pp. 251 and 269.
[23] RG, p. 293, 30–32.
[24] JB, p. 230, n. 5.
[25] MR, pp. 37–8.

been the occasion for the reëmergence of the heavenly Adam, and for the creation of the name Adam Rabba, the figure itself is certainly older, and that for a number of reasons.

In the first place, that which is told of the Great Adam in the late strata of our texts corresponds, in part at least, to earlier tradition. Thus the partial identity of Bhaq-Uthra and the heavenly Man appears also from the Liturgies and Book 5 of the right Ginza, where as Abatur he plays the role of the Anthropos in the Poimandres.[26]

Secondly, there appears in the main body of the texts an Adam, who, while he bears no distinguishing attributive, is probably the same Adam Rabba. In the Liturgies he casts the soul into the material body of the protoplast.[27] In Book 3 of the right Ginza he is styled "King of the Uthras" and together with his wife Hawwa (Eve), who is formed in the likeness of a cloud of light," he is revered by all men.[28] Heaven is twice referred to as his garden.[29]

All this is evidence to show that the Adam Rabba of the late tradition was known at the time the main body of the texts was composed. Perhaps we can go one step further and say that in the age preceding the codification of the bulk of the tradition, even more was made of this figure than later.

There exist in the texts before us passages which owe their difficulties to the author's confusion of the heavenly man and the protoplast on earth. In Book 3 of the right Ginza we have an extended account of how Ruha, the evil spirit, tempts a member of the antediluvian household.[30] The person is identified in the introduction as one of the sons of Adam[31] and later mentioned in the text proper as "Adam the son of Adam."[32] If the paternal Adam were, as the introduction would lead one to believe, the

[26] Cf. below, pp. 70–2.
[27] ML, p. 100. That this is the sense of the passage is vouched for by RG, pp. 109–10, where Adakas accompanies the soul to the body.
[28] RG, p. 118, 22–7.
[29] JB, p. 222, 1; ML, p. 248, 10.
[30] RG, pp. 127–33.
[31] RG, p. 127, 26.
[32] RG, p, 129, 7.

mundane protoplast; the tale would introduce into the legends of the first days an entirely new and incongruous figure. It seems more likely therefore, that the tale was originally told of the protoplast himself and was later transferred to one of his sons. The Adam who is the father of Adam must then be the heavenly Man.

A similar confusion may underlie a passage in the rubrics of the Liturgies, where Adam the protoplast is represented as the father of Bihram the Great.[33] Now Bihram is otherwise a member of the heavenly host, hence his father must too once have been the Adam Rabba.

That the heavenly Man was once more important than at the time when the majority of our texts were composed, can also be shown in another way. The heavenly hierarchy as we usually find it, presents the following sequence of rank and emanation: The Life, Manda d'Haye, Hibil, Sitil, Anosh and the Uthras. In this form it represents the coalescence of two distinct theologies. The one embraces The Life, The Knowledge of Life and The Treasures (of Life). It is complete in itself. The other is represented by the Hibil-Sitil-Anosh group of messengers and is incomplete. It demands at its head the heavenly Adam, for without him the trio of his descendents could scarcely have aspired to the prominence they hold. Of the two superimposed theologies, the latter is probably the earlier, first, because it takes us into the proximity of Judaism, whence the Mandean sect sprang, secondly, because it has been mutilated and adapted in the newer order.[34] The Great Adam who here and there appears in our texts was therefore at one time the most important person in the Mandean pleroma. The statement that the name Adam is the exclusive property of the Life, must be an echo of this conception.[35]

Adam Rabba and his descendents, are of course, the corresponding Biblical antediluvians in that celestial character which they acquired in the legends of the post-canonical period of Jewish thought.[36] Yet there is something that places them all one step

[33] ML, p. 120.
[34] The other must belong to the Mesopotamian period of Mandean development.
[35] Cf. above, p. 60.
[36] Cf. below, pp. 153–7.

in advance of the Jewish development. That is in the first place their elevation from the rank of "heroes" to that of bona-fide divinities, as shown by the supreme position assigned to Adam, and by the element "il" in the names of Sitil (Seth) and Hibil (Abel). It is evident also from Adam's activity in connection with the creation of the protoplast. In spite of the fact that in the case of the Great Adam, in whom we are interested at present, we have so few particulars by which to judge, it does not seem amiss to say that the transforming influence was the identification of the Jewish protoplast with the Anthropos. In name, position and activity he corresponds to the Anthropos of the earliest Syrian Gnostics, and Syria is the territory whence he is sprung.

4. We come, now, to the other Adam, Adakas. He is described in two distinct ways. In the left Ginza we are told that he reposed in the secret treasure-chambers of Life[37] until sent forth into the world to fall or be thrown into the body,[38] more specifically the body of the protoplast.[39] He is ignorant of the reasons for his being sent and fears lest he be cut off from the house of his father.[40] But by the intervention of divine agencies, the messengers, he is informed of his destiny and finally released from his bonds to return to his heavenly home.

The context in which this Adam stands in the left Ginza stamps him as the personification of the divine element which resides in the world and in each individual man.[41] But Adakas is more than merely an immanent element of human nature. Even in the left Ginza the epithet "hidden" no longer is determined by his indwelling in the human frame. It refers to the nature of the place whence he came, namely the "concealed treasure-house of God."[42] In other texts he functions as a free agent among the heavenly beings. The Liturgies name him as one of the Uthras

[37] LG, p. 487, 29–30.
[38] LG, p. 480, 16–17.
[39] LG, p. 432, 6–8.
[40] LG, p. 499, 18.
[41] IE, pp. 43–59.
[42] RG, p. 244, 14; LG, p. 459, 23; p. 487, 25–9; p. 493, 6–7.

who are to be praised and revered by all men.[43] He accompanies the soul in its descent to the body of Adam the protoplast.[44] Together with Anana d'Nhura he produces the messengers of salvation,[45] in fact he himself functions as an ambassador of Life.[46]

That we have here one and the same person described in two distinct ways is guaranteed by the name common to both representations as well as by Book 10 of the right Ginza, where an attempt has been made to merge the two descriptions into one account of the creation and salvation of the protoplast.[47]

A number of reasons indicate that Adakas is a manifestation of the Anthropos. In the left Ginza he stands in that peculiar relation to the messengers characteristic of the Manichean system and its conception of the Primal Man's divided personality.[48] The duality of his role, moreover, shows that there has been a *rapprochement* between him and Adam Rabba. Particularly, we note that he corresponds to the "inner Man" of the pagan Naasene document of Syria.[49] Together with Adam Rabba he must therefore belong to the earlier stage of Mandean theology and to the Anthropos tradition of Syria which this stage represents.

5. In a number of Gnostic systems previously examined, the saviors were considered the manifestations of the one transcendent Anthropos. Is there evidence of such a conception among the Mandeans?

Of messengers of salvation the Mandeans know four, Manda d'Haye, and the trio Hibil, Sitil and Anosh. The first we have already rejected from among the number of those figures connected with the Anthropos. Our attention will therefore be confined to the trio.

The first thing to be noted in this connection is that nowhere

[43] ML, p. 145.
[44] RG, pp. 109–10.
[45] RG, p. 118.
[46] RG, pp. 236–7.
[47] RG, pp. 240–49 and Lidzbarski's preface to the Ginza.
[48] Cf. above, p. 22.
[49] Cf. above, p. 50.

do we find direct statements indicating that Hibil, Sitil and Anosh are three manifestations of one and the same transcendent person. Statements like those of the Liturgies "blessed be our father Hibil, Sitil and Anosh" cannot be considered evidence to the contrary.[50] Whatever weight they might have is offset by the syncretizing tendency manifested in the texts as a whole, and by such statements as make them descendents one of another, and of Adam Rabba or Adakas.[51] The question we have raised can be answered only by determining whether the character and actions of the messengers are such as to be intelligible only if they are the manifestations of one transcendent person.

The Mandeans divide the course of the world's history into four ages. Each of these ages has its messenger. Originally the messengers allotted to these periods must have been Adam, Hibil, Sitil and Anosh. The elevation of Adam to a position superior to that of the rest, the introduction of the "Life" theology and Manda d'Haye upset this scheme, caused the almost entire disappearance of Sitil and made Hibil vie with Manda d'Haye as the messenger to the first generations of humanity. Through this collocation with Manda d'Haye, Hibil has gradually come to assimilate the characteristics of the former. Thus he appears as the one who at the beginning wrested from the powers of darkness the secret of their strength.[52] In other texts he creates the world order,[53] chastizes the recalcitrant stellar potentates,[54] and finally acts as judge.[55] If in certain phases of his activity he coincides with the Anthropos this coincidence is due not to his personal relation to that figure, but rather to his assimilation to Manda d'Haye.[56] Together with Sitil, of whom we know almost nothing, he merits no further consideration.

In the case of Anosh, matters are at a different pass. Of all the four messengers, he alone has preserved his original position,

[50] ML, pp. 41 and 106; cf. also Lidzbarski's note ML, p. 41.
[51] RG, p. 251, 13–4; p. 269, 10.
[52] RG, bk. 5, part 1.
[53] Ibid., bk. 10.
[54] Ibid., bk. 5, part 2.
[55] JB, pp. 169–70; p. 218.
[56] Brandt, MR, p. 216; Kessler, PRE (3rd ed.), vol. XII, p. 182.

and that because he is the one sent in the last period of the world's history. That period extended, originally from the flood to sometime shortly after the downfall of Jerusalem. Anosh is therefore the messenger to the age of the Hebrews. Of his activity we have an extended account, of remarkable antiquity. It shows us Anosh in conflict with Jesus the false Messiah. Coming with the clouds of heaven, Anosh heals the blind, the dumb and deaf, the lepers, the crippled and the lame (Is. 53, 5), routs the falsifier Jesus and sending forth from Jerusalem his disciples, returns heavenward. His ascent is followed by the destruction of the city.[57] The man who composed the account undoubtedly regarded this event as a sign of the consummation of Anosh's activity. Since that consummation meant the conclusion of the last period of the world's history, the account cannot have been written at a time far removed from that of the downfall of Jerusalem.[58]

Reitzenstein to whose brilliant analysis of the account we owe these observations finds in the Anosh of the early document a soteriological manifestation of the Anthropos. Three reasons are given in support of this contention:

1. That the literal significance of Anosh is "man," Anthropos.
2. That Anosh is also termed Malala, "word" a name properly that of Adakas.
3. That Anosh is in many respects similar to the New Testament Son of Man (whom Reitzenstein also derives from the Anthropos) though independent of Gospel tradition.[59]

Of the reasons here given, the first two require little discussion. The relations between Anthropos and Anosh, if such there were, can have been determined fundamentally only by traits common to each and all of the trio to which he belongs. The name Anosh,

[57] The account is contained in apocalypse preserved in two versions, as Books 1 and 2 of the R. Ginza.
[58] Reitzenstein, Das mandäische Buch des Herrn der Grösse, Sitzb. Heidel. Akad., 1919, No. 12, pp. 37–8; cf. Lidzbarski, Introduction to the edition of the Ginza, p. xii.
[59] The third contention forms the thesis of MB, the others are mentioned therein on pp. 45–6.

THE MANDEAN ANTHROPOS

even if its literal significance was appreciated by the Mandeans,[60] cannot be used to prove that he is a manifestation of the Anthropos. The cognomen Malala indicates nothing more than that Anosh belongs to a group of heavenly powers associated with the promulgation of truth, a group the limits of which extend far beyond the pale of those whom it would be possible to connect with the Anthropos.[61]

The third contention of Reitzenstein, to which we are thus reduced, necessitates both investigation and elucidation, and in so far as it involves his conviction that all of the elements of the Manichean Anthropos theology are equally old, cannot be fully treated even here.

It is well known to students of Christian tradition that the New Testament Son of Man diverges from the current Jewish Bar Nasha in that he represents not only the apocalyptic Messiah, but a messenger of the Kingdom as well. Anosh in the Mandean apocalypse corresponds to the New Testament type of Bar Nasha. But the description of Anosh can be shown to be independent of New Testament tradition at the two points where there is greatest propinquity of thought. One involves a quotation from the *Sophia* (Wisdom) (Lc. 11, 49), the other a quotation from Isaiah 53, 5 in Lc. 22.[62] Now the Jewish Bar Nasha, Reitzenstein contends, is not a spontaneous development on Jewish soil. He represents a Hebrew adaptation of the ancient Oriental Anthropos. The plus of the New Testament Son of Man over the Jewish Bar Nasha, unintelligible as it is in the light of Jewish sources alone, should have its origin in the prototype of which the Jewish Bar Nasha is an adaptation, namely the Anthropos. Since in its plus, the New Testament figure coincides with Anosh, since Anosh is independent of Gospel tradition and since the Mandeans harbor the Anthropos, therefore Anosh is the soteriological manifestation of the Anthropos.

As in so many other instances, Reitzenstein has here again clearly perceived the problems and possibilities presented by a

[60] MB, p. 45.
[61] Malala is applied also to Jawar, RG, p. 291, 31; and Jokabar, ML, p. 35.
[62] MB, pp. 41–72.

new text. Indeed it may be necessary to accept his contention that in the two points where the Synoptic and Mandean tradition meet, the latter is actually independent of (but not necessarily prior to) the former. It does not follow, however, that because in its description of Anosh it differs together with the Gospels from the known Jewish tradition the Mandaic document is a pure reflection of the third and ultimate source from which both were taken. Anosh and the New Testament Son of Man, where they agree, may be two independent developments from a common stock which is not directly the Anthropos tradition.

As far as the Mandean messengers are concerned, that stock may be the conception of the Adamites current in Jewish circles of the post-Maccabean period. It is a familiar fact that Jewish religious literature of this period embraces many works bearing the names of Adam, Seth, Enoch, Noah and others. The production of these pseudepigrapha requires that the antediluvians as a whole be considered capable of revealing to men the hidden oracles of God. Moreover, some, if not all of the antediluvians were believed destined to return again and to act as forerunners of the consummation.[63] Anosh, together with Hibil and Sitil, may be just such a revealer and forerunner, transferred to a Gnostic sphere and elevated there to a transcendent position.[64] Whether any importance attaches to this supposition in connection with the Son of Man inquiry is a matter to be discussed later. Suffice it to say that the argument connecting Hibil, Sitil and Anosh directly with the Anthropos is not convincing.

The matter of the savior's identity has been approached from yet another angle in the study of the Mandean texts. In the left Ginza we meet a conception of the messenger which in some respects coincides with that already considered, but in other respects goes beyond it. The designations applied to the messenger in the left Ginza are usually the generic terms savior and helper.[65] This savior not only informs the soul of its heavenly origin, he returns at the death of the particular person and at the

[63] Volz, *Jüdische Eschatologie* (1903), pp. 193–4.
[64] This is presupposed by the addition "il" to the names Hibil and Sitil.
[65] Cf. Lidzbarski's introduction to LG, bk. 2.

end of the world, to lead the individual and world soul upward to its home.[66] Twice we are given to understand that he is related to the soul in a peculiar manner, so for instance in the passage where the soul on leaving the body declares:

> I go to meet my image
> And my image come to meet me;
> It fondles and embraces me
> As though I were returning from captivity.[67]

Reitzenstein has given special attention to the words of this text. Soul and messenger are to each other, says he, as the soul and the "maiden in its likeness" in the Fihrist, or as the "self" and Zarathushtra in the Zarathushtra Fragment.[68] All have their common origin in the Anthropos theology where messenger and soul are the two manifestations of the one divided personality.

Now the term "image" as used in the Mandean texts in connection with individuals, has a variety of connotations.[69] It is true, however, that no one of them is as applicable in the passage under discussion as that which Reitzenstein has quoted from the Fihrist. As we have previously seen, the "maiden in the likeness of the soul," who according to An-Nadim meets the departing spirit, is probably the Iranian *daena*, the hypostasized conscience, a being independent of the Anthropos theology even in the Manichean tradition.[70]

At first glance the interpretation of the Fihrist thus adopted, might seem to set aside a possible relation between the messenger of the left Ginza and the Anthropos. Such is not the case. There is a difference between the soul's image in the left Ginza and the "maiden" of the Fihrist. The former is more than merely the spiritual complement of the soul. It is also the messenger of salvation.[71] In this respect, then, the Zarathushtra Fragment

[66] Cf. for instance LG, pp. 472–3.
[67] Ibid., pp. 559, 29–32; 461, 31.
[68] IE, pp. 43–59 and its place in the scheme of the book.
[69] Cf. the glossary in the index of the Ginza under "Abbild." The closest parallel is RG, p. 178, 5, where the evil powers say to their God, "thou art our image and we are thy image" and demand protection for this reason.
[70] Cf. above, p. 35, n. 101.
[71] LG, p. 461, 31.

furnishes a closer parallel. We should therefore be inclined to regard the passage from the left Ginza that is under consideration, as one the thought of which is determined by the Anthropos theology. In origin and character, however, it is late, for it shows us the Iranian *daena*, which to Mani was still an independent theological element, drawn into the vortex of the conceptions centering around the Anthropos. Hence it can shed no light upon the ultimate identity of the Mandean saviors themselves.

6. Though the heavenly Adam and Adakas are, strictly speaking, the true and original elements of the Mandean Anthropos theology (which here again lacks the soteriological element), there are in the Mandean system a number of other figures into the description of which have been refracted elements of that particular form of the Anthropos tale previously encountered only in the Poimandres and the Gospel of Mary. Of course both the name and the original associations of the heavenly man have long since been lost from view, but the situation presented in the Egyptian texts is still clearly preserved.

Abatur, the man with the scales, the Iranian Rashnu,[72] is one of the figures affected by this story. In the first part of the fifth book, right Ginza, when Hibil returns from his primordial conflict with the king of darkness, he is addressed by his superior with the words:

> Hail, Hibil, pure Mana. Joshamin has called into being three sons. One guards the nest of his father, one dwells with his father, and one, Abatur, goes to that world in which thou hast been and perceives his image in the black waters, and his image and son is formed for him from the black water.

Hibil then relates:

> When the Life, my father, had thus spoken, Abatur arose and opened the gate and gazed into the black water and at the same hour his likeness was formed in the black water and Ptahil was formed and ascended to the borderland. Abatur considered

---

[72] JB, introduction, pp. xxix-xxx. For Zoroastrian and Manichean references as to the "balance," see Prof. Jackson's observation in Pavry, *The Zor. Doct. of a Fut. Life*, p. 68, n. 42; p. 81, n. 44.

Ptahil and said to his son Ptahil: Come, come Ptahil, thou art
he whom I perceived in the black water.[73]

The episode is referred to also in a part of the last book of the right
Ginza where we read:

> ... then Abatur ... reflected and perceived himself and
> perceived his likeness and he created Adam the man and created
> for him Eve.[74]

The motif recurring in these passages, namely, creation by the
perception of one's image, is clearly that which characterizes the
Poimandres form of the Anthropos tale. In the first it is employed
to explain the creation of the demiurge, a fact that shows why
Abatur's expected descent to the water has been replaced by
Ptahil's ascent to the borderland, but in the last it is still associated
with the creation of man.

The Qolasta, describing Josmir and Sam Smir, two genii
ultimately resolving themselves into the one "protected Mana,"
seems to give us a further glimpse of this peculiar story.

The believer in one instance asks the Life "whose son am I?"
The answer explaining the divine origin of the soul is given in the
following words:

> The protected Mana, ... the great effulgence of the First
> Life, the Son of the great First Life, he who reflected and having
> considered, sought his own, from him came the stock of souls.[75]

The protected Mana is here Josmir, but the identical statement
"he reflected and considered and sought his own" is made also

[73] RG, pp. 173–4.
[74] Ibid., p. 408. The first words of the passage read: "Then Abatur and
Ptahil reflected and perceived himself." As Lidzbarski has noted, one of the
two subjects is superfluous, here as well as in a passage immediately previous
(p. 407 and n. 2), because of the singular of the verb. Lidzbarski, however,
incorrectly chooses to omit Abatur in both cases. Ptahil should be omitted
here because of the parallel passage RG, pp. 173–4, while Abatur should be
omitted, p. 407. The doubling arose from the fact than a Mandean editor
failed to comprehend the distinction between the creative activity of Ptahil
and Abatur. Incidentally, LG, p. 568, 31–4 "the man who perceived himself"
may be another echo of the situation here recorded. The text requires adjustment.
[75] ML, p. 86.

of Sam Smir. How shall we interpret the cryptic utterance? It seems to represent Abatur's or the Anthropos' consideration of and desire for his image. The interpretation is justified by the fact that both of the figures of which the Qolasta speaks are otherwise also associated with the primordial deep. Sam Smir resides "above the billows of water"[76] while Josmir is described as "the man who was joined to the waters,"[77] the description recalling the ascent of Ptahil to the borderland and the descent of Abatur to the deep.

If then, Josmir and Sam Smir in part reflect the Anthropos of the Poimandres, significance may attach to another passage of the Qolasta, where it is said of Sam Smir, that:

> The stock of souls which has come forth from him, will at the last day rejoice in him and will embrace him and they go and behold the outer air and the resplendent dwelling.[78]

The words recall nothing so much as the reappearance of the Manichean Primal Man in company with the world soul at the end of time. How old this bit of the tradition may be it is difficult to say. Certainly the Mandean echoes of the Poimandres tale are later than that tale itself. The final reunion of the souls with the one from whom they have sprung cannot therefore be the original ending of the Poimandres account.

Looking back over those portions of the Mandean theology which we have considered, we gain the following picture of its development and of the place of the Anthropos tradition within the development. The Mandeans began as a Jewish sect which regarded the antediluvians, Adam to Anosh as men who knew the counsels of God and who were destined to return at specified times to reveal these counsels to men. The coming of Anosh they experienced in the period of Jesus' activity in Jerusalem. Furthermore, like the Essenes they regarded the soul as a divine element imprisoned in the body. Brought into contact with the Anthropos tradition, they transcendentalized the first of the messengers,

---

[76] Ibid., p. 16.
[77] Ibid.
[78] Ibid.

Adam, and were taught to consider the soul as something related to him. The deification of Adam led naturally to the transcendentalization of those of his earthly descendents who like him had previously been looked upon as messengers of truth. Their identity and office was preserved to them, but they functioned henceforth as deities. At some time during this stage of the development the Mandeans became acquainted with an approximation of the Poimandres' account of the Anthropos, an account into which they injected Gnostic and Iranian deities at a later time. Subsequent to the period when they were subject to influence from the Anthropos tradition, the Mandeans were familiarized with a "Life Theology" which introduced a new cosmogony, dislocated and finally obscured Adam Rabba and confused the sequence of the messengers' appearance and their character. Finally under Manichean influence they learned to think of a relation of soul and messenger in terms of the Anthropos Theology of Mani.

The knowledge of the Anthropos must have come to the Mandeans while they were yet in Palestine, for Adakas, though he represents the Soul, is really an immanent double of Adam Rabba, after the analogy of the Syrian Son of Man. The value of the Mandean evidence relating to the Anthropos is slight. It serves as a check upon our interpretation of the earlier Syrian sources, and, since the Mandeans must have quit Palestine before or during the campaigns of Hadrian, shows that the Anthropos tradition had, at the beginning of the second century, completed a period of extensive expansion.

CHAPTER V

THE ORIGIN AND ANTIQUITY OF THE ANTHROPOS

THE apocalyptic Son of Man is one of the phases of the ubiquitous Oriental Anthropos. That is the contention advanced by Reitzenstein as a premise to his solution of the Son of Man problem in its New Testament aspects.

We have pursued the Anthropos through the Gnostic maze and found him taking many different shapes. It is by no means impossible that still other manifestations of this figure once existed. Before it will be possible to accept the contention of Reitzenstein, however, it will be necessary to inquire, first, whether the origin and antiquity of the figure are such as to permit his appearance in the sphere of time and place occupied by the Bar Nasha, and secondly, whether and to what extent the comparison of Bar Nasha and Anthropos is necessary and illuminating. The former of these questions will occupy our attention for the present.

1. At first glance it might seem as though Reitzenstein's statement were a contradiction of the obvious, and as though the Anthropos were really a Christian development. Two facts appear to point in this direction, first, that the Anthropos becomes visible on our horizon only after the synoptic Son of Man, and secondly, that the Christian Bar Nasha has formatively influenced the Gnostic Anthropos. The first of these facts is evident from the chronology of the sources already examined, the second from the Gnostic use of the name Son of Man and the presence of the theological Christ in the number of the Anthropos' soteriological manifestations. One might therefore be tempted to conclude that the "Man" is a Gnostic invention, the postulated father of the Christian "Son of Man."

THE ORIGIN AND ANTIQUITY OF THE ANTHROPOS

If we regard the matter more closely, however, the Christian origin of the Anthropos becomes quite impossible and that for a number of reasons:

1. Because our earliest information concerning the Anthropos comes from channels independent of all Christian thought,—the Chaldean tale, the Pagan Naasene Document and the Poimandres.
2. Because his contemporary appearance at the beginning of the second century in Mesopotamia, Syria and Egypt, presupposes for him a far greater antiquity than that evinced by the sources.
3. Because what the earliest documents mention are his anthropogenetic and heroic activities, that is those capacities in which he is distinct from the Jewish and Christian Son of Man, and which, if he were a Christian product would necessarily be later agglutinations, not primary manifestations.
4. Because among pagan Gnostics and Christian syncretists he is reputed to be of "Chaldean" origin and is known most intimately from Mesopotamian theologies.

The evidence for Christian influence upon the Anthropos can therefore do no more than raise the question, is his *soteriological* capacity a product of Christian thought? The answer to this question can of course be given only after the origin of the underlying pagan figure has become reasonably clear.

The discussions of the last years have given rise to a number of hypotheses concerning the source from which this Gnostic personage has sprung. Between them they have utilized virtually all the avenues of approach in any way promising for a solution of the problem. The hypotheses may be divided into two classes, completely divergent one from another. Such a divergence in the analysis of a Gnostic figure is by no means surprising, indeed it is typical of the interpretation of almost every phase of Hellenistic civilization and culture. As in the discussion of Hellenistic art "Orient or Rome" are the poles of opinion concerning its origin, and as in the analysis of Gnosticism as a whole Harnack's "acute Hellenization of Christianity" and Bousset's "predominantly Oriental character" vie with one another, so too, East and West, myth and philosophy, hoary legend and modern speculation are invoked to explain the genesis of the Anthropos.

Four attempts, at least, have been made to show that the Anthropos is the product of philosophic speculation, by H. Leisegang, E. Meyer, W. Scott and E. Bevan, respectively. Of these the first has its place in a fruitful and illuminating discussion of Gnosticism as a whole. Gnosis, Leisegang believes, is a religious development in which Greek metaphysics are translated into mythology by the use of oriental imagination and ancient eastern symbols, for the production of a more vivid and colorful interpretation of the character and destiny of the world and man.[1] As early as the days of Philo, he says, the correspondence between macrocosm and microcosm gave rise to a peculiar interpretation of the ideal world of the metaphysicians. The Alexandrine philosopher describes the conception in the following terms:

> Some have been bold enough to assert that man, the insignificant creature, is equal to the whole cosmos, seeing that both are composed of a body and a rational soul. Thus they speak alternately of man as a small cosmos, and of the cosmos as a large man.[2]

The Gnostic Anthropos is none other than this large or great Man, the personification of the cosmic Logos, says Leisegang.

As a matter of fact that is exactly what the supreme Anthropos does amount to in the Christian strata of the Naasene document. Shorn of his cosmic content the same Logos is associated with the Anthropos, as we have seen, in the system of Valentinus, as his father, and in the Poimandres as his brother, while in the Gospel of Mary, the Man is none other than the sum of Nous and Ennoia, whose manifestation the cosmic Logos represents.

There is then ample evidence for the connection of western metaphysics and the Anthropos, yet it is highly problematic whether this speculation was actually the formative agency responsible for his existence as Leisegang holds, or merely a secondary influence transforming his character.

[1] H. Leisegang, *Die Gnosis* (1924), pp. 1–59.
[2] *Quis Rer. Div. Haeres*, par. 155 (ed. minor, ed. Cohn-Wendland), cf. Leisegang, op. cit., pp. 117–8.

THE ORIGIN AND ANTIQUITY OF THE ANTHROPOS

It is not difficult to perceive that there is a distinct difference between the "large Man" of Philo and the Anthropos. The former is a figurative representation of the material cosmos, while the latter is a transcendent being, at best the cosmic Logos. The "large Man" is thus no nearer the Anthropos than the Iranian Gayomart whom Reitzenstein proposes as the Anthropos' prototype, because the Iranian figure, similarly endowed with macrocosmic significance, has also to be transcendentalized before it can be considered the origin of the Anthropos.[3] If the question at issue is to be decided on the basis of the Anthropos' macrocosmic role, a choice between the hypotheses of Leisegang and Reitzenstein would depend upon the answer given to the broader question, as to whether the basic elements and figures of Gnosticism are western and metaphysical, or eastern and mythological? Of this more presently.

Perhaps the opinion advanced by Leisegang in connection with the Ophite Anthropos, is to be considered not by itself but in connection with the earlier investigations made by him into the nature of Philo's "heavenly Man."[4]

Philo, it will be recalled, discourses at length, in a number of his treatises, and particularly in the tracts "On the Creation of the World" and "The Allegories of the Sacred Laws," concerning a "heavenly Man," for the existence of whom he finds evidence in the Old Testament.[5] This "heavenly Man" Reitzenstein and Bousset first considered a further echo of the pagan, and for them ultimately Iranian Anthropos, in fact an important link in the Anthropos tradition.[6] A subsequent reëxamination of the material upon which this interpretation was placed, conducted by Bréhier and Leisegang, showed quite conclusively that what is actually said concerning the "heavenly Man," disorganized and inharmoni-

---

[3] Cf. below, p. 89.

[4] Leisegang's article *"Zum iranischen Erlösungsmysterium"* in which the consequences of his position must appear we have not been able to consult, since the periodical in which it was published, "Ztschrft f. Missionskunde u. Religionswissenschaft," vol. xxxvi (1921), pp. 257-64, 289-99, is not accessible to us.

[5] Particularly, *de Opif. Mundi*, §§ 69 and 134-5, *Leg. Alleg.* I, §§ 31-43.

[6] Bousset, HP, pp. 194-6, cf. Reitzenstein, *Poimandres*, p. 110.

ous as it is, can be satisfactorily explained as having been evolved from the Old Testament by the use of Platonic and Stoic speculation.[7] The only question raised by the "heavenly Man" is thus, what was it that interested Philo in developing him. Surely Platonic metaphysics placed no greater emphasis upon the preexistent idea or type of man, to which he corresponds in part, than upon the types of all the other genera of material existence.

Now in other instances where Philo dwells with special care upon a point arising only incidentally in his exegesis of the Old Testament, his expatiations are likely to be inspired by apologetic motives. So, for example, his discussions concerning the nature of Time, though they follow the reasoning of Plato, owe their repeated appearance to a polemic against some form of the Aion cult.[8] One might therefore consider the "heavenly Man" an attempt to offset the pagan Anthropos speculation. While this view seems tenable, it is not the only possible explanation of the phenomena. As we shall have occasion to observe in the next chapter, the Jewish people had, since the second pre-Christian century developed a growing interest in matters primordial, particularly in the protoplast and his immediate descendents. This interest eventually produced what we may call the "Adam Literature" a group of narratives concerned with a "celestial Adam."[9] Now there is good evidence to show that Philo was familiar with the "celestial Adam" of Jewish legend.[10] His interest in the protoplast, therefore, does not need to be accounted for by his supposed knowledge of the Anthropos. Indeed his "heavenly Man" may be no more than a metaphysical interpretation and adaptation of the Jewish "celestial Adam."

Whatever influence the denial of the identity of Anthropos

[7] Bréhier, *Philon d'Alexandrie* (1907), pp. 121–6, Leisegang, *Pneuma Hagion* (1919), p. 78, note 5, and pp. 102–12.

[8] Cf. the harmless statements of *de Opif. Mundi*, §§ 26–7 (= Plato, *Timaeus*, 37D–38C), and *Leg. Alleg.* I, § 2, with *Quaestiones*, § 100 where it is said: "Time under the name of Chronos or Saturn is looked upon as a God by the wickedest of men who are desirous of losing sight of the one essential Being."

[9] Cf. below, Chapter 6, pp. 151–56.

[10] Cf. *de Opificio Mundi*, §§ 77–88 where Philo suddenly deserts his metaphysical man and begins to glorify the protoplast himself.

THE ORIGIN AND ANTIQUITY OF THE ANTHROPOS

and Philonic "heavenly Man" may have had upon Leisegang's ideas regarding the origin and development of the Anthropos, it has led E. Meyer and W. Scott to the conjecture that the Anthropos is but a pagan echo of the Philonic figure.[11] The position of Reitzenstein has thus been reversed.

In both cases the conjecture referred to was suggested by the analysis of the Poimandres. It is not difficult to understand how anyone confining his attention to the Anthropos tradition of the Hermetic tract might be led to such a conclusion. There are in the Poimandres distinct echoes of the scriptural narratives of creation and possibly also of the interpretation placed upon them by Philonic exegesis.[12] Yet if we regard the Anthropos tradition as a whole, there are eminent reasons why the ultimate origin of the pagan figure cannot be found in metaphysical postulates such as the "heavenly Man" of Philo.

If the former were truly developed from the latter it would mean that all the elements embodied in the description of the Anthropos' activity are secondary accretions syncretistically inspired, for the "heavenly Man" lacks all the mythological plasticity and vitality that characterizes the Anthropos. That is quite improbable for two reasons.

In the first place, wherever, as in Syria, we have a number of superimposed strata of Anthropos traditions, the metaphysical are secondary to the mythological. Our earliest traditions from Syria speak of the "great, most glorious and perfect Man." They tell of many hymns glorifying him.[13] Only the later strata speak of the Anthropos as "the All" or the "unmoulded Mind." Even in the Poimandres there is presupposed something more than the metaphysical Man, namely the mythological "heroic" Anthropos.[14]

In the second place the sequence of elements postulated by

[11] E. Meyer, *Ursprung des Christentums*, vol. II (1921), pp. 371-7. W. Scott, *Hermetica*, vol. II (1925), pp. 4-5 and notes on Libellus I, §§ 12-17.

[12] Meyer, op. cit., pp. 375-6, admitted with qualifications by Reitzenstein, *Studien*, pp. 23-4.

[13] Hipp. V, 6, 5; 7, 7.

[14] Cf. below, p. 97.

the conjectures of Meyer, Scott and Leisegang is contrary to the normal course of development in Gnostic theology, or at least insufficient as an explanation of the phenomena involved. We have in Gnosticism many examples of Oriental mythological figures that paled and lost color as they came into contact with Hellenistic rationalism. On the other hand, there are to our knowledge no examples of metaphysical postulates that traveled eastward and became mythologized while keeping their identity intact, save where there already existed in the Orient similar figures and concepts with which they were and could be identified.[15] The origin of the Anthropos can therefore hardly be found in the "heavenly Man" alone. It requires a similar Oriental personage in addition.

Finally the metaphysical interpretation of the Anthropos fails to take note of the fact that our Gnostic sources explicitly mention Chaldea as the home of the figure, and that the oldest tradition that we have concerning it, is the "Chaldean Tale" embodied in the pagan Naasene document. Chaldea is the last place where one would expect speculative forces to have been operative in his production.

It appears, therefore, as though the metaphysical interpretation of the Anthropos is the work of secondary forces brought to play upon him at his introduction into circles familiar with both oriental myth and Greek philosophy.

Bevan, in "Hellenism and Christianity," has recently thrown out a further suggestion regarding the origin of the Anthropos. The Christian Christ, he finds, is distinctly a *novum* in the field of ancient thought. To him the Hellenistic and Gnostic Soters owe their character. The Gnostic Soter, in so far as he differs from the Christian Christ, represents but the Pythagorean-Platonic conception of the heavenly soul's descent to and reascent from the material world, assimilated to the Christ in the achievement of salvation.[16] As we have seen, the Anthropos plays in the world a dual role. He is the divine element residing in man and the cosmos, and simultaneously the savior who, as its complement,

[15] The Logos is an example of the exception.
[16] *Hellenism and Christianity* (1921), pp. 104–5.

comes to the world for its redemption. In the latter capacity he has distinctly come under the influence of Christian thought. Is he not then an excellent example of the truth of Bevan's contention, particularly in view of the fact that his name, Anthropos, might be explained as a derivative from the term "inner Man" used of the divine element in man by Paul and Plotinus?[17]

The hypothesis is captivating, but it involves real difficulties, not the least of which is to be found in the premise upon which it is constructed.

It is quite true that in many respects the Christian Christ represented an innovation to the people of the ancient world. The avidity with which syncretistic minds availed themselves of his person is the best evidence for this fact. Yet to say that he is entirely new, and that the Gnostic Soters, in so far as they differ from him, owe their character to the assimilation of the Soul in the Soul Drama is hardly plausible. In the first place, the concept of redemption is not a Christian product and redeemers in a higher or lower sense existed before the advent of Christianity at least in Hellenistic transformations of the eastern fertility cults.[18] Without them the Christ of Paul would have been unintelligible and undesirable to the syncretists. Not because he was completely new, but because he was in many respects superior to current types, for instance in his historical appearance, did he become the dominant force in Hellenistic syncretistic soteriology. In the second place the use of the soul in this connection is unnecessary. The descent from and ascent to a forgotten heavenly home, which she serves to explain, according to Bevan, can be accounted for in a much simpler way. True, the vegetational deities of the pre-Hellenistic fertility cults from whom the pagan savior appears to have developed show no traces of such an ascent or descent. Yet the change in the religious atmosphere of the East which accounted for the increase of their prominence naturally brought with it a new conception of their relation to the physical cosmos. The change in atmosphere was occasioned by the confluence of

[17] 2. *Cor.* 4, 16; *Enneads* V, 1, 10 (ed. Volkmar).
[18] Cf. Hans Lietzmann, *Der Weltheiland* (1909), and P. Wendland, *Die hellenistische-römische Kultur*, 2nd ed. (1912), pp. 154-5.

Greek and Iranian dualism. The material world became the expression of all that was bad. A deity that was thought to foster on earth the beneficent processes of vegetational growth, of life itself, therefore could readily take on increased significance, and be considered capable of re-creating life in its human form. What is more to the point, such a deity must represent the manifestation of a power belonging to a world other than this material cosmos. It must descend to and reascend from the world of evil existence.

The real question which we must ask ourselves in connection with Bevan's hypothesis, is, can the Anthropos be explained as a type of the Gnostic-Hellenistic savior. Only a negative answer is possible because none of the Soters, so far as we know them, function, as the Anthropos, in the capacity of both primordial champion and father of mankind.[19] Secondarily Bevan's words might lead one to ask, can the Anthropos be explained as a peculiar form of Psyche in the Soul-myth? Either the Western philosophical or Gnostic mythological form of the Soul Drama might serve as a basis of comparison. The latter has been invoked already by Scheftelowitz.

Mani's Primal Man, Scheftelowitz finds, is essentially a Gnostic product. He has developed from the Mandean conception that a "heavenly, spiritual being, sent to combat the material powers of darkness and captured by them, is held imprisoned till redeemed by a divine savior and finally guided back to the world of spirit."[20] This Mandean idea has been evolved, it is claimed, through the medium of Gnostic theologies such as those of Marcion, Apelles and Justin, systems that furnish the *dramatis personae* of the action in the nature of a Good God, an Evil God and a mediator between them.[21] Eventually it may be traced, however, to the Essene conception of man as a mixture of celestial and terrestrial elements and the soul as a heavenly being imprisoned in earthly surroundings.[22]

[19] Bousset, HP, pp. 238–76.
[20] *Entstehung*, p. 66.
[21] Ibid., pp. 67–9.
[22] Ibid., pp. 31–2.

THE ORIGIN AND ANTIQUITY OF THE ANTHROPOS

It was comparatively simple for Scheftelowitz to determine the origin of the Anthropos, first because he considers only the Manichean phase of the figure and in addition even differentiates between the Manichean Primal Man and Ormuzd, thereby lessening the scope of the Primal Man tremendously, and finally because he is able with utter disregard of the governing forces in the religious development of the syncretistic East, to make original causes out of such final products as the theology of Marcion and the Essene sect.

We, on the other hand, find it impossible to distinguish between Primal Man and Ormuzd in the Manichean texts, partly because of what the Manichean texts themselves show and partly because the Anthropos appears in the capacities of champion and savior over a century before Mani.[23] Any endeavor to find in the Soul Drama, Eastern or Western, the origin of the Anthropos myth, therefore seems doomed to failure. It fails to account for the Anthropos' primordial role, and for the properties that make him a personality even more distinct than the oriental Psyche. It would be far more natural to assume that the capacities of some highly individual mythological champion had been secondarily extended by influence from the Soul Drama, than to suppose that enough energy had radiated from the passive and placid figure of Psyche to cause the agglutination of foreign traits in a quantity sufficient to transform her into the Anthropos. What the inherent value of the first of these assumptions may be, is a question the discussion of which will need be reserved until after the quest for the ultimate basis for the Anthropos has been completed.

The examination of the efforts to derive the Anthropos from the Soul Drama has led us from the hypotheses that link him with the West, to those which seek his home in the Hellenistic Orient. With this transition we find ourselves in general accord. The ultimate origin of such a figure as the Anthropos can scarcely be found in those elements of its religious life which the littoral Near East acquired from the West. After all, the influence of Greece upon the religious life of the Orient was far more a matter

[23] Cf. above, pp. 42-3, 50-1.

of new view points, new modes of expression, of the liberalization and universalization of current views and their use toward higher and more personal ends, than it was an inculcation of new forms, and the introduction of new symbols and figures. In the East we have therefore to continue our search for the origin of the Anthropos.

Among the designations applied to the Anthropos, that of Adam frequently appears. Indeed, it asserts itself prominently in those sources which lay greatest claim to antiquity, the Pagan Naasene Document and the early Mandean theology. Was the Anthropos called Adam because that was the natural name for the people of Syria to associate with a person considered the prototype of humanity, or does he actually represent the Adam of Genesis 1–2 in a Gnostic mode, transformed, let us say by the influence of the Soul Drama and the Gnostic Soter? With only the stories of Genesis to work upon, such a combination would scarcely have been possible of achievement, but, as we have already heard, and shall have occasion to hear more at length, the figure of Adam had in Jewish times been elevated to a level far transcending that of the protoplast in the Old Testament.[24] Such a celestial Adam, carried over into a dualistic atmosphere might well be considered capable of assimilating a number of traits and capacities. Yet there seem to be at least three reasons why the influence of even the Jewish Adam upon the Anthropos, shown in the use of the name and elsewhere, should be considered secondary rather than formative.

In the first place, a combination such as that projected would fail to motivate the fact that the Anthropos appears in a primordial conflict. In the second place, the Jewish origin of the Gnostic figure would make the joint appearance of Anthropos and celestial Adam in the Mandaic theology unintelligible. Finally the difficulty of considering the celestial Adam himself a rectilinear development from Hebrew conceptions may possibly necessitate a reverse derivation and thus offer an equally acceptable explanation of the similarities between the Jewish and the pagan figures.

To our knowledge no one has as yet endeavored to derive the

[24] Cf. below, pp. 151–6.

Anthropos either from orthodox Jewish sources or directly from some Babylonian prototype.[25] In both spheres points of contact undoubtedly exist. Marduk, particularly, might furnish the victorious champion and cosmogonal agent whom we miss in the other fields, but here as there, the differentia are such as to prohibit our finding in him the ultimate origin of the Anthropos. There is no reason for instance, why Marduk should merit the name "man," especially since the possibility of his being identified with the Hebrew protoplast is entirely out of question.

What we need as the prototype of the Anthropos is a figure quite distinct from any of those hitherto examined. It will needs belong to the divine sphere, have some ulterior significance and yet be capable of being identified with humanity or more specifically with the ultimate ancestor of the human race.

2. Bousset and Reitzenstein believe to have found in Iran a mythological personage, Gayomart, that will supply the necessary basis for the growth and development of the Gnostic Anthropos. The two scholars originally associated with this hypothesis have done little more than point to and describe the proposed prototype and certain incidental or basic similarities between him and the Anthropos in some of his manifestations.[26] This does not signify that they have not given their theory careful consideration. It merely shows that they have exercised scholarly caution in the use of the Iranian sources, since they were not Iranologists, and as a consequence have never analyzed the development of the Anthropos in all its scope. For any one but a specialist in the field to consider the Iranian origin of the Anthropos more in detail would scarcely be feasible, were it not that since the hypothesis was first promulgated three independent inquiries have

[25] Of course the Chaldean Tale, Zosimus and perhaps Aristides (*Apology*, ch. 3 and 7) connect the Anthropos speculation with Chaldea, but this signifies merely that the speculation came from Mesopotamia westward, not necessarily that Chaldea was its home ultimately. Besides the name Chaldean is loosely employed by Westerners in the Hellenistic age. To Aristides, so his editors felt, Chaldean was anything not Greek, Jewish, Egyptian or Christian, hence, Barbarian. Hippolytus speaks of Zarathushtra as a Chaldean (I, 2, 12).

[26] Bousset, HP, Chapter 4; Reitzenstein, *Poimandres*, pp. 81–114, recently also, *Studien*, parts I–VII.

been made into the traditions concerning the Indo-Iranian protoplasts by competent scholars.[27] While these inquiries do not register complete agreement, they present the available material and serve the outsider as a guide in venturing into the Iranian sphere of thought.

The multiform traditions of Iran, we are told, present a number of figures associated in one way or another with the beginning of the human race. Of this number, Gayomart, and doubtlessly he alone, merits serious consideration as the prototype of the Gnostic Anthropos. At first glance it might appear as though the consideration of the hypothesis of Bousset and Reitzenstein, involved no more than a plain recital of the nature and character of Gayomart as drawn from the Iranian sources. But such is not the case. In Gayomart we happen to have an enigma. That enigma can be solved only by constant reference to the bulk of the Iranian and Indo-Aryan tradition.

The most extensive account of Gayomart is found in the Pahlavi Bundahishn, a work that is based on a lost Avestan text and has come down to us in a longer and shorter recension.[28] At the beginning, we are told, there existed two spirits, a spirit of good and a spirit of evil, a spirit of light and a spirit of darkness. The former, Ahura Mazda, being omniscient, was aware of the latter's existence, and of a conflict destined to take place between them in the realm of air which separated their individual spheres. In consequence of his foreknowledge, Ahura Mazda produced in his proper territory the host of his creatures, the beings necessary to the accomplishment of his end, namely the victory over Ahriman, the evil spirt. These creatures belong to the realm of spirit exclusively. Among them is "the righteous man," probably

[27] Most recently Schaeder, in Reitzenstein u. Schaeder, *Studien*, section II, Iranische Lehren. Also, A. Christensen, *Le Premier Homme et le Premier Roi dans l'Histoire Legendaire des Iraniens*, in Archives d'Etudes Orientales, No. 14 (1918), and H. Guentert, *Der arische Weltkönig u. Heiland* (1923). Cf. A. J. Carnoy, *Iran's Primeval Heroes and the Myth of the First Man*, Indo-Iranian Studies in honor of Shams ul ullema Dastur, etc. (1925), p. 203ff.

[28] *Bundahishn*, translated by West, in Sacred Books of the East, vol. XI, and the Great Bundahishn, not accessible in translation in its entirety. Relevant passages are quoted by Christensen and by Schaeder.

THE ORIGIN AND ANTIQUITY OF THE ANTHROPOS

the heavenly Fravashi, or spiritual prototype of Gayomart.[29]

At the end of the first period of existence, the first of four aeons of 3000 years each, Ahriman rises from his sphere of darkness, bent on the conquest of the territory of light. His first effort proves a failure, and for its outcome two reasons are given, first, Ahura Mazda's utterance of the Ahunavar formula, and his revelation (to the enemy) of the lasting possession of his creatures, secondly, Ahriman's fear of "the righteous man."

As the result of his initial effort, the evil spirit remains impotent for a space of three thousand years, a period which Ahura Mazda utilizes to fashion in the realm of air a material creation embracing the earth and many of its diverse forms of life. Among the latter are the primeval (sole-created) ox and Gayomart, "mortal" or "human life."

Material creation effected, the second period of the conflict, marked by the intermingling of the "wills" of Ahura Mazda and Ahriman, as well as of their creations is at hand. It begins with the resuscitation of the evil spirit and his attack upon the vegetation, the ox, Gayomart and the heavenly fire in the order mentioned. The hostilities take various forms. Noxious creatures are introduced into the world. Impurities, sickness, disease and darkness corrupt its ethical and physical perfection. Desire need, pain, hunger, appetite and sleep overcome the ox and Gayomart. When the former has passed away under the effects of the trial and the other creatures have been rendered useless (to the ends of the good spirit) Gayomart bears the brunt of the attack. Asto-vidad, the demon of death, together with a thousand of his kind are let forth against the prototype of humanity. Gayomart remains faithful, "his eyes looking toward the great one."[30] Pursuant to divine command, his life and reign are continued for thirty years, but at last he too passes away, even as the primeval ox before him.[31]

---

[29] A spiritual creation precedes the formation of the material world. *Bund.*, 1, 8. *Bund.*, 3, 1 presupposes that Gayomart as he first existed was a part of that creation. Cf. the note of West to *Bund.*, 3, 1.

[30] *Bund.*, 3, 14–17. For the quotation, ibid., 24, 1. Cf. *Yasht* 13, 87.

[31] *Bund.*, 3, 22–3.

From Gayomart there issued at the moment of his death his seed, two thirds of which were received by the sun to be purified, the other by Spendarmad, the earth. After a period of forty years the earth produced from it Mashya and Mashyoi, the first human couple. The two sprang forth from the earth in the shape of a Rivas plant. Finally, however, they changed from the shape of a plant to the shape of man and the soul entered into their bodies.[32]

Of Gayomart we hear but once more. In a later chapter of the Bundahishn it is said that at the final resurrection "first the bones of Gayomart are roused up, then those of the rest of mankind."[33] Of the light accompanying the sun at this juncture, "one half will be for Gayomart, and one half will give enlightenment among the rest of men."[34] Even as he was at the beginning, such also is Gayomart at the end of the world, the first and foremost of his race.

To this account as preserved in the Bundahishn the longer recension of the work, the Great Bundahisn, has little to add. It tells us that Gayomart was created of two elements. His body was fashioned of earth, while his sperma or soul was of the nature of heavenly fire.[35] Because of the heavenly fire within him, Gayomart shone like the sun, a conception reëchoed in the Pahlavi writings of Zad Sparam.[36] Mortality was not from the beginning inherent in his nature. It was due to his final conquest by Astovidhotu.[37] That conquest was deferred for thirty years because the evil stellar powers had first to drive from their ascendency the divinely created stars.[38] Here as in the selections of the Zad Sparam and the Menuk-i-Khrat, finally, we are told that the death of Gayomart had cosmogonal as well as anthropogonal

[32] Ibid., 15, 1–5.
[33] Ibid., 30, 7.
[34] Ibid., 30, 9.
[35] *Great Bund.*, III, A. Cf. Schaeder, *Studien*, p. 223. *Gr. Bund.*, IV, A. Cf. Schaeder, p. 226.
[36] *Gr. Bund.*, I, A. Cf. Schaeder, p. 215. *Gr. Bund.*, IV, A. Cf. Schaeder, p. 225. *Zad Sparam*, II, 8 (SBE, vol. XI).
[37] *Gr. Bund.*, IV, A. Cf. Schaeder, p. 227–9.
[38] Ibid., III, A. Cf. Schaeder, pp. 221–3.

significance, since eight kinds of metals arose from the members of his dead body.[39]

One additional element of the Bundahishn tradition has yet to be mentioned. Its difficulty requires for it special consideration. At one point in the Bundahishn proper we are told that:

> before (Ahriman's) coming to Gayomart, Ahura Mazda brought forth a sweat upon Gayomart, so long as one requires to recite a prayer of one stanza. Moreover, Ahura Mazda formed that sweat into the youthful body of a man of fifteen years, radiant and tall. When Gayomart issued from the sweat, he saw the world dark as night and the earth as though not a needle's point remained free from noxious creatures.[40]

This obscure incident is reported in virtually the same words by the writers of the Great Bundahishn and the Zad Sparam.[41] It appears in a somewhat different form in the Dinkard where we find it introduced as an excerpt from the Varshtmansar Nask.[42] There are two important points of variance in the Dinkard narrative. The episode is relegated from the beginning to the end of the thirty years spent by Gayomart in conflict with the demons. The "sweat," moreover, is created by the demons, not by Ahura Mazda, and appears on the prototype to his discomfort. The enigmatic "youthful man of fifteen years" escapes mention entirely.

The episode which this double tradition presents has been the occasion for much speculation, particularly in connection with the hypothesis of the Iranian origin of the Anthropos.[43] Unemended the tale is intelligible only in the form found in the Dinkard. Here it is clearly intended to record a portion of the story of Gayomart's death. If the word "sweat" be euphemistically used, the tale will be but a variant of the Bundahishn account of the prototype's demise.[44] While this represents a possible

[39] Ibid., IV, A. Cf. Schaeder, pp. 225-6. *Zad Sparam*, X, 2. *Menuk-i-Khrat*, 27, 18.
[40] *Bund.*, 3, 19-20.
[41] *Gr. Bund.*, II, A-B, cf. Schaeder, pp. 219-221. *Zad Sparam*, II, 8-10.
[42] *Dinkard*, IX, 32, 9-10, cf. Christensen, p. 14.
[43] Particularly Bousset, HP, pp. 203-5; Christensen, pp. 35-9.
[44] So Professor A. V. W. Jackson is inclined to interpret.

form of analysis, there are good reasons for rejecting it as the correct solution of the problem, and for considering the Dinkard tradition a secondary development.[45] Best of them all is probably the interpretation of the Bundahishn passage recently given by Schaeder. It takes its clue from the context in which the incident stands. Just prior to the words quoted above from the Iranian Genesis, we are told that before the coming of the evil spirit to the primeval ox, Ahura Mazda administered to the animal a strong narcotic. The treatment was intended to ameliorate the effects of the demon's first attack. The coördination of ox and man plainly exhibited in the book as a whole, requires that a similar kindness be shown to the prototype of humanity. Our Bundahishn passage, therefore, is intended to convey the idea that Gayomart was rendered temporarily insensible and thus spared the shock attendant upon the inroad of the evil spirits. This sense becomes apparent in the passage if we replace the word "sweat" by "sleep," a substitution that is possible without altering the text, since the Pahlavi characters of the word "sleep" might also be read "sweat." The young man mentioned in the second sentence of the account is none other than the genius of sleep, familiar to the Parsee from other sources. The sentence is to be construed as parenthetical and serves to record the creation of the genius and the fact that his existence is due to the bounteous kindness of Ahura Mazda toward humanity.[46] By this interpretation, we add to our knowledge of Gayomart this detail, namely that at the coming of the demons the prototype of humanity became temporarily insensate and was overwhelmed by sleep.

Other Pahlavi texts add but little to the Bundahishn tradition. We are told in the Dinkard that Gayomart was the first to utter sublime words and that from him alone come all good

---

[45] It violates the parallelism between this incident of the life of Gayomart and another similar occurrence in the life of the primordial ox previously recounted in the source (*Bund.*, 3, 18). Moreover, it transposes the coming of darkness, which should be coincident with the first approach of the demons, to an inappropriate place at the end of Gayomart's earthly life.

[46] *Studien*, p. 217, note 1.

thoughts, good words and acts of men.[47] Thus he occupies the first place in the number of those who are "prophets, apostles and believers, who accept the (true) religion in its entirety."[48] The Dadistan-i-Dinik lists him among those who have contributed to the final renovation of the universe,[49] and frequently speaks of Gayomart, Zarathushtra and Saoshyant as the beginning, middle and end of creation.[50]

The Pahlavi tradition upon which we have drawn for our information concerning Gayomart is taken from sources the codification of which does not antedate the Mohammedan era. It might appear as though it were quite out of question to consider the Iranian figure a possible prototype of the Hellenistic Anthropos. Such is not the case, in spite of the efforts of Scheftelowitz to show that Gayomart is dependent upon the Jewish Adam.[51] The tradition embodied in the Pahlavi works is almost universally agreed to belong to a period far more ancient than that which saw its final composition. The Bundahishn and the Great Bundahishn particularly are considered epitomized forms of the Damdat Nask, one of the twenty-one books of the original Avesta as known in Sasanian times. What is true of these books as a whole is true also of their description of Gayomart, especially since, as we have seen, the prototype of humanity was mentioned in the Varshtmansar Nask,[53] and in at least two other books of the later Avesta.[54]

But even the third Christian century cannot be the *terminus a quo* in the existence of Gayomart. His simultaneous appearance in so many portions of the Sasanian Avesta demands that he be regarded as an element of the tradition current in Parthian times.

[47] *Dink.*, III, 143, 2.
[48] Ibid., V, 1, 8.
[49] *Dadistan-i-Dinik*, 36, 2.
[50] Ibid., 2, 9; 4, 6; cf. 28, 7.
[51] *Entstehung*, pp. 60–1. Scheftelowitz is refuted by Schaeder, pp. 241–2.
[52] A. V. W. Jackson, art. "*Avesta*" in ERE; Darmsteter, SBE., vol. IV, p. xxxv; West, ibid., vol. XI, p. xxiv.
[53] Cf. above, p. 89 and *Dink.*, IX, 32, 9–10.
[54] *Chitradat Nask*, quoted in *Dink.*, VIII, 13, 1–4; *Bak Nask*, quoted in *Dink.*, IX, 53, 18.

This contention is borne out by the mention of his name (if nothing more) in the Yashts of the "Younger Avesta."[55] Indeed it is possible to proceed one step further and maintain that Gayomart antedates even the Parthian period. Though there is no incontrovertible direct evidence in support of this view, a number of factors point in that direction.

In the first place, certain allusions in the Gathas, the oldest elements of Zarathushtrian tradition demand consideration. The famous third Gatha speaks of a Man (*maretan*) who was attacked by the demons in connection with the beginning of the struggle between the two hostile spirits.[56] Other Gathas mention by name Geush-urvan the soul of the ox who is in Pahlavi tradition the animal counterpart of Gayomart.[57] The passages in question appear to imply the existence of Gaya-Maretan, the prototypic man, at a very early time.

The identical conclusion seems to follow, in the second place, from the study of the relation between Gayomart and other figures of ancient Eastern mythology. In his major capacities, so the inquiries of Guentert have shown, Gayomart bears a remarkable affinity to a number of figures appearing in the remnants of Iranian, Vedic and Aryan tradition. He is but one particular manifestation of a type the character of which is determined by three basic concepts, first, that the world and its human beings arose from the sacrifice and death of a primordial being of human form, second, that man is the offspring of a single bisexual prototype, third, that the first mortal is also the first and foremost in the kingdom of the dead. Of these three ideas, the first two appear in juxtaposition in Iranian, Indic and Nordic lore, while the last is an admixture common to Iranian and Indic mythology.[58] The Indo-Iranian antiquity of the parent stock being scarcely

[55] *Yasht*, 13, 86–7, 145 et al., cf. Christensen, pp. 12–3.

[56] Schaeder considers Gatha 3, 6 (i.e., *Yasna*, 30, 6), a reference to Gayomart. *Studien*, p. 213. So too Prof. Jackson, in his translation of the passage, art. *Avesta*, in Library of the World's Best Literature, vol. 3 (1897), p. 1089.

[57] *Yasna*, 28, 1; 29, 1–11. Cf. Christensen, pp. 11–12. In the Iranian cosmogony that reached the West in connection with Mithra worship, only the ox appears.

[58] *Der arische Weltkönig u. Heiland*, pp. 315–94, particularly, pp. 392–3.

THE ORIGIN AND ANTIQUITY OF THE ANTHROPOS

open to question, Gayomart may well be a very old figure, at least to the extent to which he corresponds to type.

The character of Gayomart, however, shows not only typical but also individual traits. These presuppose a definite theological horizon and thus afford a third indication of the time of his origin in that form which the Pahlavi works indicate.

Gayomart is not merely the first man, he is the prototype of humanity, an element of the spiritual creation of Ahura Mazda. His death is allotted its appropriate place in the great struggle between Ahriman and Ormuzd. It results not because of a will to sacrifice himself, or because of the plan of God, but as a consequence of Gayomart's having been overcome by the evil powers. The ulterior prominence attaching to this prototype is determined not by his place in the succession of mortal beings, but by his essential righteousness and the contribution which he as the first believer made to the progress of the world. Even his name "mortal life" shows that he has been raised from the world of mythological beings into that of abstractions.

Of these individual traits, the abstract name and the place which Gayomart holds in the preëxistent spiritual creation, presuppose the Zarathushtrian sublimation of current mythological persons, a sublimation most clearly illustrated by the Amesha Spentas, and the equally Zarathushtrian conception of divine spirituality.[59] The other characteristics imply the division of the conflict between Ahriman and Ahura Mazda into periods, its statement in the form of a sacred history embracing the whole of existence, and the insistence upon adherence to Zarathushtrian principles as the essence of righteousness.

The first of these two groups of traits is the older and presupposes the purely Zarathushtrian theology. The second embraces principles that are more scholastic in nature and are by some scholars assigned to the period following the days of the great prophet himself. Inherently their character furnishes no more than a *terminus a quo*. They show that the way was prepared for the coming of our Pahlavi Gayomart in pre-Parthian, some

[59] Dhalla, *Zoroastrian Theology* (1914), pp. 26–45.

times called Mazdean or Magian, times.[60] Two further observations, however, make it imperative that the development of his person should actually have taken place at that juncture. The first is the fact that for the religion of Persia the Parthian era represents a period of decay rather than of development, and thus scarcely favorable to the creation of a figure of such importance as Gayomart.[61] The second is that Yima, who since he corresponds to the Vedic Yama, is the logical and probably original representative of the Indo-Iranian type from which the figure of Gayomart has been developed, has been relegated to comparative obscurity in our later Avestan and Pahlavi tradition, a thing that would hardly have happened had Gayomart been a creation of only the Parthian days.[62]

We therefore conclude that because of the allusions in the Gathas, because of the antiquity of the type which he represents, because the way had been prepared for the development of his individual traits in pre-Parthian days and because that development is scarcely intelligible as a product of the Parthian period, that therefore Gayomart in his Pahlavi form is at least a creation of pre-Parthian days and perhaps of the days of Zarathushtra himself. That being the case, he is certainly sufficiently ancient to merit consideration as the ultimate origin of the Anthropos, or for that matter, if need be, of the Jewish Bar Nasha.

3. The analysis of the other hypotheses concerning the origin of the Anthropos, has shown that to make any one trait of the figure the exclusive basis for the establishment of his origin and identity, is liable to lead to erroneous results. We came to the conclusion that it is rather the conjunction of the characteristics of man, primordial champion and father of humanity, which stamps him as an individual distinct from all those figures to which

[60] The division into periods was familiar already to Theopompus (c. 300 BC) according to Plutarch, *de Is. et Osiris*, 47. By "Magian or Mazdean" we mean that phase of Iranian religious development which follows the days of the great prophet Zarathushtra and extends to the beginning of the Parthian period.
[61] Dhalla, p. 188.
[62] On Yima cf. Guentert, pp. 370-8.

singly and in combination he has been compared. On the basis of this conjunction, then, the relation of Anthropos and Gayomart must be tested. The test involves the answer to two questions. First, are the points of similarity sufficiently specific to warrant the basic identity of the figures? Second, are the points of difference intelligible as having been suggested by some cognate trait of the proposed prototype, or as the changes resultant from the transfer of the prototype into alien spheres of thought?

Perhaps the closest approach in point of contact between the Anthropos and Gayomart is to be found in the Manichean cosmogony. Here the Primal Man appears in a great primordial conflict waged between two eternally contrary powers. The names applied to these opposing forces vary in the Manichean tradition in proportion as it comes from Eastern or Western sources, but it is certainly suggestive to find that in the East the name Ormuzd (Ahura Mazda) was attached to the Primal Man, Ahrman (Ahriman) to the Power of Evil and Zrvan to the Supreme God.[63] If names are to be an indication of the sphere from which the Anthropos in his original form was taken, we might expect to find the Eastern Manichees speaking of the Primal Man as Gayomart. To our knowledge this designation does not appear, and that for the very good reason that Mani was a Zervanist. The Anthropos was identified by him with Ormuzd and under the latter's name he appears in these circles.

Apart from the names, the nature of the conflict in which the Primal Man finds himself is suggestive of the Iranian provenience of the Anthropos. In both Eastern and Western Manichean tradition it is Light and Darkness that clash, and the King of Darkness who, rapt by the sheen of the Light, is determined to invade the upper sphere.[64] The situation clearly recalls the opening chapters of the Bundahishn. The nature and position

---

[63] On Ormuzd and Zrvan, cf. above, p. 27. On Ahrman, cf. Schaeder, p. 250 and note 4.

[64] For instance Bar Khoni, in Cumont, *Recherches* I, pp. 8–11, and the Chastuanift I.B. in a new edition by Bang, Museon, Vol. XXXVI., (1923) p. 144, quoted by Schaeder p. 250, but inaccessible to me.

of the contrary worlds as well as the motivation of the evil spirit's action are the same in both cases.[65]

In this struggle the Primal Man of Manicheism occupies a role in many respects approximating that of Gayomart in Zoroastrianism. In the first place it is he, a divinely created human being, who occupies the center of the stage and conditions the future course and final termination of the struggle, just as in Iran it is Gayomart about whom the primordial conflict rages most violently and in whose fate the rest of humanity is implicated. Like the Iranian prototype, moreover, the Primal Man becomes temporarily insensate, owing to the influence of the evil spirit,[66] and ultimately succumbs before the advances of the powers of darkness. In both cases, finally, the existence of the primordial champions and their tragic fate form the precondition and occasion of the birth of the human race.

Unquestionably the similarity between these elements of Manichean and Iranian tradition are suggestive of the interrelation of the figures in question. Two things, however, have to be considered before this interrelation may become a working hypothesis. In the first place evidence must be presented to show that the role of primordial champion is an integral part of the Anthropos tradition. The Manichean texts give us that tradition in its latest and most highly developed form. We must therefore have some guarantee that the picture which they paint has not been retouched on the basis of Iranian ideas. Secondly, a satisfactory explanation must be given for the existence, in the description of the primordial Anthropos, of traits utterly unrelated to the Iranian Gayomart.

The consideration of the first of these matters, to which we now turn, involves a slight digression.

To anyone judging superficially it might appear as though it were hopeless to endeavor to find a common ground between the Manichean Primal Man as champion and the Anthropos of the earlier western Gnostics. While it is true that the heresiologists, upon whom we are largely dependent for our information concerning

[65] So Cumont, op. cit., p. 13.
[66] Cf. above, p. 19.

the theology of these circles, frequently obscure the Anthropos in their haste to be about the business of polemics, there are found in their writings, none the less, random statements which give a clue to the real nature of the figure in its westerly and earlier aspects. These statements show that the Anthropos of the second century was not very far removed from the Manichean Primal Man.

The first passage to be noted in this connection is culled from the Poimandres. There it is said that:

> Having learned to know the being (of the Administrators) and having received a share of their nature, he (the Anthropos) willed to break through the bounding circle of their orbits and to subdue the power of the one who was set over the region of fire.[67]

The statement embodies the note of conflict current in the Manichean cosmogony, a note apparently incongruous in the Poimandres, and one which has given trouble to the editors of the tract.[68]

The identical note was sounded also in the early Gnostic theologies of Egypt, Syria and Mesopotamia. Among the Christian Naasenes, the Barbelognostics and the Manicheans, a peculiar form of the name Adam was in use. That form is Adamas, literally interpreted, "the unconquerable." It is clearly limited in its application to the Anthropos and is distinguished in the circles in question from the term Adam, a term here applied exclusively to the material protoplast.[69] Moreover, it was evidently formulated under the influence of the Greek and not the Aramaic idiom.[70] That the particular significance given the

[67] *Poimandres*, c. 13.

[68] Scott, *Hermetica* I, found the passage so difficult that he chose to prefer an easier reading for "subdue," namely "regard," and to transpose the passage bodily to another place. Admittedly the passage is out of harmony with the Poimandres cosmogony, but that is because it has come with the Anthropos from a non-Hellenic source.

[69] Evident wherever comparison is possible. For evidence concerning the Naasene usage compare Hipp. V, 6, 5 (Adamas) with ibid., V, 7, 6 (Adam). The same distinction is made by the Manicheans. Cf. Bar Khoni, Cumont I, p. 22 (Adamas) with ibid., p. 43 (Adam).

[70] The name Adamas is found in both Greek and Syriac texts. Its origin, as Brockelman (*Lexicon Syriacum*, sub voce) shows, is to be found in the

name Adam by this Hellenization was evident to the Gnostic users, appears in part from the restriction of its usage, and in part from the explicit statement of Irenaeus that the Barbelognostics called the Anthropos "Adamas" because "neither he nor those with him were ever conquered."[71] Even Mani, where he speaks of Adamas Light, a double of the Primal Man, refers to him as a "*heroam belligerum.*"[72]

Now the name Adamas, which we are using to substantiate the antiquity of the heroic role of the Anthropos, might seem to point to the West rather than the Iranian East as the place where this heroic capacity was developed. How do we know that a popular etymology of the name Adam, developed on the shores of the Mediterranean by the use of the Greek idiom, was not the very source whence Mani received the inspiration for his primordial champion? The question is readily disposed of. In the first place, the Poimandres indicates that the Anthropos was regarded as a bellicose figure even where the name Adamas was not employed and that as early as the first appearance of the Hellenized form. Secondly, in the Chaldean Tale, where as we recall, the "Great Man" has first to be "overpowered" before the present world order can be inaugurated, we have evidence that the heroic guise clung to the Anthropos prior to the use of the designation Adamas.[73] Now there is scarcely a doubt that the Chaldean Tale is really of Mesopotamian provenience. This can be asserted because there is no reason why the author of the Naasene Document should have falsified the origin of his source, and because the Mesopotamian Anthropos theology of a later period (Manichean and Mandean) echoes the note sounded in the Chaldean Tale.

Greek substantive ἀδάμας, derived from the verb δαμάω. The Syriac form *Adamus* cannot be the primary for in that case the ending *-us* would have diminutive force and would thus make the name inapplicable to a "Great Man."

[71] Iren. I, 29, 3.

[72] According to Augustine, *contra Faustum*, xv, 6 and Bar Khoni, Cumont I, p. 39.

[73] κεκρατημένος, Hipp. V, 7, 7. In Hippolytus' redaction of the Chaldean Tale the name Adamas occurs, but it cannot belong to the original account. Cf. our reconstruction, above, p. 50.

It follows, then, that whatever the origin of the name Adamas, the heroic Anthropos himself goes back, not only in time, but in place as well, to a sphere where Greek influence could not have acted formatively upon the delineation of his person and role.

To suppose that a heroic capacity is thus inherent in the nature of the Anthropos (since it is a constant factor in the tradition), does not necessarily imply the Iranian origin of the figure either in part or whole. We are, thus, one step yet removed from bringing the results of the previous argument to bear upon the question concerning the relation of Gayomart and Anthropos. By considering the evidence for the latter's heroic role from still another angle we shall, however, find ourselves brought back to that particular question.

The analysis of the Manichean sources has showed that while the majority regarded the Primal Man as essentially a defeated champion, there was an undercurrent of opinion to the effect that he had really been victorious in his conflict with the King of Darkness. The evidence just presented to prove that the earlier Gnostics of the littoral Near East were acquainted with the heroic Anthropos reflects the same two points of view. Where he is known as Adamas, the Anthropos is certainly the victorious "unconquerable" champion. Even the Poimandres, when it speaks of the Anthropos' "will to subdue" seems to echo this strain. Yet the burden of the Hermetic tale is closer to the other conception. The last thing it records concerning the heavenly Man is the union between him and his beloved Physis. That he disappears from the scene completely after this event indicates that he has lost his divine identity. Submitting to passion he has become its victim and paid the penalty that must be demanded of a divine being for such an act. Whatever the benefits are that accrue to man by reason of this primordial incident, it certainly brings the story of the Anthropos to a tragic close. What is true of the Poimandres is true of the Chaldean Tale as well, for here the Great Man is "overcome" in the course of events leading to man's creation.

Throughout our sources we thus find a twofold interpretation of the heroic Anthropos. He is both victorious and defeated champion. What, then, may be the relative antiquity of the two types and the origin of the later of the two?

Anyone familiar with the growth and development of mythological and legendary tradition will not find it difficult to answer the first of these questions. It is much more likely that the weaker, defeated champion should become a victorious hero in the course of time than that the opposite should be the case. Human nature in inherently optimistic and the traditions handed down by humanity have a tendency to be changed into conformity with that optimism.

The second question, relative to the origin of the later (victorious) type is not so readily disposed of. We have two criteria by which to formulate an opinion, first, the fact that the Anthropos and Manda d'Haye were are one time identified, second, the characteristics of the victorious Anthropos.

Among the scholars who have occupied themselves with the interpretation of the Mandean texts, those venturing an opinion upon the origin of Manda d'Haye have, with the exception of Reitzenstein, been unanimous in declaring that he represents a Gnostic form of the conqueror Marduk.[74] The correspondence between Marduk and Manda d'Haye in both outline and detail is so striking as to admit of almost no other explanation.[75] If, then, the heroic Anthropos has been considered cognate to Manda d'Haye, it may not be amiss to ascribe the existence of the victorious type of heroic Anthropos to the influence exerted upon the figure by the old Babylonian deity. The mere fact that both are primordial champions serves to motivate the rapprochement between them.

Confirmation of this contention may be gained from the analysis of the more important characteristics of the victorious Anthropos, as indicated in the Manichean sources.

[74] Brandt, MR, pp. 182–4, 213–16; Kessler, art. *Mandäer*, PRE (3rd ed.), vol. XII, p. 182, 19–22; Bousset, HP, pp. 242–51; Pallis, *Mandaeiske Studier*, (1919), pp. 23–32.

[75] Particularly in RG, bks. 3 and 5, 1. In the latter Hibil has secondarily taken the place of Manda d'Haye Brandt, MR, pp. 213–6; Kessler, loc. cit.

The sources upon which we are dependent in reconstructing the Manichean theology are agreed that in the primordial struggle the Primal Man loses a portion of his person or of the arms or powers of his panoply. They disagree, as we have seen, concerning the circumstances attending the loss. Some regard it as the tragic result of the Anthropos' defeat. The rest view it as a clever and premeditated stratagem, the idea being that absorption of the foreign material forces the powers of evil into submission.[76] This idea that the loss represents a stratagem may well have been suggested by the story of Marduk's conquest of Tiamat, for Marduk there sends the tempest, one of his helpers, into the inward parts of the monster and by this means overwhelms her.[77]

Furthermore, the conception that the five elements connected with the Primal Man form his armor, recalls the fact that Marduk too was armed in his descent to the lower world.[78] Nahashshebet, finally, the personification of the weapon carried by the Primal Man in other accounts, may well be the serpentine lightning, which in pictorial representations the dragon fighters of Babylonia hold in their hand.[79]

If our analysis of the heroic, and particularly of the victorious Anthropos is valid, it will serve not only to clear the way for the interrelation of Anthropos and Gayomart, by showing that the role of primordial champion is a constant element in the tradition, but will give us in addition a positive basis upon which to establish that connection.

Direct statements preserved in the sources, general considerations arising out of the study of Gnosticism as a whole and the impression created by the relative vitality evinced by our figure in the different streams of tradition, indicate that the home of the Anthropos is in the inner Orient, and that the geographical diffusion and inner development of the tradition progressed as he

[76] Cf. above, pp. 19-20.
[77] S. Langdon, *The Babylonian Epic of Creation* (1923), pp. 133 and 141.
[78] Ibid., p. 131.
[79] A. Jeremias, *Handbuch der altorient. Geisteskultur* (1913), pp. 26-7 and plates 15 and 17.

traveled from East to West.[80] If then we are to consider Babylonian thought as the means of his transformation into a victorious champion, the ultimate origin of the underlying and transformed figure should logically be found east of Mesopotamia, in Iran.[81] The similarity between the Iranian Gayomart and the Anthropos as defeated champion, as we have already outlined it, cannot be either secondary or fortuitous. The stratification of the Anthropos tradition and the course of the Anthropos' movement from Mesopotamia westward, demand that the two figures must be fundamentally identical.

Before the argument on this point becomes conclusive, one further step will need to be taken. An adequate basis, not in conflict with the hypothesis advanced, must be found to explain the evolution of those details in the description of the preëxistent and primordial Anthropos for which there is no immediate foundation in the person and role of Gayomart.

Between the two figures whom it is proposed to connect, there are a number of distinct differences. In the first place, Gayomart is but the prototype of humanity.[82] He struggles against the demons as one who is an element of Ahura Mazda's material creation. The Anthropos, on the other hand, is a completely transcendent person, a member of the divine pleroma. Among the Manicheans he was regarded as the third of a divine Trinity comprising Father, Mother and Son. Other Gnostics placed him in the divine Ogdoad of emanations or made of him the supreme deity.

Now of course it is true that Gayomart was a member not only

[80] Cf. above, pp. 83-4.

[81] That the change actually took place in Mesopotamia is demanded by the intimate knowledge of Marduk revealed in the characterization of the Anthropos.

[82] Guentert (p. 316) is probably correct in assuming that the Indo-Arian prototype of Gayomart was considered a divine being, and Scheftelowitz is probably also right in his contention that the Pahlavi Gayomart is not a God (*Entstehung*, p. 59). But the conclusions drawn from his observation by Scheftelowitz are incorrect. The Pahlavi Gayomart is certainly more than a normal human being, and because of this fact he could well become a God in Gnostic circles.

THE ORIGIN AND ANTIQUITY OF THE ANTHROPOS

of the material creation of Ahura Mazda, but of the spiritual and preëxistent creation as well. If that fact was known to the individuals from whom the Gnostics derived their information, it would serve to explain why they classed him among the divine beings. Yet it would not explain the prominence and preëminence accorded him in his divine form. This, together with the transformation as a whole, can be accounted for satisfactorily if we interpose between Gayomart and the Anthropos the former's identification with Marduk. Once the two champions had been identified with one another, a divine Anthropos could well result. Indeed the tendency to regard the Anthropos as one of the highest, if not the highest of the pleromatic powers cannot be disassociated from the fact that Marduk, as the son of Ea is actually considered the manifestation of the third power in the Babylonian Trinity, [83] and that by reason of his victory over Tiamat he is sometimes considered the foremost of the Gods, having the rank of Anu. [84] Minor fluctuations in the position of the divine Anthropos, such as those characterizing the diverse Valentinian schools, are of course due to the confluence of a number of distinct traditions, of which the Anthropos theology was but one. Mani's identification of Primal Man and Ormuzd has roots that extend into Zervanistic doctrines as well as into the Anthropos tradition of earlier times.

In his role as divine being the Anthropos sometimes aspires to metaphysical significance, particularly in the capacities of Nous, Logos and All. To some these capacities constitute evidence for the contention that the Anthropos is Western and speculative in origin. The fallacy of this contention we have already had occasion to discuss. Reitzenstein, on the other hand, has latterly endeavored to show that the noötic characteristics of the Hellenistic Anthropos are the correct expression of the nature of Gayo-

---

[83] HAOG, p. 23. Such trinities are, however, common in Oriental thought and might have originated almost anywhere. Cf. Bousset, III², pp. 333-8, where the effort is made to connect the trinity embracing the Primal Man with Dinkard, III, 82, Gayomart being there the son of Ahura Mazda and Spendarmad.

[84] HAOG, p. 273.

mart as a member of the preëxistent spiritual world and as the representative and embodiment of qualities inherent in Ahura Mazda.[85]

While we are not yet ready to agree with Reitzenstein that the channel through which these impressions were transmitted westward was the knowledge *in extenso* of Avestan books like the Damdat Nask (which he finds summarized in the Poimandres), the view given by the German scholar represents one distinctly possible explanation of the phenomena under discussion. Its only weakness is that the Anthropos Theology in other respects seems to reflect the impression made by the vicissitudes and the position of Gayomart, rather than by his essential qualities.

Considering this fact and the extremities to which syncretism led in the littoral Orient, where the Anthropos became metaphysical, it seems feasible to suggest a less recondite explanation of the transformation which he suffered. In his Mesopotamian phase, the Anthropos was regarded as cosmogonal agent and occupied either first or third places in the heavenly hierarchy. Such a form of Anthropos theology transmitted to Syria and brought violently into contact with metaphysics would naturally lead to the coördination of Anthropos and any metaphysical postulate correspondingly placed in the scheme of ultimates. The very range of speculative thought represented by the concepts Nous, Logos and All attached to the Anthropos, would seem to indicate that their application to him rests not upon the correct appreciation of his essential being, but rather upon the desire to syncretize.

Under these conditions it is extremely difficult to ascertain whether and to what extent the macrocosmic significance attaching to Gayomart played a part in determining the nature of individual forms of the Anthropos' metaphysical appearance in the West. Suffice it then to say, that the origin of the speculative interpretation of the Anthropos is as readily intelligible in connection with any hypothesis maintaining his Oriental origin, as the fact that, once he had been introduced into the speculative sphere, it became customary to differentiate between entirely transcendent and transcendent-immanent phases of his being,

[85] Reitzenstein u. Schaeder, *Studien*, pp. 3–37.

and thus to reduplicate the figure, using the Christian expression "Son of Man" as the designation of second manifestation.

It is a further peculiarity of the Anthropos that in his pleromatic as well as his subjective existence, he is frequently characterized as bisexual.[86] This trait he manifests only in sources that show contact with Greek speculation. It has, moreover, no direct and explicit parallel in the description of Gayomart. Hence, it has been pointed to as an argument for either the Jewish or the Greek speculative origin of an Anthropos, in proportion as attention has been focused either upon the bisexual Adam of the Midrashim[87] the super-sexual "heavenly Man" of Philo[88] or the corresponding cosmic Logos.[89]

These conclusions are based upon the examination of only a part of the relevant evidence. In a number of sources where bisexuality plays no part in the description of the Anthropos, we find him supplied with a female *paredros*. She appears under a diversity of names, either as Ennoia, Ekklesia, Anana d'Nhura or Barbelo.[90] Everyone will no doubt admit that his appearance in the company of a consort is the result of the division of the bisexual Anthropos into his component male and female elements. Since the sources that speak of the partner are relatively no older than those mentioning the hermaphrodite man, the existence of the consort might seem to shed no light on the origin of the trait of bisexuality. That is not the case.

Two of the four names applied to the consort of the Anthropos identify her as one and the same person, the famous deity, Ishtar of Arbela. The first is the name Barbelo, the best etymology of which is, we believe, "in Arbela."[91] The second is Anana d'Nhura, the Mandean designation which approximates an epithet applied to Ishtar as queen of heaven in a hymn, namely,

[86] Cf. above, pp. 44, n. 36 and p. 55.

[87] *Bereshith Rabba*, 8, 1; *Wayyikra Rabba*, 14,1; cf. Scheftelowitz, *Parsismus und Judentum* (1920), p, 217.

[88] *Opif. Mundi*, § 134; *Leg. Alleg.*, II, § 13; Leisegang, *Der Heilige Geist* (1919), pp. 78–80; Scott, *Hermetica*, II. p. 45.

[89] Leisegang, *Gnosis*, pp. 93–5; 117–8.

[90] Cf. above, pp. 41, 46, 61.

[91] A number of etymologies have been suggested. Hilgenfeld, *Ketzer-*

"fiery cloud."[92] Now we have already seen that internal and external evidence connects the Anthropos at one stage of his development with Chaldea, and that this stage antedates the period of his speculative metaphysical interpretation. It would seem that the period when he was identified with Marduk was the juncture that produced his collocation with Ishtar. In the first place, to assume that the *paredros* is a creation of the later epoch, when the Anthropos had already reached the Hellenized littoral of the Near East, is to make her (secondary) identification with Ishtar unintelligible. Ennoia and Ekklesia would be her proper names in this case, and neither suggests Ishtar as its Babylonian counterpart. Indeed the Christian influence visible in the name Ekklesia may well be thought to militate against the possibility of paganizing the figure. On the other hand, if Ishtar is the consort in her original form, the change to Ekklesia, the bride of the heavenly king, is at least feasible. But that means in turn that the consort reverts to the pre-Christian pre-Hellenistic period of the Anthropos tradition, a period represented only by the Chaldean Tale, in other words the period that saw the identification of Anthropos and Marduk. In the second place, as Zimmern has pointed out, the syzygy idea which plays such a part in determining the nature of Gnostic theology, may well have its origin in the Babylonian practise of listing deities in pairs.[93] If, as we have reason to believe, the Anthropos passed through Mesopotamia before he appeared in the West, that is both the place and the time for the addition of a consort and the formation of a syzygy.

It has already been said, that logically, the Anthropos bisexuality should precede his appearance in company with a partner. If the partner be an addition accruing to him in his passage of Mesopotamia, his bisexuality should revert to his pre-Mesopo-

geschichte, p. 233 ("in the four is God"); Bousset, HP, p. 14 (corruption of Greek παρθένος). The one we should be inclined to accept, namely "in Arbela," is that of Gressmann, ZKG, vol. XL (1922), p. 187.

[92] HAOG, p. 257. The epithet as transcribed by Jeremias is *Akukûtum*.

[93] Zimmern, *Babylonische Vorstufen der vorderasiatischen Mysterienreligion*, ZDMG, vol. 76 (1922), p. 52.

tamian prototype, Gayomart. This brings us face to face with the difficulty, that Gayomart is nowhere explicitly styled bisexual. Two facts have, however, to be noted, first, that as Guentert has shown, this trait is a current feature in the Indo-Iranian type of which Gayomart is a particular manifestation,[94] second, that because of his prototypic character, Gayomart may be said to be not alien to ideas of bisexuality. This makes possible the assertion that the type which Gayomart represents, and the solitarity of his existence could suggest his being thought of as bisexual or being connected with a partner.[95] That makes him a sufficient basis for the origin of the phenomena of the Anthropos tradition which are at present under consideration.

Manicheans, as we have seen, associate the Primal Man with five elements. These they consider fundamental to his physical structure, or adjuncts to his person in the nature of sons, armor or cloaks. In the Iranian tradition, Gayomart, through his death and disintegration, contributes seven metals to the constitution of the cosmos. The parallel is not exact, both in the number of the elements and in their nature. Yet it is incorrect with Scheftelowitz to ignore the existence of even a partial similarity, and to use the relation of Anthropos and elements in support of the hypothesis maintaining the non-Iranian origin of the figure. For this contention there is one excellent reason. Element speculation was, as Reitzenstein has shown, a widely diffused practice.[96] Canons of four, five and seven elements are found over the whole of the ancient world, from China and India to Greece and Egypt. There are infinite possibilities for fluctuation in number and character, particularly in such a religion as Manicheism, which drew upon Buddhistic, Iranian, Greek and Christian as well as Gnostic sources from the beginning. A suggestion such as that contained in the Gayomart tradition is sufficient to connect the Anthropos with element speculation. Of course it

[94] Guentert, p. 392.
[95] In the Pahlavi texts the Earth, Spendarmad, functions as the spouse of Gayomart.
[96] *Gedanken zur Entwickelung des Erlöserglaubens*, Historische Zeitschrift, vol. 126 (1922), III. Folge, vol. 30, pp. 10–14.

must be remembered, too, that the five-fold number of the Anthropos' elements is only the Manichean version of the tradition. In the Poimandres, it is seven powers with which the Anthropos is endowed. Twice six are the aeons which according to Valentinus and his school, the Anthropos produces.[97] Variation is truly the only constant factor in the element speculation. Gayomart is therefore still a sufficient beginning for the phenomena concerned.

That brings us finally to the question of nomenclature. Anthropos is a designation applied to the figure under discussion only in systems where it has lost much of its original vitality. It is almost certainly an abbreviated form of the terms "First Man," "Primal Man" or "Great Man." Gayomart, we have constantly referred to as the "prototype of humanity."[98] He is not on a level with the protoplasts of the Semitic world and Greece. Their nearest counterparts in Iran are Mashya and Mashyoi. The difficulty thus stated is not insurmountable. It arises solely from the inadequacy of the terminology current in non-Iranian circles for the expression of Iranian ideas. The Anthropos never descends in person or role to the level of a mere protoplast. He is always closer to a prototype. But what designations other than "Primal Man" and "Great Man" could people of Mesopotamia and Syria apply to a human prototype. They had, to our knowledge, no terminology to express typicality. Primal Man was the nearest approach possible. Its use in connection with the Anthropos does not separate the latter from Gayomart.

Perhaps it will be possible to arrive at a more definite conclusion from the discussion of nomenclature. Among the designations applied to our figure, only Anthropos, Adam and Adamas can be called proper names. These, however, represent a late development. The earliest terminology applied to the Anthropos is entirely descriptive, as for instance "Upper Man," "Great, Most Glorious and Perfect Man" and, perhaps, even "Primal Man." In the strict sense of the word the Anthropos is then originally nameless. The same is true of the proposed Iranian prototype.

[97] Irenaeus, I, 11, 1.
[98] With Christensen, p. 32.

If we regard the passage in the third Gatha (Ys, 30, 6) as a reference to his person, the Iranian figure bears at first the generic designation "maretan," meaning "mortal." In the Younger Avesta of the Sasanian period, the period that witnessed the growth and earliest diffusion of the Anthropos tradition, he was known by the equally descriptive term "gaya-maretan," signifying "Life-Man" or "Mortal Life,"[99] In the Pahlavi works this term is reduced to the proper name Gayomart. The designations originally applied to the Gnostic and Iranian figures differ in origin. Those applied to the former were determined by the consideration of his place and position, while those applied to the latter were determined by his nature. In kind and character, however, the two groups of designations are alike, for they are descriptive designations, not proper names. Both Anthropos and Gayomart are then originally nameless in the strict sense of the word. Perhaps this constitutes a further link between them.

The chief points of divergence between the Anthropos in his primordial role and the Iranian Gayomart can, as we have seen, be explained satisfactorily as the result of the transformation which the latter would naturally undergo when transplanted to a more westerly soil. We therefore regard the Iranian origin of the Anthropos as a working hypothesis and proceed to the discussion of the psychic and soteriological aspects of the figure, their origin and development.

4. In a number of Gnostic systems the Anthropos is considered the fountainhead of a material yet spiritual principle indwelling in mankind and the world. This principle is variously defined as the Soul, the Pneuma, Reason, or indeed as a combination of Soul and Pneuma or Soul and Mind. Where technical terminology has been evolved it is known by the names Jesus Patibilis, Inner Man, Son of Man and Adakas.

The ultimate origin of this conception is a problem of great intricacy, and one the solution of which is not entirely possible to-day. What makes it so difficult is the fact that it is inextricably bound up with the as yet unsolved problem of the origin of the Soul Drama.

[99] Ibid., pp. 12–3, quoting the Yashts.

It was a belief current in many parts of the ancient world that man has within him a divine element, a spark from the fire of the Gods. Appearing under many names, but predominantly that of "Soul" this element was more than the sum of a man's subjective processes; it was a substance that came from God and returned to him.

Attention was first directed to the question whence came this conception, by the German scholar Anz.[100] Examining the Gnostic material in so far as it was known at the time and confining his attention to the story of the soul's final journey heavenward, Anz came to the conclusion that the conception originated in Mesopotamia. The basis of his findings was the fact that in the Gnostic description of that journey, taking the soul through a hostile stellar and planetary world, much of the Babylonian astronomical theology was presupposed. Bousset, who followed Anz, broadened the field of inquiry by taking into consideration Hellenic, Hellenistic, Christian, Jewish and Iranian conceptions in addition to those Gnostic beliefs already examined. He found that the idea of the soul's heavenward journey appeared also independently of Babylonian astral theology. It need not, then, be Messopotamian in origin. Indeed it was Iranian, he believed, for in Iran it appeared in its most highly developed form. The Greek parallels from Plato on, might be either an independent product or possibly dependent in some way ultimately upon Persian theology. These Greek parallels, whatever their origin, undoubtedly contributed to the Gnostic statement of the Soul Drama, but were not sufficient to explain its peculiarities. The Gnostic form was essentially Iranian with an admixture of much Babylonian material which the conception acquired as it travelled westward to be incorporated in the Gnostic systems.[101] Bousset's investigation, accepted in its main outlines by Cumont and others, remained in favor for some time.[102]

---

[100] *Zur Frage nach dem Ursprung des Gnostizismus*, Texte u. Untersuchungen, XV, 3 (1897).

[101] *Die Himmelsreise der Seele*, Archiv f. Religionswissenschaft, vol. 4 (1900), pp. 136–69; 229–273.

[102] Wendland, *Kultur*, pp. 170–87.

THE ORIGIN AND ANTIQUITY OF THE ANTHROPOS

The inquiry entered upon a new phase with the works of Reitzenstein. What is new in Reitzenstein's treatment of the subject is not the denial of the conclusions reached by Bousset, it is the use of new material, in the shape of syncretistic cosmogonies and Manichean liturgical texts, and the discovery of new facts concerning the nature of the Gnostic Soul Drama.[103] Of new facts there are two, first, that the fate of the individual soul in the Soul Drama, is but a rehearsal of the fate of the World Soul; second, that the heavenly journey is only one element of a larger unity which includes also the primordial descent and imprisonment of the divine element.

These new conceptions serve at once to broaden and yet to limit the Gnostic form of the Soul Drama. It becomes greater and more significant, and simultaneously takes on a religious guise that distinguishes it from that view of the soul's vicissitudes current in the speculative systems of the philosophic West. Religion, says Reitzenstein, is older than philosophy. The Gnostic Soul Drama is inherently older than the Hellenic, because it is religious. Its Psyche, the World Soul, is a mythological character, not a metaphysical postulate.

Since the Manichean texts and the syncretistic cosmogonies, particularly that of Asonakes (?), embody elements that are of Iranian origin, Reitzenstein feels justified in looking to Iran as the source of the conceptions embodied in the fundamentals of the Gnostic Soul Drama.

Now Avestan and Pahlavi sources, the basis for our knowledge of orthodox Zarathushtrianism, reveal intimate acquaintance with only one element of the Gnostic Soul Drama, namely the heavenward ascent of the individual soul. Reitzenstein has thought to find in a few passages some reference to the World Soul and its primordial descent to matter, but Gressmann[104] and Wesendonk[105] are probably correct in maintaining that these passages speak only of the individual soul. Furthermore, it is by

[103] Particularly Reitzenstein, *Psyche*, and IE.
[104] ZKG, vol. XL (1922), pp. 184–7.
[105] *Urmensch u. Seele* (1924), pp. 61–3; but cf. Reitzenstein's answer, *Studien*, pp. 124–6.

no means evident that the status of the individual soul in this world was regarded in Iran as of the nature of imprisonment. Man at all times exercises free will and finds about him a world which is not inherently bad.

The hypothesis of Reitzenstein, however, does not look to Avestan and Pahlavi sources and what they have to say as the criterion of its justifiability. The "Erlösungsmysterium" built upon the religious form of the Soul Drama, is thought to be an element of popular Iranian belief, as distinguished from the formal theological convictions of Mazdaism embodied in the Iranian sources. So stated the hypothesis is difficult either to affirm or deny, the former because there are no criteria, the latter because in its character it is a step in the right direction.

If anyone not as intimately connected with the study of syncretism as Reitzenstein were suddenly to postulate the existence of an undocumented popular Iranian religious atmosphere, we might be inclined to regard it as a subterfuge. Matters being as they are, it is a monument to profound grasp of the subject. The diversity, unity and general temper of those manifold syncretistic movements that appear on the horizon at the beginning of the second Christian century demand the existence, somewhere, of a proto-Gnostic form of religious belief, popular in character and mystical in outlook. The only question upon which there can be difference of opinion, is whether that projected sphere of thought is actually Iranian.

Though it may seem to be a digression all this has a direct bearing upon the question whence comes the idea that the Anthropos is the fountainhead of a spiritual principle indwelling in mankind.

To attempt to find its ultimate source in the figure and associations of Gayomart is, we believe, fruitless. Reitzenstein and Schaeder have in recent times produced evidence which might appear to argue to the contrary. It is the Great Bundahishn's identification of the semen which flows from Gayomart at his death, with the soul.[106] Since the earth's reception of this element actually results, according to Pahlavi tradition, in the

[106] *Studien*, pp. 223-6.

birth of the first human couple, it might be said that Iran and Gayomart once more furnish a source for an element of the Anthropos tradition, this time that of the Anthropos' psychic manifestation.

The identification which the Great Bundahishn upholds, though it has earmarks of primitive thought, is at variance with the rudiments of the psychology evolved by the scholars of Iran. For the theologians of Persia the nature and origin of the soul was determined not by the fact of its being an element of Gayomart, or even by its being a portion of the world soul, but by the consideration of the immateriality and incalculability of the subjective processes and phases of human nature. Hence the complexity in the composition of the psychic and divine portion of man, as they viewed it. Simultaneously it is evident that the shorter, or Indian recension of the Bundahishn preserves no trace of the identification referred to by Reitzenstein and Schaeder, and that the Great Bundahishn, in spite of itself, tells how the offspring of Gayomart receive the soul, not as an inheritance from their father, but as something that entered into their bodies when they passed from the plant to the human stage of their development.[107] The creationistic rather than traducianistic nature of Iranian psychology reasserts itself once more. Thus it appears as though the identification upon which the Iranian origin of the psychic role of the Anthropos depends is either very late or very early (or both), but is under no conditions the expression of those ideas which were dominant in the circles to which we owe the bulk of our knowledge of Iranian thought, and played no part in the days that saw the rise and growth of the Anthropos tradition. Bundahishn XV, 1 we therefore consider no more than a reference to the fact that Gayomart at the moment of death became the father of the human race.

The only alternative to the conclusion that the psychic role of the Anthropos is a secondary element of the tradition and not connected with Iran is this, that there existed in the popular religion of Iran an ancient goddess Psyche, the similarity of whose fate as compared with that of the defeated Gayomart, led at an

[107] Ibid., pp. 230–1.

early time to the correlation of the two figures. To this hypothesis Reitzenstein until recently subscribed. Here, then, we see the bearing of the Soul Drama inquiry upon the Anthropos investigation.

In view of obtaining conditions we prefer to leave the question of the hypothetical Iranian Psyche open, till a more detailed analysis of the manifold lines of influence running hither and yon between the lands of the East in Hellenistic times shall have determined whether the proto-Gnostic atmosphere with which the Soul Drama is intimately connected had its home in Iran or elsewhere. This conclusion does not relieve us of the necessity of endeavoring to ascertain whether the superimposed and fluctuating forms of the Anthropos tradition have any verdict to render in the matter of the primary or secondary nature of the Anthropos' psychic manifestation. As a matter of fact they seem to have a verdict to give.

It is a peculiar phenomenon of Manichean theology that the Primal Man is connected in two ways with humanity. In the first place he is the fountainhead of that divine element which was lost by him in the primordial conflict, was captured by the archons and was finally deposited by them at their own volition in the human frame. In the second place, the Primal Man assisted at the very act of man's creation, by furnishing the prototype in whose image man was moulded.

This double tradition is echoed in the remainder of the Gnostic sources. On the one hand we have the Valentinian and Christian Naasene systems bearing witness to the immanence of a portion of the Anthropos' person, but failing either to presuppose or present a reason for its presence, a reason such as would root the phenomenon in the nature, character or life of the Anthropos himself. On the other hand we have the Valentinian counterpart of the Manichean account of how man was made in the image of the Anthropos.

Aside from this double tradition stands that represented by the Chaldean Tale, as interpreted by the author of the Pagan Naasene Document, and by the Poimandres. Here we are told that the divine element came to reside in man in connection with the Anthropos' assistance at the episode of man's creation, an episode in which the image of the Anthropos also plays a part.

Appearing coincidentally in the two sources that give us our earliest glimpse of the Anthropos, the last of these traditions would appear to have greatest claim to priority and relative originality. This is borne out by the fact that it connects itself most readily with the story of Gayomart, for of all the Gnostic accounts the Chaldean Tale and the Poimandres alone rehearse the Iranian conception that the moment of the death or downfall of the prototype is the moment of the birth of the human race.

The authors of both the Pagan Naasene Document and the Poimandres believed that the Anthropos furnished the protoplast with a divine element from above. To the former, this element was the Spirit, the Inner Man. If he interpreted the Hebrew account of the creation of man in the light of this conception, he no doubt found a reference to that divine element in the "image" of the Anthropos mentioned in the Chaldean Tale.

Fundamentally, we are inclined to believe, the Chaldean Tale does not support his views. The image, here, is not something which man has. It is something that man is, and the man who is the image, is in this case "the man whom the earth produced." Secondly, the Chaldean Tale represents, as we have seen, that strand of tradition regarding the primordial conflict of the Anthropos in which the latter is defeated. Where this defeat entails the loss of an element, the loss is coincidental with the defeat. But the Chaldean Tale presupposes that the Anthropos is still undefeated after the "image-man" has been produced. The image cannot then represent a lost element. Finally, the thing that is enslaved is the πλάσμα, a term applicable only to the "image-man" and not applicable to the image or the Spirit.

Nor is it possible to suppose that the soul was the Anthropos' contribution to human nature in the Chaldean Tale. Reitzenstein at one time defended this interpretation,[108] but it cannot be harmonized with the statement in the narrative that what is imprisoned and enslaved is the πλάσμα of the Anthropos. The soul should be the one to suffer at the hands of the body.

[108] *Poimandres*, p. 84, n. 7.

We must therefore conclude that in the Chaldean Tale the Anthropos contributes neither Spirit nor Soul to the nature of human existence. This constitutes an argument against the contention that the psychic manifestation of the Anthropos is a fundamental element of the Anthropos tradition. While it occupied a permanent place in all of the early Western and later Eastern forms of Anthropos Theology, it fails us when we trace the tradition back to its early Mesopotamian form. Thereby we gain a check upon our interpretation of the Iranian sources.

There is one great objection to this contention. How, if the Anthropos contributed neither Spirit nor Soul to human nature in the Chaldean Tale, can the story of man's creation therein recorded involve the defeat of the heavenly Man? It is a question concerning the real meaning of the Chaldean Tale and one which we cannot afford to avoid since in its answer lies not only the defense of our position but the key to the genesis of that whole complex of ideas associated with the creative activity of the Anthropos.

In a greater or lesser degree both the Chaldean Tale and the Poimandres' account are a fusion of the same two elements, the Anthropos tradition and the Old Testament narrative of the creation of man.[109] Both of these elements can be traced prior to their appearance in conjunction with one another. The former we have already pursued through some of its Mesopotamian and Iranian ramifications. With the latter and its development in Hellenistic times we must now concern ourselves.

The first to introduce changes into the Biblical accounts of creation were the Jews themselves. Impelled by the necessity of adapting the old narratives to the newer transcendental conception of God and finding in the plural of the words "let us make man" the justification of their views, they associated the angels in ever-increasing measure with the act of creation.[110] In certain circles the angels were even thought to have furnished the prototype in the image of which man was made.[111] The likeness

---

[109] Of the Poimandres, Reitzenstein admits this, *Studien*, pp. 23–5.
[110] L. Ginzberg, *The Legends of the Jews*, vol. I (1909), pp. 52–5.
[111] *Ber. Rab.* 21, 5; *Shemoth Rab.*, 30, 16.

between man and God or the angels, however, the Jews never stated in terms of nature or essence. Man was like God only in outward appearance or in certain faculties, characteristics or capacities such as intelligence, immortality and free-will.[112]

Philo represents an individual development from this basis. He too speaks of powers[113] about Him,[114] whom God employed in the creation of man.[115] These powers fashioned the body and soul, the elements subject to passion, while God himself made the human reason.[116] The similarity between man and God is limited to the matter of reason, but human reason is an immanent element of divine reason, the Logos.[117] In reason then man is related to a manifestation of God but the "image" which makes man like God exists also apart from man in a mode of God, namely in the Logos.

Paul, whose theology like that of Philo is an offshoot of Palestinian Judaism, clings to the traditional views where the creation of the first humanity is concerned. God and man are not related in nature. None the less he is familiar with the view which attributes to the image of God an existence independent of both man and God. To him this image is Christ.[118]

As soon as the Hebrew account of creation entered the world of the syncretists further changes were bound to be introduced. The angels who fashioned man's body here represented grossly inferior or even Satanic powers. If that was the case how could man be made in God's image? The angels could of themselves have no knowledge of that image. Consistent dualistic Gnostics of Marcion's type answered the question by the contention that the image was that of the evil God, not of the good God.[119] More optimistic interpreters found a solution of the difficulty in the view shared by Philo and Paul that the image of God was

[112] Weber, *Jüd. Theol.*, pp. 209–10.
[113] *de Fuga*, §69.
[114] *de Confusione*, §179.
[115] *de Opificio*, §75.
[116] *de Fuga*, §69.
[117] *de Opificio*, §69.
[118] *Col.*, 1, 15, et al.
[119] Tertullian, *adv. Marc.*, II, 1–5.

independent of God's person and could act by itself. This image was thought by them to have revealed itself momentarily to the inferior powers. Having perceived it, the angels made man "according to the image." Reinterpreted after this manner, the Biblical narrative of creation was incorporated bodily in the Anthropos tradition. It finds its clearest expression in the Manichean sources.[120]

According to Genesis 2, 7 man became, at God's hand, a "living soul." To the syncretists the soul was a familiar concept. It represented, as we have seen, that divine element that came down from the highest God and was imprisoned in inferior forms of existence, till at death it returned homeward. That being the case, it could not have been added to human nature by the agency that had created the body. The Soul, moreover, was regarded by the syncretists as something expressing itself not in terms of blood or breath, but in terms of action. The Soul furnished the members to the human body.[121] It followed from this, that the man whom the angels had created was a being which, lacking members, could not stand erect but moved by crawling, after the manner of reptiles.

The alterations produced in the Biblical account of man's creation by its transfer into the syncretistic sphere are best illustrated from what Irenaeus tells us of Saturninus' view of man's beginning. Here we are informed that

> Saturninus, like Menander, taught the one Father unknown to all, who made Angels, Archangels, Powers (virtutes: δυνάμεις) and Mighty Ones (potestates: ἐξουσίαι). The world, moreover and all things in it, were made by a group of seven angels. Man, too, was the workmanship of angels. (The following were the circumstances of his formation.) A resplendent image coming from the highest Power manifested itself below (i.e., outside the pleroma). When they (the angels) found themselves unable to restrain it (tenere: κρατεῖν ?) for the reason that it immediately returned upwards, they urged one another, saying: "Let us make man in accordance with the image and likeness." When the form (plasma) had been fashioned and proved unable to

[120] Cf. above, p. 23.
[121] The members belong to the soul also in the Odes of Solomon, Ode 21, 4.

stand erect, by reason of the impotence of the angels, but wriggled (on the ground) like a worm, the Power above (desuper: ἄνωθεν) took pity on it, since it had been made in its likeness, and sent forth a spark of life which set it upright, gave it limbs (articulavit) and made it live.[122]

What has already been said concerning the individualization of "the image of God" and concerning the Gnostic conception of the soul should clarify the sense and origin of most of what is recorded in the story of Saturninus. Two details alone have not been accounted for in the preceding discussion, namely that the angels wished to restrain the image and that the act of creation was inspired by this wish. We shall revert to them presently.

With the story of Saturninus before us we are in a position to analyze the Chaldean Tale. This does not signify that the latter is a derivative of the former. It means that Saturninus' story shows the range of ideas with which the Biblical account of creation was combined and the direction in which syncretists who had no direct knowledge of the Anthropos tradition were working in adapting the Bible to their needs.

That the Anthropos tradition should be combined with the syncretized version of the Biblical account of the creation of man, as in the Chaldean Tale, is but natural. Not only did the two readily lend themselves to combination, but quite aside from this any narrative that told of a similarity between man and a heavenly power must prove interesting and valuable to circles concerning themselves with a heavenly Man. After all the best likeness of a human being is another man, and the Anthropos the ideal prototype for a primal man "after the image."

The identification of the origin of a number of details in the Chaldean Tale is quite simple. The Tale begins by relating that Adam is the man "whom the earth produced." A little later we hear that he owes his origin to "the powers of the many." The first statement recalls the fact that, in the Iranian tradition which provoked the Anthropos speculation, the undivided primal couple is produced by Spendarmad, the Earth. The second recalls the creative activity of the angels in the reinterpreted Biblical narrative. On the basis of the account of Genesis these two

[122] Irenaeus, I, 24, 1.

elements could be combined, for there man is actually made (though not born) of the earth and is fashioned (though not born) of agents speaking in the plural. What the Chaldean Tale records between the two statements of which mention has been made, shows that the Anthropos has been identified with "the power that manifested itself" to the angels, an identification that is quite *á propos* in view of the fact that the Anthropos in Iran assists at the creation of man.

The next statement concerning the heavenly Man is that he is at length to be subdued and that his overthrow is to be effected in connection with the creation of man. To this extent the Chaldean Tale again runs true to the Anthropos tradition, for in its Iranian form, we recall, Gayomart is overcome by hostile powers after a long struggle, and the moment of his defeat is the moment of the procreation of man. It is peculiar to the Chaldean Tale, however, that the overthrow of the Anthropos is the result (rather than the cause) of the creation of man, and that the overthrow is accomplished by the empsychosis of the body which is his image. About this detail the controversy concerning the originality and primary character of the Anthropos' psychic manifestation turns. Reitzenstein contends that either the author of the Pagan Naasene Document or Hippolytus has misinterpreted the sense of the Tale and given us an erroneous rendition of the original at this point. We should be inclined to believe that the element in question can be made intelligible by reference to a well-known axiom of ancient religious thought. It is a commonplace that in antiquity the image or name of a deity was considered an extension of the person of the deity. He who possessed such an image or was familiar with the name could by manipulation bind or honor the God at will. Has not this idea played a part in moulding the Chaldean Tale? The Powers fashion a material image of the Anthropos. The soul is added as in the Biblical and syncretistic accounts. Its addition gives the image autonomous existence. It is separated from the Anthropos and placed under the control of the Powers. Thereby the subjection of the Anthropos is accomplished.[123]

[123] The data on the subject are most interestingly presented in F. Preisigke,

Can this interpretation of the statement that man is the cause of the Anthropos' downfall be substantiated? Two facts should be noted in this connection. In the first place the role played by the image in the story of Saturninus and in the Chaldean Tale differs. In the former the image is in the upper realms and man is "according to the image." In the latter the Anthropos is "above" and man on earth is the image. In the second place, Saturninus derives the soul from the power that originally manifested itself to the angels, while the Chaldean Tale leaves her origin doubtful. In both these details the Chaldean account departs not only from its Syrian counterpart but from the Biblical narrative. Such a departure seems to demand explanation. May it not have been caused by the introduction and operation of the magical axiom to which we have referred? Certainly the changes harmonize with the demands that would be made by the use of the axiom in connection with the story.

One difficulty remains to be considered. Not only the Chaldean Tale but Saturninus as well claims that the angels desired to restrain the image and that the creation of man resulted from this desire. Now the latter gives no evidence of direct acquaintance with the Anthropos speculation. How, then, can we connect these details with the Anthropos tradition in the case of the Chaldean Tale? The difficulty lies, we feel, in Saturninus' story. The two elements of which mention has been made do not fall into line with the changes made in the Biblical narratives by people unaware of the Anthropos speculation. Not only that, but they stand in direct conflict with the statement of Saturninus that the Power which furnished the image took pity on the lowly product of the angels and vivified it. The provenience of the Pagan Naasene Document shows that the Chaldean Tale had been transplanted to Syria in the days when Saturninus taught there. Because the details in question have their organic place only in the Chaldean Tale and since this Tale is not far removed

Das göttliche Fluidum, and *Die Gotteskraft in der frühchristlichen Zeit*, in the Veröffentlichungen des Papyrusinstitut Heidelberg, Nos. 1 and 6, 1920 and 1922. The unity between image and deity we are inclined to regard as dynamic not essential.

either in time or place from Saturninus, we should be inclined to suppose that the first of the Syrian Gnostics had been indirectly influenced by the Anthropos tradition at this point.

Our inquiry into the genesis of the Chaldean Tale substantiates the opinion that the Mesopotamian form of the tradition makes the Anthropos the father-creator of the human race and to this extent again connects the Anthropos with Iran. It serves further to show how the view that he contributed the psychic element to the human constitution arose. The Biblical account of creation identifies the one who furnished the image with him who contributed the soul. The tendency among syncretists must therefore be, to connect the Anthropos with the subjective element of man's nature. Once the connection had been established and the loss of the element had become the reason of the Anthropos' downfall the frame work of the Chaldean Tale was rent asunder and the idea of the loss imbedded in the account of the primordial conflict. The conflict and the creation of man become two distinct acts in the drama. Yet the connection between Anthropos and image survived as a mute witness to the earlier steps of the development, though, of course, the normal tendency to regard man as one fashioned "after the image" altered the old conception that man is the image of the Anthropos.

In the development of this part of the Anthropos tradition the Poimandres has an interesting but unimportant place. As in the Chaldean Tale the creation of man and the downfall of the Anthropos are elements of a single episode. The image, moreover, is still something that exists below, "in Physis" as the author of the tract says, and the Anthropos is still the father-creator of man. Yet in addition to being man's father, the Anthropos also contributes to man's constitution. To this extent we are already one step removed from the beginning of the process and one step nearer to the goal of the development. Illustrating as it does a period of transition in the course of the Anthropos tradition, the Poimandres, of course, embraces many elements the nature of which is entirely incidental. Speculative concepts such as Nous, Logos and Physis have taken the place of mythological figures. Mystical terminology such as that represented by the terms Life and Light have entered the account. An amorous relationship is established between the Anthropos and Physis. To none of these can we give a place in the earlier reaches of the Anthropos tradition.[124] Not the Poimandres but the Chaldean Tale is the key to the growth of the idea that the soul is the imprisoned "self" of the heavenly Anthropos, for "self" like "reason" and "spirit" are but variant designations of the one subjective element originally connected with the Anthropos as the soul.

5. One additional matter requires our consideration, namely the origin of the idea that the saviors are the manifestations of the Anthropos.

In Manicheism we found this conception most lucidly presented. The seven messengers are the incarnations of the Anthropos' heavenly self. With this view that of the Christian Naasenes of Syria coincided, at least approximately. In Egypt, as we have seen, the messenger was thought of as the son rather than as the remanifested person of the Anthropos. In the earliest strata of the Syrian tradition as well as in the early Mandean religion, the soteriological phase of the Primal Man was entirely lacking.

If the last of these observations be correct, it is a clear indication that the whole idea of the remanifestation is a secondary element. The Iranian sources register their agreement with this contention. Gayomart is never connected directly with the Iranian saviors. Of course there are allusions in the Avesta implying that Gaya Maretan was the first man and that the Saoshyant will be the last man, or again in Pahlavi there are statements to the effect that Gayomart, Zarathushtra and Saosh-

[124] Since Windischmann (Abh. f. d. Kunde d. Morgenlandes, ZDMG, supp. 1, 1896, p. 73ff.) and Bousset (HP, pp. 203-5) it has been customary to seek the origin of the amorous situation depicted in the Poimandres in the episode of Gayomart's "sweat," an episode which Windischmann interpreted in the light of the Narcissus myth. Schaeder has shown that this interpretation is impossible (cf. above, p. 89) yet the Narcissus myth continues to be invoked. For this we find no justification. In that form of the Narcissus myth current in the days of the Anthropos tradition, the youth did not yet descend to the lethal waters (the detail upon which the connection between him and the Anthropos is established), but pined away at the side of the pool, Cf. Pausanias, *Descriptio*, I, 10, 19; Ovid, *Metamorphoses*, III, 341ff.

yant are the beginning, middle and end of creation,[125] but these statements co-ordinate rather than connect the persons mentioned.

We have therefore but to ask ourselves, how and why was the role of the Anthropos extended to include that of the saviors? The statement just made, that Gayomart has no inherent connection with the messengers of God, does not signify that he has no ulterior significance whatsoever. As we have already seen, Gayomart is one representative of an Indo-Iranian type of figure the characteristics of which are that it is first of those to die and hence first and foremost among those who are dead. Gayomart corresponds to this type to the extent that he is not alone the prototype of humanity, but also the one whose bones are raised up at the end as the first, and for whom half of the light of the sun is reserved in the new world. The eschatological prominence of Gayomart may account in part for the prominence of the Anthropos among those who are gathered before the throne of God according to Manichean eschatology.[126] Might one then consider the soteriological manifestation of the Anthropos an extension from the idea that the prototype of humanity is the foremost in the new world? Such a view might be possible, but it is scarcely probable. Our earlier Gnostic Anthropos tradition has almost nothing to say concerning the end of the world. What little it has to report, and much of what the Manicheans believed besides, can be explained as the natural result of a tendency to bring together again the Anthropos and his lost self, the soul. It arises out of the union of Anthropos and Soul Drama.

What the basis for the identification of Anthropos and saviors may have been is difficult to say. Our tradition itself affords two clues, in the first place the fact that the Manicheans enroll Adam and Seth in the number of those manifesting the Anthropos, in the second place the fact that in Egypt the savior was considered the son rather than the person of the transcendent Man.

[125] *Yasna*, 26, 10; in Pahlavi, *Bund.*, 30, 7 and *Dadistan i Dinik*, 4, 6.
[126] His coming from the North is a detail of the tradition for which no definite origin can be given because the North played an important part in a number of Oriental religions, Persian, Babylonian and Jewish alike.

Two avenues of thought are opened by these considerations. It is possible, on the one hand, that views such as those of the Mandeans formed the occasion for the appearance of the Anthropos in soteriological guise. The Mandeans, it will be recalled, considered Abel, Seth and Anosh messengers of saving knowledge among men. The identification of their father, Adam, with the Anthropos led to their transcendentalization. They became divine messengers, the sons of the Anthropos Adam. A short distance separates them at this point from the Manichean messengers who are modes or manifestations of the Anthropos himself yet bear individual names. Another possibility is that the phenomenon at issue resulted from the correlation of Gnostic and Christian concepts, a correlation provoked by the similarity between the Anthropos and the preëxistent creator Christ or by the similarity between the names Anthropos and Son of Man.

A third possibility, the importance of which we are not inclined to underestimate, may eventually be found in the Widsom speculation such as influenced early Christian christology in Luke and the Odes of Solomon and early Gnostic thought such as that of the Ophites as well.[127]

We are not in a position to decide between these three possibilities at present. Whatever the occasion may have been it is likely that the ultimate reason for the soteriological manifestation of the Anthropos will be found in the necessity to bring the Anthropos and the imprisoned soul together once more at the end of time.

The development of the Anthropos tradition as it has been outlined, has within it a certain element of verisimilitude. The latest part of the tradition is that characterizing the Anthropos as savior. The next in order of priority is that connecting him with the soul. The earliest portions are those which view him as the creator and father of man and as primordial champion. The first mentioned accrued to him in the littoral Orient, the next in the Jewish Gnostic sphere of Mesopotamia. The tradition regarding him as victorious primordial champion, and perhaps that

[127] Cf. my article, *The Odes of Solomon and their Significance for the New Testament*, Lutheran Church Review, July, 1927.

ooking upon him as the creator of the race, presuppose his having passed through a period of Babylonian influence and his having sprung from a stock in which he represented a defeated primordial hero and the father of humanity. We have thus an unbroken line of tradition running from the littoral Orient via Jewish-Gnostic and Pagan Mesopotamia to some other place. The antecedent probability is that this place is still further east. Not only the ideas but also the course of the Anthropos tradition thus point to Iran as its ultimate home.

6. With the origin and development of the Anthropos theology thus clearly before us we can ask the final question in regard to the antiquity of the whole speculation. As we have already seen, our sources range from the end of the third to the very beginning of the second Christian century. There they stop, as do all Gnostic sources. Three observations permit us to be certain that the speculation of which they tell is decidedly older. In the first place, our Anthropos tradition appears contemporaneously at the beginning of the second century in Egypt (Poimandres), Palestine (Mandeans) and Syria (pagan Naasene Document). At least a generation must be allowed for its spread over this wide area. In the second place, the presence in our earliest Syrian source of a Chaldean Tale bearing the Anthropos story, necessitates a still longer period of diffusion. Beyond the Chaldean Tale, in the third place, lie Babylonian and Iranian stages of development. These argue for an even further extension of the time limit.

How long the whole process of the growth and diffusion actually took cannot be stated even in round numbers, for we have no knowledge of how swiftly the wheels of syncretism were running in the first Christian and the pre-Christian centuries, and whether their speed was actually the speed of the growth of the Anthropos tradition. Co-ordinating our general findings at this point with the results of our investigation into the antiquity of Gayomart, we cannot but say that the doors must be left open to all who would attempt to make the Jewish and Christian Bar Nasha intelligible as a development from the Oriental Anthropos. The

THE ORIGIN AND ANTIQUITY OF THE ANTHROPOS

Anthropos tradition permits no *a priori* conclusion one way or another. The matter must be decided on its own merits entirely. To connect the Christian Son of Man as savior with the Anthropos directly seems foredoomed to failure because of the fact that in his soteriological manifestation the Anthropos is definitely a product of the second Christian century. This part of his growth we have been able to watch. Whether there is any common ground between the eschatological Bar Nasha of the Jewish apocalypses and the primordial champion Anthropos is another question. To that we now turn.

CHAPTER VI

THE ANTHROPOS IN JEWISH THOUGHT

1. THE analysis of the subject matter contained in our Gnostic sources has shown that the Anthropos when he first appeared on the shores of the Mediterranean, had passed through a long period of extensive development, and that his origin is probably Iranian, as Reitzenstein has surmised. Is it true, then, that in this ancient figure may be found the key to the Son of Man problem?

The influence of Iran and Iranian thought upon Judaism is a moot question. It is not that the possibility of such influence can well be denied, for the Jews were long under Persian suzerainty, but rather that it is extremely hazardous to enumerate explicit instances. From Asmodaios to the doctrine of the resurrection the ground has been so insistently contested that incontrovertible proof for some one definite point of contact between the two religions has yet to be found.

The effect of this clash of opinion has not been to discourage even cautious scholars from further efforts to connect Iran and the Jew.[1] It has led them rather to qualify the nature of whatever influence they may see, and to consider it "an aid to the development of Jewish thought, rather than a controlling factor."[2]

In the case of the book of Daniel, where the Son of Man first appears, the problem of Iranian influence becomes acute. Here

---

[1] A. V. W. Jackson, art. *Zoroastrianism*, Jewish Encyclopedia; cf. also A. J. Carnoy, art. *Zoroaster*, Encyclopedia of Religion and Ethics, esp. p. 866; R. H. Moulton, Journal of Theological Studies, 1902, pp. 514-27; H. P. Smith, American Journal of Theology, 1910, pp. 337-360; G. F. Moore, Harvard Theological Review, vol. V (1912), pp. 180.

[2] Schuerer, *Geschichte des juedischen Volkes*, etc., 4th ed. (1907), vol. II, p. 587.

we have a work composed in times when the Near East was a medley of cross-currents in cultural and religious matters. Here, too, is the first mention of the "mechanical doctrine of the resurrection" which an authority like Charles believes to have been shapen by Mazdean forces.[3] Above all, Daniel together with a number of later Jewish works, is the representative of that intensified and phantasmagorical eschatology which is usually termed "apocalyptic" and constitutes a peculiar innovation in the religious literature of the Jews.

Apocalypses and apocalyptic are a problem in themselves. Whence came the riot of symbols, illusions, images and mysterious actions? Whence too were drawn the dominant ideas that determine their interplay? The efforts of countless willful interpreters, especially among Christian enthusiasts, have proven no help in solving the riddle; nor could we even by the wildest stretch of the imagination credit to any one man the invention of all the imagery which one such document embodies. Only since the mythological cosmogonies of the ancient Orient and the idea of a cyclic movement in history were discovered, have the origin and the axioms determining the use of apocalyptic symbols become intelligible.[4] Cheyne may therefore well have been correct when he said that in apocalyptic "Persian influence upon Judaism may most surely be recognized."[5]

These considerations place the mythological and Iranian origin of apocalyptic figures such as the Son of Man distinctly within the range of possibility. To convert this possibility into a probability, however, it will be necessary to show:

1. That the Jewish figure in question cannot be explained adequately as a product of Hebrew thought.

2. That it and the proposed foreign prototype are basically homogeneous, and

3. That the suggested prototype was actually adaptable to the expression of those Jewish ideas which it served to convey in the new environment.

[3] *Eschatology Hebrew, Jewish and Christian*, Jowett Lectures (1899), p. 136.
[4] Cf. Gunkel, *Schoepfung und Chaos*, 1895.
[5] Encyclopedia Biblica, vol. IV, p. 5439.

2. The Bar Nasha appears first in the vision recorded in the seventh chapter of the book of Daniel. The seer, we are told, beholds four winds stirring up the sea, and four beasts rising from the depths. The first is like a lion, the second like a bear, the third like a leopard and the fourth an incongruous monster the identity of which is not established, but which, from its description, must be the most horrible creature imaginable to the apocalyptist.

From the monsters the prophet turns to see thrones erected and the Ancient of Days seating himself in judicial capacity amid a host of ministering powers. While the seer's mind dwells now on the majesty of the divine presence, judicial sentence is passed, for when he turns to the beasts again, it is to see the fourth slain and the others deprived of their power and circumscribed in the period of their existence. Thereupon we read:

> And behold with the clouds of heaven,
> There came one like a man;
> To the Ancient of Days he came,
> Before Him they brought him.
> And to him dominion was given
> And glory and kingdom,
> And all peoples, nations and tongues
> To him will do homage;
> His power is a power eternal
> That never will perish,
> And his kingdom . . . [6]
> That ne'er will be shaken.

To this vision the remainder of the chapter in Daniel endeavors to give a satisfactory interpretation. Actually there are two such interpretations, one a succinct statement that is complete in itself (vss. 17-8), the other a more extensive rendering connected with the analysis of the fourth beast and its significance (vss. 26-7). The first comprises three tetrastichs, as follows:

> Of kings four will arise from the earth.
> But the Saints of the Highest will obtain dominion;
> And possess the kingdom for . . . [7] ever and ever.

[6] Lacuna with Marti, Kautzsch, *Heilige Schrift des A.T.*, 3rd ed.
[7] Omit "ever, even for" as a gloss with Kittel, Biblia Hebraica.

The second is couched in exultant distichs, the irregular strophes ending in tristichs.

> And the court shall sit.
> And its [8] power be taken
> To consume and destroy it to the end.
>
> And the kingdom and the power
> And the majesty of dominions
> Beneath all heavens
> Shall be given to the people
> To the Saints of the Highest.
> His kingdom is an everlasting kingdom.
>
> And all dominions
> To him shall do service and homage.

Before we can consider the relation of the Anthropos to the "man-like" one of this vision we must ask ourselves whether the latter is at all intelligible as a product of Jewish thought.

To put this question to the text of Daniel is neither to deny or affirm the reality of the visionary experience involved, for whether reflection or religious intuition have moulded the elements of the tale, its narration was of necessity dependent upon the writer's intellectual horizon. Upon its answer, however, a great deal else depends. Other writers in Jewish circles have utilized and even augmented the figure of the Bar Nasha, but all invariably harken back to Daniel's description of him. This indicates that he is traditional and Jewish only in so far as he may be said to be the creation of the author of Daniel.

According to the authoritative interpretation that follows the vision, the man-like one represents the Saints of the Most High. To embody a group in the form of an individual after this fashion, was but natural under the circumstances. Groups are inherently difficult to handle, and besides, the Hebrew mind was well versed in the use of personifications, as the Ebed Yahwe [9] and certain

---

[8] i.e., the beast's power.

[9] Of course only in the prophecies of Deutero-Isaiah proper. The Ebed of the Servant Lyrics (*Is.* 42, 1–4; 49, 1–6; 50, 4–9; 52, 13–53, 12) is probably an individual.

patriarchs who play the part of Israelite clans in Hebrew story, demonstrate.[10]

Two explanations are usually offered to show how the author of Daniel determined the identity of his symbol. In the first instance the matter is said to be decided by the contrast which the writer saw between the kingdoms of this world and the kingdom of the Saints. The first he considered brutish, the second he thought of as "the typically human power among the nations of the world."[11] Hence he placed beast and man in opposition to one another. Again, it is said, that the Bar Nasha in Daniel is none other than Michael, chosen to represent the Saints because he is the guardian angel of the Jewish nation, and described as "man-like" because Daniel frequently speaks of angels as "having the appearance of a man."[12]

If either of these hypotheses were entirely adequate the Bar Nasha might be intelligible as the spontaneous creation of Daniel. But such is not the case. The former entails a number of difficulties, particularly that of projecting into the writer's mind an idea which is scarcely Jewish. Of course the Hebrew differentiated sharply between those of his people and other nations, but certainly there was in his religious exclusiveness nothing that would lead him to restrict the possession of humanity to himself. The very world outlook which such a vision as that of the four kingdoms presupposes, forbids a denial of the basic identity of human nature wherever it appears. The contrast which determined the symbols in question can therefore be only that between degenerate and typical humanity. But this in turn is unsatisfactory, for not only are the ideas of type and correspondence to type the product of western abstract thought, but, what is more, the beasts upon whom the comparison depends are anything but an expression of

[10] Especially *Gen.* c. 10; cf. Gunkel, *Genesis*, 3rd ed., pp. xvi-xix.

[11] So characterized by E. F. Scott, *The Kingdom and the Messiah* (1911); p. 37; frequently found, so Bertholet, *Biblische Theologie*, II (1911), p. 37, Marti, Kurzer Handkommentar, *Daniel* (1901), p. 52-3; J. A. Montgomery, International Critical Commentary, *Daniel*, 1927.

[12] So latterly Bertholet, op. cit., pp. 222-3, N. Schmidt, Ency, Bibl., art. *Son of Man*, and Grill, *Untersuchungen zur Entstehung des vierten Evangelium*, I (1902), p. 54.

"degenerate" humanity. Their description embodies too many details arising neither out of the note of degeneration nor out of the situation in which the writer found the kingdoms which they represent.[13] Besides, the kingdom which the Saints and the Bar Nasha exemplify is for Daniel still the *Malkuth Yahwe*, the prime characteristic of which is not its humanity but its divine authorship.[14]

The similarity in the terminology used of angels and of the Bar Nasha by Daniel is certainly striking and deserves further attention, but it fails to establish the angelic identity of the man-like one. The angel of whom Daniel speaks as "man-like" is in most cases surely, and in all cases probably Gabriel.[15] Of course angels are endowed with human form in other portions of Jewish religious literature.[16] Yet the fact that human qualities are ascribed by Daniel only to Gabriel, shows that the designation "man-like" arose not out of a popular concept so much as out of the name of Gabriel himself.[17] The Bar Nasha would then logically have to be the angel Gabriel. With Michael functioning as the protector of the Jewish nation, Gabriel, however, could hardly be chosen as the symbol of the Saints. In other words, Michael lacks the name and Gabriel the calling to become the Bar Nasha.

Furthermore, both Gabriel and Michael are well-known persons, active continually in bringing to their consummation God's plans concerning his people. By contrast, the Bar Nasha is a new factor on the horizon.[18] He has no connection with the ministering hosts (vs. 10) to which archangels must belong. Like the beasts he has but one specific purpose to fulfill.

It appears, then, that the hypotheses advanced to show how

[13] Most nearly akin are the hybrid monsters of which even Berossos took notice. Cf. Zimmern, *Das alte Testament im Lichte des alten Orient* (1916), p. 20.
[14] Cf. *Daniel* 7, 27.
[15] So both Marti, Kurzer Handk., and Behrmann, Goettinger Handkommentar (1894), on the passages quoted above.
[16] *Tobit* 5, 4; cf. also Weber, *Juedische Theologie*, 2nd ed. (1897) p. 173.
[17] So Marti, Kurzer Handk. on *Daniel* 8, 15.
[18] Volz, *Juedische Eschatologie* (1903), p. 11.

the apocalyptist arbitrarily determined the nature of the symbols in Daniel c. 7, are unsatisfactory. The reason is by no means difficult to discover. The figures here employed as symbols and the situation in which they stand are not basically related to the idea which they serve to convey. The writer has employed a tale current in his day as a means to depict his vision of the consummation of God's reign. Hence there is a clash between the statement that the saints were in conflict with the fourth beast prior to the appearance of the Ancient of Days and the fact of their subsequent arrival in the person of the Bar Nasha.[19] Hence, too, the description of the Bar Nasha gives no hint of past sufferings and purifications such as one might expect to characterize the people, judging from the rest of the book.[20] For this reason, finally, the vision contains elements not organically connected with the supposedly dominant idea, such as the winds' stirring up the sea and the issuance of the beasts from it.[21]

Now it is true that certain details of the vision arise solely out of the historical situation confronting the author of Daniel, and out of his interpretation of history and tradition. The ten horns and the little horn (vss. 7–8), the human heart given to the first beast (vs. 4), and perhaps even the clouds of heaven with which the man-like one comes (vs. 13) belong to this category. But in the final analysis these details represent merely the fruit of efforts to adapt to his purpose a tale otherwise not entirely suited. The very controversy raging about the interpretation of Daniel's Bar Nasha shows that he is as much an element of that adapted entity as the beasts that rise from the sea. Since nothing in Jewish tradition serves to identify and render intelligible the materials adapted by Daniel in the description of his vision we are not only privileged but compelled to look outside the Jewish sphere to determine their origin and significance.

The Bar Nasha appears a second time in the Similitudes of the Book of Enoch, that portion of the composite work comprising

[19] Vs. 21.
[20] *Daniel* 7, 25; 11, 35; 12, 1; cf. Porter, *Messages of the Apocalyptical Writers* (1905), p. 131.
[21] So the winds, vs. 2, and the coming of the beasts from the sea, vs. 3.

a group of visions from approximately the beginning of the first century B.C.[22] In the second of these visions the seer describes how he saw:

> ... one who had a head of days,
> And his head was white as wool,
> And with him was another being whose countenance had the appearance of a man,
> And his face was full of graciousness like one of the holy angels.[23]

Questioned "concerning that Son of Man, who he was, and whence he was and why he went with the head of days"[24] the *angelus interpres* accompanying the seer replies:

> This is the Son of Man who hath righteousness,
> With whom dwelleth righteousness,
> And who revealeth all the treasures of that which is hidden,
> Because the Lord of Spirits hath chosen him,
> And whose lot hath pre-eminence before the Lord of Spirits in uprightness forever.
>
> And this Son of Man whom thou hast seen
> Shall raise up the kings and the mighty from their seats,
> (And the strong from their thrones)
> And shall loosen the reins of the strong
> And break the teeth of sinners.[25]

The identity of the mysterious Son of Man has thus been established, but his origin remains obscure. Another portion of the vision throws light on this point.

Before the throne of the Lord of Spirits the seer beholds an inexhaustible fountain of righteousness. The reader soon realizes that this fountain is but a symbol of the "Son of Man who hath all righteousness,"[26] an impression that is corroborated by the statement: "at that hour (i.e., the moment when he beheld the fountain) the name of that Son of Man was named in the presence

---

[22] Charles, *The Book of Enoch*, 2nd ed. (1912), pp. xlviii-liv.
[20] C. 40, 1, translation by Charles, in *Apocrypha and Pseudigrapha of the O. T.*, vol. II (1913).
[24] C. 46, 2.
[25] C. 46, 3-4.
[26] C. 46, 3.

of the Lord of Spirits."[27] Then follows a vivid description of the significance and origin of the Son of Man.

> Yea, before the sun and the signs were created,
> Before the stars of heaven were made,
> His name was named before the Lord of Spirits.
> He shall be a staff to the righteous whereon to stay themselves and not fall,
> And he shall be the light of the Gentiles,
> And the hope of those who are troubled of heart.
> All who dwell on earth shall fall down and worship before him
> And will praise and bless and celebrate with song the Lord of Spirits.
> And for this reason hath he been chosen and hidden before Him
> Before the creation of the world and for evermore.
> And the wisdom of the Lord of Spirits hath revealed him to the holy and righteous.[28]

In the third and last vision the Son of Man again appears. What is said of him in this case assures us that not only his name, but he himself is pre-existent.

> For from the beginning the Son of Man was hidden
> And the Most High preserved him in the presence of his might
> And revealed him to the elect.[29]

It further reaffirms the opinion that he will judge the righteous and sinners,[30] and gives in addition an interesting description of the communion of the Son of Man with the blessed in the new world.

> And the Lord of Spirits will abide over them,
> And with that Son of Man shall they eat
> And lie down and rise up for ever and ever.
> . . . .
> And they shall have been clothed with garments of glory
> And these shall be the garments of life from the Lord of Spirits
> And your garments shall not grow old,
> Nor your glory pass away before the Lord of Spirits.[31]

[27] C. 48, 1–2. The statement serves to convey the authoritative interpretation of things seen.
[28] C. 48, 3–7.
[29] C. 62, 7.
[30] C. 62, 9ff; 63, 11; 69, 26–9.
[31] C. 62, 14–16.

That the Son of Man of Enoch is identical with the Bar Nasha of Daniel cannot be questioned. Two such figures could hardly exist side by side in the same environment without being related. Besides, the Son of Man when first introduced in Enoch, appears in juxtaposition to a "Head of Days, whose head was white as wool" thereby distinctly recalling his associations with the Ancient of Days in Daniel.[32]

In so far as the Son of Man of Enoch is but a rehearsal of Daniel's figure, that which has been said about the latter's origin applies here as well. But greater than the common ground between them, is their dissimilarity. Instead of a mere symbol of the Saints, the Son of Man of Enoch is the pre-existent Messiah. The question then confronts us, is the difference between them due to the transforming influence which Jewish ideas have exercised upon the traditional Bar Nasha? Two explanations of the change might be offered in favor of an affirmative answer. The Son of Man in Enoch might be Daniel's figure messianically misinterpreted and described in terms of the traditional kingly Messiah[33] or he might be the newer transcendent Messiah bearing merely the nomenclature of the Bar Nasha.

The first of these possibilities gains support from the observation that there are in the description of the messianic Son of Man elements which harken back to the current conception of the messianic king. Like the latter he is characterized by righteousness;[34] like him, too, he vindicates the righteous and is a light to the gentiles.[35] But it should be noted that there are even more elements in his characterization that lack all parallel in previous and contemporaneous messianic prophecy, especially his pre-existence, his concealment by God, his capacity as revealer of things hidden and as judge of all flesh. Some of these other traits might possibly have been called forth by a misinterpretation of

---

[32] C. 46, 1; cf. *Dan.* 7, 9.

[33] Bousset, *Religion des Judentums*, 3rd ed. (by Gressmann for Lietzmann's Handbuch, section 21) (1926), pp. 265–8. Cf. also Bertholet, *Bibl. Theol.* II, p. 446.

[34] *Book of Enoch*, 46, 3; cf. *Is.* 9, 7; *Jer.* 23, 5; *Zech.* 9, 9.

[35] *Book of Enoch*, 48, 4.

Daniel's Bar Nasha, but certainly not the one most prominent in Enoch, the capacity of judge.[36] In Daniel as everywhere else, it is distinctly Yahwe who enacts judgment over mankind. Only to an already heavenly and transcendent Messiah could this activity of Yahwe have been transferred.

The second possibility leads to even greater difficulties. When the similitudes of Enoch were composed, the transcendent Messiah was as yet a new figure in Jewish thought.[37] Appearing for the first time in the days of the Maccabees, his manifestation is undoubtedly due to a number of causes. Among them were probably the realization that to expect the fulfillment of national hopes through human agencies was useless, the individualism and universalism which at that time were transforming the outlook of the people, and the attention focused in trying times upon those things which are above and beyond the sphere of the merely human.[38] Yet all these taken together and brought to bear upon the current conception of the kingly Messiah, could not have produced the transcendent Christ as we know him from the Testament of Levi (c. 18). There is a plus both in coloring and in the expression of idea and action that is not the result of reflection but rather of the ancient mythologoumena which all of the ancient near East derived from the land of the rivers. It is therefore usually assumed that in this respect the transcendent Messiah represents only the Jewish rendering of some figure given in the mythological interpretation of the world and its destiny, a foreign person used as the vehicle for the expression of conclusions derived from personal experience.[39]

Now the messianic Son of Man is actually the most concrete, complete and colorful form of the transcendent Messiah that we know. What would our impressions of this Messiah amount to

[36] Ibid., 46, 3–4.
[37] Cf. *Ps. Sol.*, 72, 5; *Sibylline Oracles* III, 49f, 286f; *Testament of Levi*, 18.
[38] Volz, *Jued. Eschat.*, pp. 58–60.
[39] So Bertholet, Rel. in Geschichte u. Gegenwart, art. *Messias*; Bousset-Gressmann, *Religion*, pp. 259–62; Gressmann, *Ursprung der israelitisch-juedischen Eschatologie*, (1905) pp. 286–94; 334–65; Volz, *Juedische Eschatologie*, pp. 61–2.

if we were to omit all references to the Bar Nasha? It would seem to follow, then, that we are at this point closest to that foreign source which moulded the picture of the transcendent Messiah in the first place.[40] To explain the difference between Daniel's Bar Nasha and the Son of Man of Enoch by reference to the heavenly Elect as we know him from other more indistinct manifestations, appears unreasonable.

Here again we must, therefore, conclude that the problem represented by the altered significance of the Bar Nasha, cannot be solved by recourse to the influence exerted by Jewish ideas. The solution must lie in the nature of that non-Jewish figure which Daniel introduced and which must have been familiar to the author of the Similitudes in a different form.

Our third and last glimpse of the Son of Man in Jewish apocalyptic comes from the book known as IV Esra. The sixth of the visions recorded in its pages reads as follows:

> And I beheld and lo! there arose a violent wind from the sea and stirred all its waves. And I beheld and lo! the wind caused to come up out of the heart of the sea as it were the form of a man. And I beheld and lo! this man flew with the clouds of heaven. And wherever he turned his countenance to look everything seen by him trembled; and whithersoever the voice went out of his mouth, all that heard his voice melted away as wax melts when it feels the fire. And after this I beheld and lo! there was gathered together from the four winds an innumerable multitude of men to make war against the man that came up out of the sea. And I beheld and lo! he cut out for himself a great mountain and flew upon it. But I sought to see the region or the place from whence the mountain had been cut out; and I could not. And after this I beheld and lo! all who were gathered together against him to wage war with him were seized with great fear; yet they dared to fight. And lo! he neither lifted his hand nor held spear nor any war-like weapon; but I saw only how he sent out of his mouth as it were a fiery stream and out of his lips a flaming breath and out of his tongue he shot forth a storm of sparks. And these were all mingled together—the fiery stream, the flaming breath and the stormy mass, and fell upon the assault of the multitude which was prepared to fight, and burned them all up, so that suddenly nothing more was to

---

[40] Bousset-Gressmann, *Religion*, p. 262.

be seen of the innumerable multitude save only dust of ashes and smell of smoke. When I saw this I was amazed. Afterwards I beheld the same Man come down from the mountain, and call unto him another multitude which was peaceable. Then drew nigh unto him the faces of many men, some of whom were glad, some sorrowful; while some were in bonds, some brought others who should be offered.[41]

As though to fight fire with fire and to offset the despair of his people in those tumultuous times after Jerusalem's fall[42] by pointing to a still greater tribulation that would soon befall the enemies of their God, the author of this vision has painted the picture of the Son of Man with all the colors of his palette.

Unquestionably the figure thus outlined is identical with the one that inspired the authors of Daniel and Enoch. It has the "form of a man" and "flies with the clouds of heaven"[43] yet represents the transcendent Messiah. But the Son of Man of IV Esra is one step removed even from his counterpart in Enoch and thus the question whether indigenous or foreign traditions have moulded the character arises once more.

What particularly differentiates the Son of Man in IV Esra from his earlier manifestations, is his combat with the hostile nations. The conception of such a final conflict in which all the nations of the world send their hosts against the chosen people at Jerusalem is nothing new. It goes back to the days of Ezekiel, whose prophecies concerning Gog and Magog found a permanent place in later Jewish thought and are probably reflected here once more.[44] True, the credit for the destruction of the enemy, formerly attributed to Yahwe exclusively, has here been given to the warrior Son of Man. The change, however, is intelligible and natural since the latter was already before the days of IV Esra an element of the transcendent world and an agent of God

---

[41] C. 13, 1–13. Translation and numbering by Box in Charles, Apocrypha and Pseudigrapha, II, 616–17.

[42] Accepting the data of· *circa* 100 A.D. with Bruno Violet, *Griechische christliche Schrifsteller der ersten drei Jahrhunderte*, vol. 32, 3, p. xlix.

[43] C. 13, 3.

[44] *Ezek.* c. 38–9; cf. *Joel* c. 3. Later traces of Ezekiel's conception gathered by Volz, *Jued. Eschat.* pp. 174–5.

himself. In this respect, then, as champion in the final conflict with the enemy nations, the Son of Man of the last apocalypse is an indigenous product.

A number of other particulars betray Jewish origin. The statements that everything trembled before his gaze and melted like wax before his voice, expressive as they are of judiciary capacity, directly recall the description of Yahwe in the Old Testament, especially in the book of Psalms.[45] The fiery stream, the flaming breath and the storm, though their juxtaposition is new and unexplained, are individually stereotype in theophanic descriptions and have their closest parallels in Isaiah.[46] From Daniel the later work has borrowed the winds that stir up the sea, and the "coming forth from the heart of the sea," which he now associates with the arrival of the Son of Man.[47] Even the mountain cleft from nowhere can be explained from Jewish sources as a combination of the mysterious stone of Daniel with the mountain of Zion featured in Joel's prophecy of the final conflict of the nations.[48]

Given the individualized, transcendent and preëxistent Son of Man, we may therefore conclude, there is little or nothing of note in IV Esra c. 13 that cannot be explained as an accretion from indigenous Jewish ideas. This is as it should be. In the days of the Book of Enoch the figure to which Daniel first referred might conceivably yet have been known in its original foreign form. Two centuries, yes a century later, its origin must have been so entirely obscured that to the Jew the Son of Man was intrinsically Jewish. However much the force of circumstances might lead Judaism to change its views regarding this figure, the alterations could not be stated in terms of the foreign original and its associations. They must of necessity be Jewish.

3. The preceding pages have shown that while many of the associations and activities of the Bar Nasha are intelligible as products of Jewish tradition, this tradition and the mentality it

[45] *Ps.* 97, 5; 104, 32; cf. also *Micah*, 1, 4.
[46] 11, 4; cf. Box's note on *IV Esra* 13, 10.
[47] *IV Esra* 13, 2; cf. *Dan.* 7, 2 and Gressmann *Ursprung*, p. 354.
[48] *IV Esra* 13, 6, combining *Dan.* 2, 34 with *Joel* 3, 15–6.

presupposes furnishes no adequate explanation of the genesis of the figure, of its dual role as symbol and personality, and of its connection in the latter capacity with the messianic hope. As it happens, the residuum of the unexplained includes elements the origin of which must be determined, if the Bar Nasha is to be revitalized. To endeavor to find in pagan thought a type, the supposed influence of which might clarify these difficulties, is therefore not only permissible but necessary.

From what has already been said the limitations of such hypotheses as that connecting Anthropos and Bar Nasha are evident as well. Only such material the Jewish origin of which is doubtful can serve to identify his supposed foreign prototype. On the pagan side only evidence of sufficient antiquity may be used to establish comparison, that is, in the case of the Anthropos, only those elements of the Anthropos tradition that belong to the Persian and Mesopotamian portion of his heritage.

In seeking to determine the origin of the Man-like One and his ultimate identity, we cannot proceed from the analysis of his capacities, for they are not uniform, but solely from the descriptive designation applied to him and the situation in which he appears in Daniel.

Much has already been said on the subject of the words "one like a man." Gressmann and Volz maintain that the "like" found in the phrase has no inherent value, but belongs to the apocalyptic terminology and serves merely to develop the atmosphere of the mysterious essential to a vision.[49] If that were the case, the true designation of the Man-like One would be either "a man" or "the man," the equivalent of "the Anthropos." The reference made by Gressmann and Volz to Ezekiel c. 1, shows that such an interpretation is possible, but further consideration indicates that it is improbable. In the first place, neither the author of Enoch nor of IV Esra so interpret it, for they continually use demonstratives and modifiers with the designation "Man," and in each case introduce the figure with the whole cumbersome phrase found in Daniel.[50] Secondly, while the beasts

[49] Gressmann, *Ursprung*, p. 342. Volz, *Jued. Eschat.*, pp. 10–11.
[50] The passages are listed by Bousset-Gressmann, pp. 262–3.

of Daniel c. 7 are all (save the fourth[51]) described with a "like," the beasts of c. 8, as well as the visionary image and the visionary tree of earlier chapters, lack this supposed bit of visionary machinery. The conclusion would seem to be, that the use of "like" is dictated not by visionary technique, but by the demands for a comparison.

Now a comparison such as that indicated in Daniel 7, 13 may be made either upon the basis of the fundamental nature or with an eye to certain of the attributes of the things concerned. The "one like a man" may therefore be either a member of the *genus homo* with certain differentia distinguishing him from other members of the genus, or he may belong fundamentally to an entirely different group of beings, and, by certain of his qualities, recall the human kind. Marti and Bertholet, each in his own way, hold to the latter conception. Marti, if we may so state his view, holds that the figure's genus is that of a kingdom, and that the typically human qualities of the kingdom of the saints have determined the phraseology of the description.[52] Bertholet maintains that the figure is basically that of an angel, and that the designation is intended to show that the angel in question has a human form like certain other angels mentioned in Daniel.[53]

The way in which the comparison is meant is not difficult to determine if we contrast the symbols of c. 7 with those of the rest of the book. The latter have nothing highly unusual in their description. The names ram, goat, tree and image applied to them cover all that is said quite adequately. The former differ in this respect. Eagles' wings and multiple heads are not characteristic of lions and leopards in general. Bears do not normally eat flesh. There would seem to be a connection between this fact and the respective absence and presence of "like" in the nomenclature. In the first case the comparative is not used because it is not necessary. In the second case it is used to allow for the superadded peculiarities of the beasts, not to distinguish

[51] Its genus is indeterminate hence it needs no "like" to express approximation.
[52] Kurzer, Handk., p. 52.
[53] *Bibl. Theol.*, pp. 221-2.

them generically from the animal whose name they bear. If the other symbols of Daniel c. 7 are then true members of the genus with which they are associated, we should by analogy expect that the "man-like one" is fundamentally a human being, but one who manifests certain peculiarities that set him apart from the rest of mankind.[54]

If this be truly the significance of the words "one like a man," it at once establishes a possible point of contact between Bar Nasha and Anthropos. From the beginning the latter is, as we recall, a human being. His very origin depends upon his humanity. Yet he was, at the same time, more than an ordinary man. He was the prototype of humanity and a member of the spiritual creation of Ahura Mazda, standing above and beyond the sphere of the normally human. This peculiarity of human and extra-human character the Anthropos never lost. It finally produced the anomaly of a "man" in the pleroma of the dualistic Gnostics.

But as we have already noted, the Anthropos even when he appeared in Mediterranean lands had as yet no proper name. The appellatives "first man," "great man," "great, most glorious and perfect man" were all the result of efforts to identify and localize in some way the person of the equally nameless "mortal life," Gaya-maretan, in the form which that person had taken while passing through Mesopotamia. The designation "one like a man" therefore serves to connect the bearer and the Anthropos, because it harmonizes with the sort of terminology applied to the pagan figure.

But more important than the matter of the designation is that of the situation in which the Bar Nasha first appears. It presents in a graphic way the fate of kingdoms. To what has been said of the mythological origin of apocalyptic symbols and situations, those of Daniel form no exception. But while Burkitt has succeeded in establishing the zodiacal origin of the ram and the goat of Daniel c. 8, as the representatives of Persia and Syria,[55]

---

[54] Gressmann and Volz arrive at this conclusion but from a false premise.

[55] Meyer, *Ursprung des Christentums*, vol. II (1921), p. 194 quoting Cumont, Klio, vol. IX (1909), p. 273.

the origin of the material found in Daniel c. 7 as a whole is still in many respects the subject of discussion.

The first step toward the partial solution of the problem is the realization that the first three beasts have been secondarily introduced into the situation in which they now appear together with the fourth. A number of indications point in this direction. In the first place the four kingdom conception which here multiplies the monsters is something not bound up exclusively with the vision of Daniel c. 7. It appears also in c. 2. Next, as we have already noted, there is a difference between the first three and the fourth beasts. The first three are generically identified, but the last is so horrible as to be in a class by itself. Thirdly neither lion, bear, nor leopard belong in the watery deep whence they appear. Finally too, it must be remembered that only one of the four beasts is slain at the judgment of God, and that a distinction thus arises for which there is no motivation in the historical circumstances which the prophet is depicting.

There is admittedly little that would serve to identify the first three beasts, yet the fourth has two characteristics, its coming from the sea, and its description as the most horrible monster imaginable, which reveal its nature and origin. Only one creature will serve to cover these traits, the great chaos-monster Tiamat that dwelt in the deep (with Apsu) at the beginning of things, a figure far famed in ancient story, long familiar to the Israelites in other forms[56] and worthy of finding a place in such a vision as that of Daniel. The identification can be verified. The fangs and talons of the monster, which Daniel treats as though they were among its most pronounced features, are also accentuated in pictorial representations of Tiamat dragons found on Babylonian seals.[57]

Of Tiamat there is one and only one important story, that of her conflict with Marduk in primordial times. If Tiamat is really the prototype of the fourth beast of Daniel's vision, and if the fourth beast is really determinative of the action there unfolded,

[56] The fullest presentation is still to be found in Gunkel, *Schöpfung und Chaos* (1895).
[57] Jeremias, *Handbuch d. altorient. Geisteskultur* (1913), pp. 26–7, pl. 15–7.

we must necessarily conclude that the situation in which the Bar Nasha appears is an adapted form of the tale recounting the overthrow of the dragon. Of this again there are verifying indications. The four winds that stir up the sea prior to the arrival of the beasts also play a part in the Babylonian story.[58] In fact the process of "stirring up" the deep has its counterpart there as well.[59] The motif of the conflict itself, though it has been well nigh obscured by the idea of the judgment and omnipotence of the Ancient of Days, still lingers in the statement made in the course of the interpretation of the vision and in the words that tell us that the fourth beast and the Saints (i.e., the Bar Nasha) have been at war with one another.[60]

If, then, the situation presented by the vision of Daniel c. 7 recommends itself to us as an adaptation of the well-known myth of the overthrow of Tiamat, what shall we say of the Bar Nasha? Does he belong to the *dramatis personae* of the myth or has he been introduced secondarily like the additional beasts and the idea of judgment? In the Tiamat myth there is but one other person of importance beside the monster itself, namely her slayer Marduk. In Daniel's vision the fourth beast is slain by reason of the judgment pronounced by the Ancient of Days. This would seem to indicate that Yahwe had here as in other places stepped into the place of the mythological hero.[61] In this case the Bar Nasha must be a later addition to the situation. Yet it must be noted that while Yahwe's judgment forms the occasion for the execution of the beast, the identity of the executioner is not revealed. Simultaneously the interpretation of the vision, as we have remarked, discloses that the Saints were at war with the monster prior to the arrival of the Ancient of Days, and that Jahwe's coming gave the judgment to the Saints, that is, crowned their struggle with victory.[62] This would make it seem as though the

---

[58] S. Langdon, *The Babylonian Epic of Creation* (1923), p. 133.
[59] Tiamat who not only dwells in the deep but personifies it is "troubled" or "disturbed" by the winds, cf. Langdon, op. cit., p. 133, Tablet IV, 48.
[60] *Dan.* 7, 22.
[61] *Schöpfung und Chaos*, p. 88.
[62] *Dan.* 7, 22-3.

THE ANTHROPOS IN JEWISH THOUGHT

Bar Nasha represented the conqueror Marduk, and with this a number of other observations concur. In the first place the Bar Nasha lacks, in the vision proper, a role in harmony with his prominence and with the benefits conferred upon him. In the second place the preëminence which Yahwe and his judgment hold can be explained as the natural result of the adaptation of the situation to the demands of Jewish Monotheism.

If the Bar Nasha is to represent the conqueror Marduk of the adapted situation, how then can he simultaneously be the Iranian Anthropos? Here is after all the crux both in the analysis of the situation and in the problem of Anthropos and Son of Man. The prototype of the Bar Nasha must be at once a man above men, and a conquering deity. No other person will fit. And here our analysis of the Gnostic evidence for the Anthropos serves us well, for it has shown conclusively that as he passed through Mesopotamia the Iranian figure was identified with Marduk and consequently changed his character. He ceased to be merely the prototypic man sacrificed in the primordial struggle with Ahriman, and became instead the Great Man who signalized and prepared the victory of the heavenly powers over those below, Adamas, the unconquerable. True, the conquering Anthropos, whom Daniel may have adapted, is not the conquering Anthropos of our Gnostic sources. Yet the difference between them is a matter of the proportionate strength of the concurrent elements. Among the Gnostics (save the Mandeans) it was the dualistic cosmogony of Iran that furnished the rudiments of the setting in which the Anthropos appears, and thus determined a preponderance of Iranian elements in his characterization. In Daniel it is the Babylonian cosmogony that underlies, and hence it is Marduk who most nearly but not completely approximates the Bar Nasha.[63] In both cases, however, the same two elements are fused, and after all it is this particular fusion that determines the origin of the figure in question.

If such be the case, how could the Anthropos become a symbol of the Saints? Was it because of some quality inherent in him?

[63] It is the fundamental dependence upon Babylonian tradition that makes the Mandean figures like Manda d'Haye often so similar to Jewish figures.

Probably not. Of course, the Anthropos in his Iranian form is the prototype of humanity and the first of the righteous, but it would require a combination of these two ideas to make him exemplify righteous humanity, a combination with which we have no right to credit the author of Daniel since neither of the two ideas are necessarily carried by that form of the Anthropos myth which he used and adapted. More properly one might therefore ascribe the introduction and interpretation of the Anthropos to the appeal made by the situation in which he appears and the circumstances attending its adaptation.

Since the days of Ezekiel the Israelites had been told to expect, and as Joel shows, did anticipate that all the enmity which their nation had experienced, would in the last times kindle a conflict in which the mightiest forces of the world would be allied to blot out the chosen people, but would themselves be vanquished by the power of Yahwe. As an echo of this view, the notion that the execution of judgment was to be immediately preceded by the most terrible moments in the world's history, with God arrayed, as it were, against the unbridled forces of iniquity, remained in Daniel's day. Daniel was sure that the days of Seleucid oppression represented the beginning of the prophecy's fulfillment; he dared to say so in symbolic fashion. What more fitting vehicle for the apocalyptic expression of this thought than some form of the stories that recounted a similar climax in the developments of primordial times? Of course, a man of Daniel's temperament was bound to refashion any such story in accordance with his own ideas, like that of the fourfold nature of the world powers. His sublimated idea of God, particularly, was sure to affect the presentation. Where the staid and placid Ancient of Days was concerned, there could be no struggle for the enforcement of divine will. His judicial sentence effects the suppression of the enemy, no matter how great the threat. Any narrative, such as that of the Anthropos' primordial conflict, when utilized by Daniel to express a similar dénouement in eschatological matters, must of necessity suffer the introduction of judgment executed by the Ancient of Days. The original champion, because of his heroic qualities, could not be identified with the transcendent

Yahwe and was thus left to be discarded or put to other use. Daniel, it seems, has chosen the latter course and by analogy with the beast has interpreted him as the representative of the chosen people.

If the symbolic role of the Bar Nasha fails to conflict with the hypothesis that in the Anthropos we have the origin of the enigmatic figure, then certainly the messianic significance attached to him in Enoch cannot. Given the presence of those forces which were in the days of the Book of Enoch changing men's outlook and pointing to the inadequacy of the older messianic ideas, the Anthropos might well suggest himself as a means toward the recreation of the ancient hope on a higher and nobler plane. As the representative of God, his champion and protagonist in the clash with contrary forces, as one who is connected in some way with humanity, and contributes toward its advancement, he is sufficiently akin to the older national Messiah to preserve continuity of thought, and lend himself to description in the traditional terminology. His extra-human position, his transcendence and preëxistence, on the other hand, when coupled with the current figure of the Messiah, could serve to raise that figure above the national, the material and ephemeral. It is exactly this combination of elements that the messianic Bar Nasha of Enoch represents.

In the guise of a victorious champion the Anthropos belongs to primordial history. His conflict with the powers of the deep stands at the very beginning of things. The Son of Man, on the other hand, is an eschatological person. A broad gulf might thus seem to separate them one from another and to tear asunder the threads which appear to connect them. Yet such is not the case.

Apocalypses endeavor to unveil the trend and nature of the future. A thorough knowledge of the present and its relation to the immediate past may furnish a man with intimations concerning the trend of events in the future, but it supplies no knowledge concerning the nature of those events. Since the apocalyptists actually described the future, they must have a second source of information to add to their knowledge of the present. This source is to be found in the Oriental axiom of the cyclic movement of history, the axiom according to which the events leading to the establishment of the new world are a rehearsal of those connected with the primordial creation. Cosmogony is thus the substratum of eschatology, and the Anthropos of primordial history the necessary prototype of the eschatological Son of Man.

The discussions of the preceding pages have had as their focus the question, Does the Anthropos serve to explain those elements of the Bar Nasha which are not intelligible as the product of Jewish thought? Led, even as we have been, to an affirmative answer, Reitzenstein has proposed to connect with the Anthropos tradition a number of incidentals in the description of the Son of Man, which may also be regarded as Jewish in origin, and have so been listed by us.[64] It so happens that in our estimation the details referred to by Reitzenstein, such as the "coming from the sea" and the "fiery stream, the flaming breath and the storm of sparks" found in IV Esra, are truly of Jewish origin.[65] Yet it must be admitted that hypothetically a given trait of the Bar Nasha might be doubly accounted for. The "coming with the clouds of heaven" may be an instance of this kind. It is certainly devoid of all mythological associations and simultaneously intelligible as a trait which the Bar Nasha received from Yahwe, and which is intended to convey the idea of his divine authority or of his celestial character. Now Daniel, who first mentions the detail, carefully distinguished, as we were led to believe, between the role of Yahwe as judge and that of the Bar Nasha. It hardly seems as though he would have borrowed from the description of Yahwe under the circumstances, without additional reason. This reason may be supplied by the connection of the Anthropos with a "cloud of light," a connection that appears to go back to the Mesopotamian period of his existence.[66] Given a mythological

---

[64] Reitzenstein, IE, p. 123.

[65] The Anthropos connection with the primordial deep as found in the Poimandres, is as we have seen late cf. above, p. 123. The fiery phenomena of the Son of Man do not even remotely recall the five elements of the Anthropos; cf. above, pp. 18–19.

[66] Cf. above pp. 105–6.

cloud in the retinue of the Anthropos, the author of Daniel might more conceivably have borrowed from Yahwe a trait used for the embellishment of the Bar Nasha. Speculation along these lines, however, is as good as useless, for even probability can never be attained. We feel at liberty, therefore, to forego the discussion of other details with a similar background.

4. The Anthropos, as we have seen, is a figure that even in its earliest forms has predominantly primordial significance. The Bar Nasha, on the other hand is exclusively eschatological. To say that the latter represents an adaptation of the former, implies that the Anthropos was familiar to the authors of the first two apocalypses in his original form. Why, then, has he left us no traces of his presence in that guise?

It will of course be evident that the traditional theology of Judaism imposed severe restrictions upon the introduction of such a figure as the pagan Anthropos into its midst. Of the three capacities in which he might have been employed, as cosmogonic agent, as victor in an initial conflict between two hostile powers, and as ultimate progenitor of the race, two could not by any chance have been of service to the Jew. Hebrew monotheism absolutely prohibited the introduction of a second creator alongside of Yahwe, even in a limited sense, and had in addition long since obliterated the traces of the old conception, shared too by the Jew, that a tremendous conflict preceded the creation of the world. Only in an adapted form could the Anthropos as primordial champion find a permanent place in Jewish thought. In the third of his early capacities, as ultimate progenitor of the race, he must, however, have been unobjectionable. We are justified, then, in searching for traces of his presence in this form. The Jewish conceptions of the primal man are the sphere within which the search must be conducted.

Preëxilic Israel, with which we must begin in order to comprehend the course of developments, appears to have had no idea of a Primal Man, *proprie dictu*. What it told of the creation of man, it said of man in the generic sense. The account of

Genesis c. 2, which echoes its views, is essentially the story

> Of man's first disobedience and the fruit
> Of that forbidden tree, whose mortal taste
> Brought death into the world and all our woe.

It is inspired not so much by the admiration of the creator and his creation, as by the observation of man's present woeful existence and the endeavor to explain its origin.[67] Thus interpreted in the light of the present, even the beginning of the race was to the older Israelite a "sad story."[68] It remained so, undoubtedly, for the preëxilic prophets as well. For, though the majesty and righteousness and love of Yahwe now entered as further themes into their religious compositions, the sad tale of man lingers on, so that as Davidson has aptly said: "the greatness of God and the sinfulness of man are the two poles between which the messages of the prophets moved."[69]

With the exile matters begin to change. A badly mutilated passage in Ezekiel,[70] which describes as paradisiacal the luxury of the prince of Tyre, and which has often been pressed to furnish evidence of the idea of a divine primal man with whom the prophet is then supposed to compare the ruler in question, can be employed legitimately to show that interest was beginning to attach independently to ideal conditions such as those originally projected into the remote past merely as a foil to the woeful condition of the present.

The priestly account of creation (Gen. 1) leads us one step further. Appearing here for the first time certainly as a concrete personality, the first man, Adam, enjoys the advantages of being created in the image of God (an image which he hands down unsullied to the generations that follow),[71] of having power over the living creatures of the land[72] and residing in a garden which is God's own dwelling place.[73]

[67] Kautzsch, *Biblische Theologie* (1911), p. 177.
[68] Gunkel, *Genesis*, 3rd ed., p. 32: "Die Stimmung des Mythus ist traurig."
[69] Davidson, *Old Testament Theology* (1912), p. 203.
[70] *Ezekiel* 28, 12ff.
[71] *Genesis* 5, 3; 9, 6.
[72] *Gen.* 1, 28.
[73] Gunkel, *Genesis*, 3rd ed., p. 35.

From this time on, there seem to appear slight traces of two distinct conceptions of man's beginning, running side by side. The majority of writers continue in the older pessimistic strain. Nowhere is the frailness, helplessness and hoplessness of human existence more clearly documented than in Job,[74] and yet Gunkel is probably correct in quoting the passage where Job's wisdom is ironically questioned in the words "art thou the first man that was born, or wast thou brought forth before the hills,"[75] as an indication that even to the author of Job the idea of an "all-wise" protoplast was known.[76] Perhaps, too, Psalm 8, modelled as it is on Genesis c. 1 (P), embraces in its two statements, first, that man is but a little lower than Elohim, and is crowned with honor, perfection and dominion, and secondly, "what is man that thou art mindful of him," an attempted reconciliation of two current opinions concerning man's origin and destiny.

However this may be, the extra-canonical literature of Judaism not only gives excellent testimony to the co-existence of two evaluations of the protoplast,[77] but shows that the condemnatory is losing favor to the laudatory. IV Esra and II Baruch are the prime representatives of the former. They are pronounced in their verdict that through the fall of Adam sin has come upon the whole world, and that even before the fall,[78] Adam had a kernel of evil within him,[79] and as a consequence an evil heart.[80] Opposed to them stand the books Wisdom, Jubilees, the Enoch literature, Sirach and the Sibylline Oracles. The first three without exception transfer the blame for the present degraded state of man, a state once determinative of the nature of man's beginning, to the shoulders of Cain,[81] the demons,[82] or the angels.[83] Together

[74] Bertholet, *Bibl. Theol.* II, p. 133.
[75] *Job*, 15, 7.
[76] Gunkel, *Genesis*, 3rd ed., p. 33.
[77] Even the pessimistic interpreters now deal no longer with man in general but with an individual protoplast.
[78] *IV Esra* 3, 7; 7, 11; *II Bar.* 23, 4; 48, 42.
[79] *IV Esra* 4, 30f.
[80] Ibid., 3, 21f.
[81] *Wisdom of Solomon*, 10, 3.
[82] *Jubilees* 5.
[83] *I Enoch* 6.

they give a highly ennobled picture of the first man. His glory when created was above that of every living thing.[84] From his abode in Paradise, which was in the third heaven,[85] he could see the angels before God's throne.[86] Indeed, he was himself an angel, a ruler of the earth.[87] Wisdom guided him to the last and delivered him from transgression.[88] He is a symbol of the cosmos,[89] a perfect microcosm.[90]

Even Philo may be adduced as a witness for the newer interpretation of man, for, though what he says of the "heavenly man" is stated in Platonic and Stoic terms, his interest in that figure cannot be explained save in the light of the apocrypha and the "Adam Literature."[91]

The term "Adam Literature" we apply to that group of accounts of the lives and vicissitudes of the Adamites and Adam, that has come down to us in Syriac, Ethiopic, Greek, Latin, Armenian and Slavonic versions.[92] They represent for the most part, imaginative expatiations and Midrashim upon the stories of Genesis. But imagination alone is not sufficient to account for the favorable impression of Adam gained from them, and many of the elements utilized in his description. A definite tradition, such as that which we have followed in the apocrypha, must have been incorporated in these works. Now most of the works, as we have them, are of a late date, and show unmistakably the imprint of Christian thought.[93] Still, the tradition which they embody cannot be said to be Christian, for those whose opinion

[84] *Sirach* 49, 14–16, and note.
[85] *II Enoch* 8; cf. 2. *Cor.* 12, 3–4.
[86] Ibid., 31, 2.
[87] Ibid., 30, 11–2.
[88] *Wisdom* 10, 1; cf. *Jub.* 2, 23–4.
[89] *Sibyl. Oracles* III, 24–5.
[90] *II Enoch* 30, 8–13; cf. E. Meyer, *Ursprung*, II, pp. 350–1.
[91] Cf. Gressmann, *Ursprung*, p. 362.
[92] The works in question are (1) the cognate *Apocalypse of Moses, the Vita Adae et Evae*, and the *Life of Adam and Eve*, edited and reconciled in Charles, Apocrypha, II, pp. 123–54; (2) the *Conflict of Adam and Eve*, translated by S. C. Malan (1882); (3) the *"Adamsschriften"* translated by Preusschen, in *Festgruss für B. Stade* (1900), p. 165ff.
[93] Charles, Apocrypha, vol. II (1913), pp. 126–9.

guided the development of Christian ideas, built their interpretation of the protoplast upon the words of Paul "as in Adam all sinned," and upon the older pessimistic view of man's beginning which Paul as a former Pharisee represents.[94] That the Adam Literature, none the less, achieved among Christians the popularity evinced by its manifold form and preservation, is evidence that it formed part of the precious inheritance which the nascent Church received from Judaism before the ties binding them together were finally sundered. It becomes thus, with certain limitations, a source for our inquiry.

The initial state of Adam these texts regard as a form of heavenly existence not comparable in any way to that of later humanity. The Ethiopic text describes it as a condition of spiritual effulgence, or luminous spirituality akin, perhaps, to that of the Homunculus of Goethe's "Faust."[95] The fall, it considers a lapse from this state into incarnation. A cognate conception appears in the Armenian documents, where the disobedience of Adam is followed by the loss of his "garment of light,"[96] and where the fall appears as a downward precipitation from realms of everlasting brilliance.[97] Here, too, we find the peculiar idea, that the protoplast fell first from absolute light to absolute darkness, and after six days was redeemed and brought to the land of intermittent sunshine and shadow.[98]

Though the fall, as is apparent, plays an extensive part in the Adam Literature, it fails to stamp Adam as a woeful subject. Gifted with the powers of divine intervention, he performs miracles

[94] *Rom.* 5, 12–4. Of course there were fluctuations of opinion even among the Christian writers. Tertullian speaks of Adam as a prophet. (*de Anima*, 11, 43.) Tatian condemned him to Sheol (Iren. I, 28, 1) and Origen was rebuked for comparing Adam and Eve to Christ and the Church. (Socrates, *Ecclesiastical History*, III, 7). But these fluctuations are of minor significance. The main trend of thought goes over Paul, Tertullian (*de Carne Christi* 16), Ambrose (*in Luc.* VII, pars. 164, 234) to Augustine (*Quaestiones*, 66, 3–5; *de Libero Arbitrio* 20, 56 et al.) cf. Harnack, *Dogmengeschichte*, 4th ed. (1909), pp. 137–8.)
[95] Malan, pp. 10; 15.
[96] Preusschen, p. 191.
[97] Ibid., p. 193.
[98] Ibid., pp. 192–3.

upon earth, even after the lapse.[99] He is privileged in visions to behold the heavenly realms and to commune with God.[100] At the close of his life, his soul is borne aloft and seated upon the throne with God[101] or upon the throne of Satan;[102] for throughout his life Adam is himself the great antagonist and opponent of the powers of evil.[103]

In rabbinical theology the two interpretations of Adam current in the religious literature of later Judaism and nascent Christianity find a further echo. Though they never saw fit to deny the freedom of the will nor the possibility of sinlessness, in other words to establish a doctrine of original sin, the great teachers of the later centuries granted that Adam's fall was of fatal consequence for mankind. By it the evil inclination, the Yezer hara, previously dormant, was awakened and became man's actual master and king,[104] so that "there is no one who has not sinned and there is no creature that has not incurred guilt before God."[105] Thus through Adam, guilt and death have actually come to all generations.[106] Yet, Adam is to them more than the author of guilt. He is set upon a plane superior to that of normal humanity. He lived in purity, beauty and wisdom,[107] as the monarch of all creation.[108] Heavenly light surrounded him[109] indeed he was himself the light of the world.[110] Male and female were united in his person,[111] and his body thus became a symbol of the Torah under which man was destined to live.[112] His stature and size were those of a giant, filling both heaven and earth.[113]

[99] Charles, Apocrypha, II, p. 135.
[100] Ibid., pp. 139–40.
[101] Preusschen, p. 187.
[102] Charles, II, p. 150.
[103] Ibid., p. 137.
[104] *Nedarim* 32b.
[105] *Wayyikra rabba* 14.
[106] *Pesikta* 1b; *Bammidbar rabba* 13; cf. Weber, *Juedische Theologie*, p. 224.
[107] Tal. jerushalmi, tr. *Shabbath* II, 3; *Pesikta* 37a, 34a.
[108] *Ber. rabba* c. 25; cf. 19 et al.
[109] Ibid. 11.
[110] Tal. jerushalmi, tr. *Shabbath* 1I, 3, cf. *Pesikta* 37a, I01a.
[111] *Ber. rabba* 8.
[112] Targ. jerushalmi I, *ad Gen.* 1, 27.
[113] *Ber. rabba* 8, the "golem."

In the Zohar and the cabalistic writings these speculations find their last echo. The difficulty of distinguishing between Palestinian and Philonic tradition in the description of its Adam Kadmon,[114] bids us refrain from following the development to its final conclusion. We turn, therefore, to the question concerning its ultimate origin: What may the forces have been that produced side by side with the traditional pessimistic interpretation of man's beginning, the picture of a superior protoplast? A distinction will probably need to be made between the factors operative in the canonical and the post-canonical periods respectively, partly because of the differences in religious and intellectual horizon, and partly because of the necessity of accounting for the sudden bound into preëminence taken by the newer interpretation in the later period.

What the priestly writers thought about the protoplast can be explained with satisfaction as the result of the importance attached since the exile to Yahwe as the creator. What Yahwe created "was good." Hence man, though he came to grief and brought grief to others must have been created in a higher state and for other ends.

Those who contend that Ezekiel was acquainted with a divine protoplast dwelling on the mountain of God,[115] might point to the Barbelognostic Adamas and the celestial mountain Harmozel on which he lived as a parallel to their rendering of Ezekiel's the prophecy.[116] But even though the parallel were exact, the ultimate source of the conception could scarcely be Iran and the Anthropos, for the prophecy against Tyre antedates the days when the Persian religion became a factor in the Fertile Crescent, and the mountain of God, together with the regal splendor of the protoplast who dwells there, recall the Babylonian-Sumerian ideas of divinity and celestial existence rather than the Persian.[117]

To account for the character and prominence of the superior

---

[114] Karppe, *Études sur les Origines et la Nature du Zohar* (1901), pp. 431–4.
[115] Cf. Gunkel, *Genesis*, 3rd ed., p. 35, but cf. *Book of Enoch*, 24, 2.
[116] Irenaeus I, 29, 3; cf. above p. 42, n. 31.
[117] Jeremias, *Handb. d. altor. Geisteskultur* (1913), pp. 53–7, Bousset-Gressmann, p. 489.

Adam in the period of post-canonical Judaism is more difficult. Of those influences that first moulded his form in earlier days, some probably continued to be effective. Though Ezekiel's sentiments find little response,[118] the ideas of the priestly writers were now the dominant forces in Jewish religious life. The inclusion of the West in the cultural horizon of Palestine bids us allow, too, for the influence of the optimistic interpretation of human existence current in Greek circles. But while these factors help us to understand and explain certain of the characteristics ascribed to the superior protoplast, his wisdom, perfection and beauty, they fall short of accounting for all of his traits and for the genuine interest suddenly attaching to him.

The difficulty is not solved by supposing that the ever-present "Lust zum Fabulieren" had fortuitously seized upon the protoplast as an excellent subject of fictional elaboration. It seems to call rather for the presence of a cognate figure affecting and helping to transform the character of the first man, and for the ascription of some ulterior significance to his person.

To gain an opinion concerning the identity of the figure in question we must concern ourselves with the more difficult of the traits characterizing the celestial Adam. Among them none recurs with greater consistency than his description in terms of "Light." Now "Light" is used metaphorically in connection with Yahwe as early as the Book of Isaiah and the post-exilic portion of the Psalter.[119] It remained, however, for the late apocalypses to give the term preëminence and to use it as the expression of the nature and being of God, the angels and the blessed.[120] This newer significance, with which it is employed, too, where attached to the protoplast, appears to require particular motivation. It is but natural to think of its being inspired directly or indirectly by Iranian tradition, for Light is here one of the current expressions of the nature and essence of deity.[121]

[118] *Pesikta* 37a; cf. Weber, *Jued. Theol.*, p. 215.
[119] *Isaiah* 2, 5; *Ps.* 104, 2.
[120] *Dan.* 11, 2, and for Enoch the references in Volz, *Jued. Eschat.*, pp. 328–9, 358.
[121] Bertholet, *Bib. Theol.*, pp. 462–3; cf. Gressmann, *Ursprung*, pp. 343–7.

It is a further peculiarity of the celestial Adam that, even where we are told of his lapse and consequent death at the end of a thousand years, he functions really as a protagonist of God and the race in their common struggle against the power of Satan, and that, keeping his life unsullied, he is able to hand down to his descendents the model of a godly life. This conception stands in intimate connection with the dualistic trend that was making itself felt in the thought of later Judaism. Now this dualistic impress, noticeable particularly in the importance attached in the period of the apocrypha to Satan and to the kingdom of darkness in its opposition to the Kingdom of God, is hardly typical of Hebrew ideas. It is usually said to be the result of Iranian influence.[122] Thus two important particulars point to Iran as the ultimate home for such phenomena as characterise the celestial Adam.

Gayomart, who therefore again furnishes the point of comparison, might indeed have served as the figure that aided the transformation of the Biblical protoplast. He belongs, in the first place, to the spiritual creation of Ahura Mazda, a creation fashioned in the sphere of "endless light,"[123] and constantly described as "light" or "shining."[124] When created, we are told, he was brilliant and white,[125] brilliant, in fact, as the sun.[126] Even at the end of the world, one half of the sun's light will be radiated upon him, while the other half will serve the rest of humanity.[127] In the second place, Gayomart, as we have seen, plays an important part in the conflict of Ahriman with Ormuzd. The coming of the tempter to Gayomart is the climax of the first phase in the struggle between opposing forces.[128] The death of the prototype, ensuing from the conflict, is not the result of his submission to the temptations with which he is confronted. He

---

[122] Bousset-Gressmann, p. 515, E. Meyer, *Ursprung*, II, pp. 95–120.
[123] *Bundahishn* 1, 2.
[124] L. H. Gray, Ency. Rel. and Ethics, art. *Light and Darkness* (Iranian).
[125] *Bundahishn* 24, 1.
[126] *Zad Sparam* 10, 3.
[127] *Bundahishn* 30, 9.
[128] Ibid., 3, 12–19, *Zad Sparam* 4, 3.

is till the last a doer of good works.[129] The pure propitious liturgy which he spoke aided him.[130] Through him, however, the outlook for humanity's future is assured, for all men are to be of his race, and have been furnished in advance by him with the example of good works and the command to perform them.[131] Thus the faithful of the later generations revere his homonym, the "fravashi of Gaya-maretan, the righteous."[132]

The similarity between the Iranian prototype and the celestial Adam may extend still further. Even as Adam is said to go from light to darkness at his fall, so Gayomart is enshrouded in darkness at the coming of the tempter.[133] The bisexuality ascribed to Adam is not remote from the Iranian protoplasts.[134] Even the garment of light which Adam is clothed quite in contrast to the Biblical conception of his nakedness, may together with the garments ascribed to the blessed, be derived from Iran.[135] Finally the immense, world-encompassing size ascribed to the protoplast may be an echo of Gayomart's macrocosmic importance.[136]

Should the character of the celestial Adam have truly been moulded in these respects by the figure of Gayomart, as it was carried westward in the form of the Anthropos, a number of phenomena in Jewish, Christian and Gnostic traditions would become intelligible. We should be able to understand, in the first place, why the superior protoplast begins to attain preeminence in the second pre-Christian century. That is the time when the Anthropos as Bar Nasha, too, makes his first appearance. In the second place it might supply the necessary basis for the origin of the Adam-Christ speculation.

At first glance it appears as though there can be no connection between the Adam-Christ speculation and the common origin of

[129] *Zad Sparam* 4, 6.
[130] Ibid., 10, 1.
[131] *Bundahishn* 3, 23.
[132] *Yasna* 13, 7 et al., *Dinkard* 3, 35.
[133] *Bundahishn* 3, 20.
[134] Cf. above, p. 107.
[135] Cf. *Enoch* 62, 16; cf. above, p. 136, and note of Beer in Kautzsch, Apokryphen, vol. 2. and Reitzenstein, IE, p. 147.
[136] *Zad Sparam* 10, 2.

celestial Adam and Bar Nasha. Neither the Adam Literature nor the apocalypses in which the Bar Nasha occurs show any acquaintance with this speculation. First and last man appear together for the first time in the letters of Paul.[137] But Paul, it is quite certain, was not presenting to his readers a new theologoumenon. He introduces the Adam-Christ speculation as though it were traditional.[138] If traditional it belongs undoubtedly to his Jewish heritage. Paul thus leads us back to Judaism, and in our sources for the religious life of the immediately pre-Christian centuries the conception to which he gave utterance can again be found. In the Testament of Levi the Messiah's activities are described in part as follows:

> And he shall open the gates of paradise
> And shall remove the threatening sword against Adam,
> And he shall give to the saints to eat from the tree of life,
> And the spirit of holiness shall be on them.
> And Beliar shall be bound by him
> And he shall give power to his children to tread upon the evil spirits.[139]

That paradisiacal conditions are to obtain at the coming of the Messiah, is a thought already expressed by Isaiah.[140] But the prophecy here takes a new form. The Messiah now reënacts the life of Adam in a reversed sequence of events, each event having a significance opposed to that originally connected with it. That actually presupposes a contraposition of protoplast and Messiah identical with the one to which Paul gave utterance.

To ascribe the origin of such a connection between first and last man, to the common origin of the Bar Nasha and the celestial Adam may appear unwarranted, and that for two reasons, first, because the relation of the two figures is antithetical rather than complementary and thus draws upon the older pessimistic view of Adam, secondly because the Messiah in this case is not the Bar Nasha.

[137] *Romans* 5, 12–14; 1. *Cor.* 15, 45–7.
[138] Lietzmann, notes on the passages above, in Lietzmann's Handbuch, vol. III (1913).
[139] *Testament of Levi*, 18, cf. Bousset-Gressmann, pp. 260–1.
[140] *Isaiah* 11, 6–8.

ANTHROPOS AND SON OF MAN

Neither of these reasons has decisive force, because, if we mistake not, there is evidence also of a connection between first and last man, in which both the Bar Nasha and the celestial Adam play a part. The evidence is a bit awkward and difficult, yet by no means negligible. It is found in Enoch's elevation to the position and role of Bar Nasha.

The 71st chapter of the Book of Enoch in which this elevation is recorded, has for some time been a matter of dispute. Charles, in twice editing the book, has voiced the opinion that the sense which the chapter at present conveys is due to the loss of a reference to the Son of Man (between vss. 13 and 14), and a scribe's substituting a pronoun of the second person for one of the third, to the number of eight times.[141] Textual conditions in the Book of Enoch being what they are, it must be admitted that such a change could possibly have occurred. And yet, it must also be admitted, that if the chapter makes sense in its present form, the antecedent probability is for an unvitiated text.

What has argued against the originality of the passage more than anything else, is the nature of the sentiments conveyed. There is at first glance no possible basis for the identification of Enoch and Bar Nasha. A number of scholars have pointed to the prominence which Enoch enjoys in other texts, as a religious personality, as the author of science and the agent of revelation, and on this basis they have sought to defend the originality of the present reading.[142] While this seems to be a step in the right direction, it fails to clinch the matter. A few words may serve to show how the relation of Anthropos and celestial Adam will clarify the difficulty.

The rise to prominence which the celestial Adam experienced in the apocryphal period of Jewish religious literature, is not an isolated phenomenon. Together with him, his descendents to the days of Noah suddenly take on new significance. Pseudepigrapha appear under the names of Seth, Enoch, and Noah. On the borders of Jewish lands arise many sects, Adamite, Sethite, Ophite,

---

[141] Cf. the note on *Book of Enoch* 71, 14–17 in Charles, Apocrypha, vol. II.
[142] So Beer, in Kautzsch, Apokryphen, vol. II in note on *Enoch* 71, 24, and Bousset-Gressmann, pp. 353–4.

Melchisidecian, which give great prominence to the antediluvians. Abel, Seth and Anosh find a home in Mandean lore in the capacities of prophets. Mani includes Adam, Seth and Noah in his catalogue of the great teachers of the world. The development to which these facts testify is by no means late. It goes back, as the apocalypses of Enoch and Noah, and random references in other non-canonical books show, to at least the very beginning of the first pre-Christian century. But why should all these antediluvians suddenly become inspired prophets, men in whose names the occult may be revealed? In the case of Enoch there is an element of predisposition, but the majority, certainly, have no inherent capacity for their role. There is but one reason that adequately explains the development. It is through the change in the character of the protoplast that they have taken on a new form. The glamor surrounding the celestial Adam has passed over to those who are his immediate offspring, and who, through their association with him during his life of one thousand years,[143] may well be thought to have learned his wisdom and shared his divinity. Enoch's elevation to the office of Bar Nasha is thus but another expression of the connection between Adam and Messiah. This time it is not merely that the Christ reënacts the role of Adam. The Messiah is here in his person an Adamite.

If our interpretation is correct, the text of Enoch chapter 71 is irreproachable, because there is nothing impossible in the sentiments which it conveys. Simultaneously, however, we gain from the Book of Enoch evidence for an interrelation of first and second man that is not antithetical in kind. It is similar to that found in the "*Adamsschriften*," where the mediating person of the glorious trinity arises from his throne to make room for Adam at his return from the earth.[144]

From the discussion of the elevation of Enoch, the origin of part, if not all of the efforts to connect first and last man, should be evident. No matter how we may explain the genesis of the sentiments of Paul and the Testament of Levi, Enoch has as its

---

[143] This conception appears very early; cf. *Jubilees* 4, 30.
[144] Preusschen, p. 187.

prerequisite a unity of the persons of the celestial Adam and Bar Nasha such as can have arisen only on the basis of their common origin in the Anthropos figure.

From the preceding discussion we have gained the impression that the Anthropos speculation can be employed to furnish an eminently satisfactory explanation of the origin of the Jewish Bar Nasha, of the character of the celestial Adam and of the latter's association with the Messiah. Since this speculation can be shown to have existed in an early proto-Gnostic form in Mesopotamia and since there was frequent intercourse between the communities, Jewish and Gentile, of Mesopotamia and Palestine, there is no improbability attaching to the use of the Anthropos as a means of clarifying the development of these elements of later Jewish thought.

The establishment of such a connection between Anthropos tradition and Jewish religious belief, moreover, furnishes a means of testing our interpretation of the Gnostic records. In the first place, we gain a corroboration of the contention that in his proto-Gnostic form the Anthropos was primarily a primordial champion, adapted in part to the figure of Marduk, and the celestial father-prototype of humanity. Secondly we are able to confirm our suspicion that the soteriological manifestation of the Anthropos is a late element of the tradition, for had it played a part in determining his proto-Gnostic character, it, and not the Anthropos' capacity of primordial champion, would have moulded the figure of the Bar Nasha. The Jewish sources show no knowledge of a connection between Anthropos and a divine element in human nature, but we are not at liberty to suppose that this, their silence, represents a proof of its absence in the early form of the Anthropos speculation, since, contrary to the matter of the soteriological manifestation, it was not amenable to Jewish ideas in general. None the less, the silence of the records would serve to support our view of the relation of Anthropos and Soul. Finally the Adam-Christ speculation, as developed in Judaism, and particularly the importance attached to the Adamites furnishes a basis for the origin in Jewish and Christian circles for ideas approximating the later syncretistic Anthropos Theology, but not directly related to it,

THE ANTHROPOS IN JEWISH THOUGHT

and a possible basis for the construction of the relation between Anthropos and Soter.

The growth of the Anthropos speculation is as much indebted to Jewish religious thought as Jewish ideas are indebted to the Anthropos tradition.

CHAPTER VII

THE ANTHROPOS AND THE NEW TESTAMENT SON OF MAN

Is the Anthropos whom we have followed through Gnostic speculation and Jewish apocalyptic capable of throwing new light upon the problem of the New Testament Son of Man? This is the last of the questions to which we must seek an answer. The answer will be found by determining whether the Anthropos as he existed outside of Judaism can be made to account for the excess in ideas and associations which the New Testament Son of Man and Jesus as Son of Man manifest over and above the measure of those connected with the "man-like one" of the apocalypses.

In three distinct spheres of New Testament tradition scholars have recently thought they perceived the influence of the pagan Anthropos, in the Fourth Gospel, in the Pauline Theology and in the Synoptic Gospels. To the contentions advanced with respect to the first and second of these spheres it is a necessary presupposition that the Anthropos was familiar to the religious communities of Syria in the first Christian century, to the third that he was simultaneously known directly to sects in intimate contact with the people of Judea and Galilee. Our study of the Anthropos tradition has shown that in the first two cases the presupposition is justifiable and does not lack corroboration, for the Anthropos was almost certainly in Syria before the end of the first century. In the third case we cannot consider the presupposition entirely impossible, since we granted the possibility of a relation between the Anthropos and Daniel's "man-like one," but we must consider it less probable by reason of our view that the Mandean Theology in its earliest form lacked the contact with the Anthropos tradition. It will be necessary to enter upon a discussion of the various elements of New Testament tradition involved in the controversy and to seek from the analysis of the material itself a verdict to the question at issue.

1. The name Son of Man is employed or alluded to in the Fourth Gospel some twelve or thirteen times. It designates Jesus as the complete revelation of the Godhead, the ever-present, the one dependent upon the Father, the giver of life, the preexistent in heaven, the one who ascends to heaven, the judge, the one glorified on earth, the Messiah, the incarnate, the one who was crucified and died, the one exalted at death, the Savior and object of faith.[1]

Two facts must be emphasized in this connection. The first is that the Johannine use of Son of Man is rooted in the Synoptic tradition. Both traditions stress the Messianic character, suffering, death and glorification of the Son of Man, and what is more, similarly divide their attention between his transcendent or heavenly and immanent or earthly relations. The second fact to be noted is that it is a long step forward from the original Synoptic position to that stage of the tradition represented by the Fourth Gospel. This is evident from the way in which the judicial capacity of the Son of Man is minimized, and from the emphasis which is placed upon his transcendent nature and origin, his relations to the Godhead and his place in the life of the believer as an object of faith.

The question which we must ask ourselves is whether this change has been brought about by influence exerted by the pagan Anthropos conception?

[1] 1. The revelation of God, 1, 51; 3, 13; o, 27; 8, 28; (12, 34); 13, 31.
2. Ever present, 6, 27; 6, 53.
3. Dependent upon the Father, 5, 27; 6, 27; 8, 28.
4. Giver of Life, 3, 14; 6, 27; 6, 53.
5. Preëxistent in heaven, 3, 13; 6, 62.
6. Ascends to heaven, 3, 13; 6, 62; 8, 28.
7. Judge, 5, 27 (implied).
8. Glorified on earth, 12, 23; 13, 31.
9. Messiah, 1, 51; 9, 35; 12, 34.
10. Incarnate, 3, 13; 3, 14; 6, 53; 6, 62; (9, 35); 12, 23; 13, 31.
11. Crucified and died, 3, 14; 8, 28; 12, 23; 13, 31.
12. Exalted at death, 3, 14; 8, 28; 12, 23; 13, 31.
13. Savior and object of faith, 8, 28; 9, 35; 12, 34.

In the second edition of his commentary on John, Bauer has recently answered the question in the affirmative. The Johannine Son of Man, he says, "clearly reflects the conception of the Heavenly Man as redeemer, a conception which must have enjoyed extensive popularity in the time of John and is still visible particularly among Gnostics, Mystics of the Hermetic circle, Mandeans and Manicheans."[2]

With this conclusion we find ourselves in disagreement. An analysis of the Fourth Gospel shows without shadow of a doubt that the ideas associated by the author of this document with the name Son of Man are simultaneously employed also in connection with the names Son of God, Only-begotten, Logos, Christ and Son, and appear as well entirely apart from the use of titular and descriptive nomenclature.[3]

If we are to assume that the Son of Man of the Fourth Evangelist owes his character to the Anthropos it will be necessary to suppose that the whole Johannine Christology has been influenced from this angle, and that so far as the ideas connected with all the many designations are concerned, a process of nivellization has been in operation, the moving force of which is the Son of Man—Anthropos. This conclusion is manifestly erroneous for two reasons. In the first place the name Son of Man is of less importance in the Fourth Gospel than the names Son, Son of God and Christ, and is restricted in its use to fewer passages than in any of the Synoptic Gospels where it actually has determining force. In the second place it is evident that the ideas associated with the Johannine Son of Man are connected with the Christ of the Odes of Solomon by a writer who stands in a line with Ignatius and Barnabas in their use of Son of Man, who in other words has not the slightest inkling of its original and derived significance and who, therefore, scarcely employs the designation.[4]

---

[2] Lietzmann, Handbuch zum N.T. 2nd ed., pt. 6 (1925), p. 40.

[3] Cf. Holtzmann, *Neutestamentliche Theologie*, vol. II, pp. 444–508.

[4] The name "Son of Man" is applied to the Messiah only in Ode 36, 3 and is there taken as a term expressive of Jesus' humanity; cf. Ignatius, *Ephesians* 20, 2. Comparison between the Christology of the Odes and that connected

If then the designation Son of Man can boast of no particular prominence in the Fourth Gospel, and if the ideas associated with the Son of Man by the Fourth Evangelist are to be found in the Christology of a cognate document where the name has lost all its pristine significance, it would seem fairly certain that the forces which produced the Johannine Christ were not connected with or related to the name Son of Man.

To this conclusion there will be one great objection. It transfers the issue to the Odes of Solomon without an attempt to solve it, and disregards the fact that much light has recently been shed on the problems of the Fourth Gospel by comparison with the Mandaic Liturgies and the Odes, a comparison that is said to bring the Odes directly into line with the Anthropos tradition. In the present context we can state our answer to this objection with but a few words. We believe that the comparison between the Fourth Gospel, the Odes and the Mandaic Liturgies is a step in the right direction, but that it is incorrect to assume that that which connects the three documents is the Anthropos Theology. In Mandean theology there are three essential elements, Jewish speculation, Anthropos Theology and Life Theology.[5] The tie that binds the Mandean Documents to the Odes and the Fourth Gospel is the last of these,—the Life Theology.

in the Fourth Gospel with the name Son of Man is afforded by the following list, the sequence of items being that of the list of note 1.
    1. *Ode* 7, 12; 36, 4–6; 41, 13.
    2. 8, 21; 42, 4.
    3. 22.
    4. 3, 8.
    5. 41, 9.
    6, 22, 1.
    7. 33, 11. The Odist does not distinguish between the person of Wisdom and the person of Christ.
    8. 17, 7*b*.
    9. 9, 3; 29, 6.
    10. 7, 12; 28, 8–18.
    11. 28, 8–18; 42, 3–17. Christ dies but does not remain dead.
    12. 17, 7; 22, 1; 38, 10; 41, 12.
    13. 15, 6; 17, 14; 39, 13.
[5] Cf. above, p. 73.

This contention, which cannot be substantiated further at this point, we hope to be able to demonstrate at some later occasion. Suffice it to say that we cannot see either in the Fourth Gospel or in its associations evidence that its Son of Man has been transformed by the influence of the Anthropos.

A further attempt to connect the Anthropos Theology with the Fourth Gospel has recently been made by Schaeder in connection with the reconstruction of the Aramaic original of the famous Prologue of John. With the efforts of Burney,[6] Montgomery,[7] Bultmann[8] and Schaeder to determine the Aramaic original of portions of the Fourth Gospel, particularly the Prologue, we find ourselves in complete sympathy. Schaeder, with whom we are exclusively concerned at present, follows the lead of both Burney and Bultmann in supposing that the Prologue as we have it to-day is a hymn or ode adapted by the author of the Gospel by translation and by the addition of prose elements to serve as the introduction to his work. Schaeder's hypothesis differs from the rest in the contention that the original hymn was one which celebrated the identity of the heavenly messenger Anosh (of Mandean fame) with the divine Memra. The Anosh of this hymn the disciples of the Baptist connected with John as in the Mandean Book of John. The Fourth Evangelist reflects their point of view when he says that "the 'man' sent from God was John," but differs from them when he distinguishes between Memra and "man" and uses this distinction to minimize the importance of the Baptist.[9] If tenable this hypothesis would prove the literary dependence of a Christian writer upon a document coming from circles identified with the Anthropos Theology. Schaeder's contention hinges upon the assertion that in the two instances, verses 6 and 9 where the Fourth Evangelist uses ἄνθρωπος, he read in the Aramaic original אנשׁ and that this אנשׁ he interpreted as a form of אנשׁ, either by reason of his Hebraic heritage or because the form was actually current in his circles as it was in Nabatean communities.[10]

[6] *The Aramaic Origin of the Fourth Gospel*, 1922.
[7] *The Origin of the Gospel according to St. John*, Philadelphia, 1923.
[8] *Eucharisterion*, Festschrift für H. Gunkel, pt. 2 (1923), pp. 1–26.
[9] Reitzenstein u. Schaeder, *Studien*, pp. 306–41.
[10] Ibid., p. 326.

THE ANTHROPOS AND THE NEW TESTAMENT SON OF MAN

In dealing with Schaeder's hypothesis we shall endeavor to do no more than to show that the assertion upon which it hinges is not essential or necessary to the reconstruction or interpretation of the Prologue. We are then concerned particularly with vss. 6a and 9. Here the Greek text reads:

Ἐγένετο ἄνθρωπος ἀπεσταλμένος παρὰ θεοῦ
[. . . . .]
Ἦν τὸ φῶς τὸ ἀληθινόν, ὃ φωτίζει πάντα
ἄνθρωπον ἐρχόμενον εἰς τὸν κόσμον.

The words intervening between these two sentences Schaeder considers a prose addition of the Evangelist, somewhat after the analogy of Burney.[11] What remains he translates into a stanza of three lines with three beats to the line, as follows:

הוא אנוש משדר מן אלהא
הוא נהורא דכושטא דמנהר כל
אנוש אתי בעלמא

In our analysis it will be best to begin with Schaeder's reconstruction of vs. 9. What he has done is evident. He has placed the cesura after πάντα and construed ἄνθρωπον with ἐρχόμενον. In so doing he has preserved the rhythm of the earlier portion of hymn, has rescued the passage from the obscurity of the prose addition to which Burney had consigned it and found an Aramaic basis for defending the construction which earlier exegetes placed upon the difficult Greek sentence of John. This, together with the fact that the Mandean Anosh "comes into the world," and that the Evangelist has just been minimizing the importance of the Baptist whom the Mandeans identified with Anosh, forms an immediate justification for the supposition that what the Evangelist translated ἄνθρωπος actually read אנוש not אנש.

While we are willing to agree to much of Schaeder's construction, to the idea that the sentence represents a couplet of the original hymn, and that the ἐρχόμενον κτλ. should be preserved, we cannot accept either his division of the sentence or the introduc-

[11] *The Aramaic Origin*, etc., p. 41.

tion of אנש as the only feasible rendering of the original Aramaic. It is equally possible, we believe, that the Aramaic couplet originally read:

הוא נהורא דכושטא
דמנהר כל אתי בעלמא

In this rendering we have followed both Burney and Schaeder in connecting ἐρχόμενον εἰς τὸν κόσμον with Talmudic בוא לעלמא equivalent to Aramaic אתא בעלמא. Schaeder has pointed out the fact that Burney's translation כל אנש אתי בעלמא is pleonastic.[12] That is correct, for the Talmudic idiom by itself can signify "man." We must therefore either follow Schaeder and substitute אנש, or omit the equivalent of ἄνθρωπον and show why the translator introduced this element into the Greek translation. Of the two, the latter is the simpler. Connected with כל, the words אתי בעלמא can signify either "all men" or "all created things."[13] In the present context the sense "all men" is required. For the Evangelist to have translated them with φωτίζει πάντα ἐρχόμενον εἰς κτλ. would have meant to leave the sense of the phrase ambiguous, for then πάντα could have been construed as a neuter plural, and ἐρχόμενον could have been connected with φῶς. To the exegetes of to-day the sentence even with the word ἄνθρωπον presents these possibilities of interpretation. The scholars of the ancient Church, who were more closely connected with the living speech of the Greek New Testament, recognized in the ἄνθρωπον a burdening element tying πάντα and ἐρχόμενον together and interpreted accordingly. By inserting ἄνθρωπον in the passage, the writer of the Fourth Gospel did as much as he could, and for his day sufficient, to convey to his readers the actual sense of what he was translating without going too far afield from the idiom of the original hymn. Of interpretative additions such as the ἄνθρωπον then represents, Schaeder makes the Evangelist quite capable in connection with his discussion of vss. 3–4 of the Prologue.

[12] *Studien*, p. 328.
[13] Strack-Billerbeck, *Kommentar z. N.T. aus Talmud u. Midrasch*, vol. 2 (1924), p. 358.

THE ANTHROPOS AND THE NEW TESTAMENT SON OF MAN

While it is possible to exclude an equivalent of ἄνθρωπος from the Aramaic original of vs. 9, it is not possible to do so in vs. 6. Here the word "man" is rooted in the text. But, while we are willing to follow Schaeder in his contention that in translating vs. 6 Burney's נברא is less acceptable than אנש,[14] we cannot agree even here that אנש must be preferred to אנש.

Our first objection is a matter of general considerations. The main theme of the hymn of the Prologue is not essentially Mandaic. The Logos played no important part in Mandaic theology. True, Anosh is given the cognomen *Malala*, Word; but, as we have seen, this signifies little more than that he was one of the powers connected with the revelation of truth. To connect Anosh with the Logos in the sense in which that word is used in the Prologue requires special motivation. If Anosh were actually introduced in vs. 6, it would require, moreover, that he remain the subject of all that was said in the original hymn up to vs. 14. That would make Anosh the creator of the world and one who was rejected by his adherents. There is nothing in the Mandean description of Anosh or the Baptist to warrant his being regarded in this way.

The second objection is that Schaeder's reconstruction is reasonably intelligible even if we preserve the אנש which the Greek text demands. It might in this event be translated "and he became a man (namely), one sent from God." The reference would be to the Logos, of whom it might well be said that the world was made by him and that he was rejected by his own. The thought of vs. 6 would be parallel to that of vs. 14 and the words "the Logos became flesh," a thought which would necessarily require expression before vss. 9 and 11. In addition, it would accord with the fact that to the Fourth Evangelist Jesus is "the one sent from God" *par excellence*. In the face of the unity which would thus be established in the hymn as a whole, it would not be difficult to defend the repetition of the fact of the Logos' incarnation.

It will not be profitable to follow the ramifications of the discussions connected with the reconstruction of the Aramaic original of the Prologue any further. Suffice it to say that we find no

[14] *Aramaic Origin*, p. 41.

cogency in the reasoning that would introduce Anosh into that original and no direct contact between this part of the Fourth Gospel and the Anthropos tradition.

2. Leaving the world of the Fourth Gospel we come now to Paul, and to the efforts that have been made to connect elements of his thought with Anthropos speculation. The name Son of Man was never employed by Paul, at least not in the letters that have come down to us. That does not signify that the name was not applied to Jesus in his day or that he was unfamiliar with it, as Schmiedel was the first to demonstrate.[15] Neither does it set aside the question whether Paul was familiar with the Anthropos theology and whether it affected his views.

The antecedent probability that he was influenced from this angle is greater in the case of Paul than in the case of any other writer of the New Testament. In the first place, the tradition of which he is the classical exponent has no limited horizon, like that of the Gospels, but one that is in many of its elements world-wide. It was formulated first by Hellenized Jews in Jerusalem, developed in Syria and Arabia and enriched in its contact with a religious genius of the first rank, a man with a universal outlook. In the second place, the Pauline Theology embraces as one of its characteristic and universal elements a conception which plays an important part in the later Anthropos Theology. This is none other than the Pauline idea of the Spirit. It is true that Paul's views on the Spirit were not gained apart from the impression created by the Old Testament tradition and early Christian experience, but their formulation and a large number of the metaphors employed in their presentation have their origin in a theology identical with or similar to that found in documents of the Mystery Religions such as the Mithraic Ritual and the Corpus Hermeticum.

If it could be shown that the conception of the Spirit as it existed in these Oriental cults was of Iranian origin, and that the idea of a divine pneumatic or psychic element indwelling in man formed an essential part of the Anthropos tradition, Paul's view of the Spirit might be used as an argument in favor of his knowledge of the Anthropos tradition. Since this is not as yet apparent, we

[15] Prot. Monatshefte, 1898, pp. 291–308.

must base our judgment in the matter entirely upon the two statements of Paul regarding the "inner man" and regarding Christ as the "spiritual" or "heavenly man."

Paul places Adam and Christ into juxtaposition in two distinct ways. In one instance, in Romans 5, they are contrasted by reason of the nature and result of their actions. Adam remains Adam, Christ remains Christ, the fact of the incarnation of Christ plays but a subsidiary part. Since the contrast is determined by Adam's sin and fall from grace on the one hand and Christ's sinlessness and grace on the other, there can be no question of the direct influence of Anthropos Theology at this point. Quite on the contrary, it is evident that Paul is here dependent upon Jewish speculation such as that found in the Testament of Levi, whatever its origin may have been.[16]

In the second instance, 1. Cor. 15, 44–9, the juxtaposition is rooted in a similarity between the natures of Adam and Christ; for only if both are in a real sense beings of the human type can the verses in question become a proof of the introductory contention that there are two kinds of human bodies, psychic and pneumatic. Moreover, this similarity cannot be temporary, a result of the incarnation, for then there would be no guarantee of the permanence of the believer's spiritual body, but must be permanent. Christ is therefore in an absolute sense a type of man, a conception which is one step in advance of the Adam-Christ speculation underlying Enoch c. 71, and which, therefore, raises the question of the influence of the Anthropos Theology once more.

The inquiry into the origin of this view of Christ turns about the discussion of the proof-text quoted by Paul with the words: "and so it is written, the first man, Adam, was made a living soul, the last Adam a life-giving spirit." The quotation is evidently in the nature of a Targum. Its first half represents the text of Gen. 2, 7 to which the words "first" and "Adam" have been added.[17] Its second part is scriptural only in a relative

---

[16] We are inclined to consider the Adam-Christ speculation of the Clementine Literature a product of this line of thought and have therefore omitted it from the discussion of the Anthropos tradition in which it was first included by Bousset, HP, pp. 171–5.

[17] Three steps are involved in the genesis of the expression "the first man

sense, since it is an expression not of any one Biblical passage but of the truth which the exegete sees behind the words of Scripture.

It is customary and natural at once to think of Philo in connection with the origin of this interpretation. Philo saw in the first two chapters of Genesis two accounts not of the same but of different creations. The first creation was that of the world of ideas, the second that of the physical cosmos. There are then, as we have seen, two "men" in Philo's theology, the one an idea or type, the other its material counterpart. This being the case it has been thought likely that the basis of the second portion of Paul's Targum is the Hellenistic, Philonic exegesis of Genesis 1, 27.[18] Paul's speculation concerning the heavenly man would then require for its origin only the subsequent identification of the "man of the idea" with the Messiah and would owe its character to current metaphysics.

There are a number of difficulties in the way of this solution of the problem. In the first place it is not certain whether Paul would have regarded a metaphysical postulate as something "real" in the sense in which he regarded the preëxistent man as real. Furthermore, Paul employs Genesis 1 at other occasions as the account of the creation of the present visible cosmos. Finally Christ is to him in no sense an element of creation. He is not made but is the instrumentality of creation.[19]

Because of these difficulties it seems preferable to suppose that not Philo directly but some third source upon which Philo too is dependent forms the basis of the Pauline speculation. In the last analysis this third element is for Reitzenstein the Anthropos Theology. Here we have undoubtedly such a preëxistent, pneumatic, non-metaphysical Man at once distinct from the protoplast and connected by late writers with the saviors.

Adam" (1) the expression "man" used in the LXX of Gen. 2, 7; (2) its rabbinical interpretation "the first man" *'adam harishon*; (3) Paul's interpretation of the rabbinical expression for the benefit of his Corinthian readers, "the first man Adam." Reitzenstein's constructions are unnecessary; cf. *Hellenistiche Mysterienreligion*, 2. ed., p. 198.

[18] Holtzmann, *Ntliche Theologie*, vol. II, pp. 85–6.
[19] Ibid.

The analogy is very nearly perfect and must therefore not be dismissed lightly. The only reason why it cannot of itself satisfy the demands of the passage under discussion lies in the fact that Paul's heavenly man is introduced as a Biblical character. This difficulty Reitzenstein has sought to offset by the use of Philonic testimony. The Alexandrine philosopher, he contends, was dependent in part upon an ancient Jewish tradition in which by reason of the influence of the Anthropos Theology a distinction was made between the protoplasts of the two Biblical accounts of creation. This tradition Philo has Platonized in the tract on the "Creation." In its original form he presents it in the first book of the "Allegories," where in connection with Gen. 2, 7 he remarks "the races of man are twofold, for one is the heavenly man, the other the earthly man."[20] For Paul to introduce the heavenly man, who is essentially the Anthropos, in connection with Gen. 2, 7 was therefore the natural result of his use of a Jewish tradition. He takes care, however, to differentiate his own interpretation from its Philonic counterpart when he says "not first is that which spiritual but that which is natural."[21]

Since this construction satisfies the problem of the Pauline quotation, since it does not connect Philo directly with the Anthropos tradition and since we have already admitted that the Anthropos may have affected the Jewish conception of the protoplast, it will not be possible to deny it a certain measure of plausibility. But it is by no means satisfactory in all respects. The "heavenly man," even though he is introduced by Philo in connection with Gen. 2, 7, remains the "man according to the image," a creature and hence a being quite distinct from the uncreated Christ.[22] Furthermore, neither Paul, nor to the best of our knowledge the Rabbis of Palestine, differentiated between the creation recorded in Genesis 1 and that of Genesis 2. This would seem to make the tradition upon which Philo was dependent Alexandrine and thus separate it from Paul.

These difficulties make it necessary to admit that Professor

[20] *Allegories*, bk. I, §31, ed. Cohn-Wendland.
[21] IE, pp. 104–11.
[22] Holtzmann, pp. 85–6.

L. Ginzberg has found at least an equally suitable explanation of the origin of Paul's speculation concerning Christ as the "heavenly man." He calls attention to a Midrash in the two extant forms of which we are told that the "Spirit of God moving upon the face of the waters" is the "spirit of Adam" and the "spirit of the Messiah."[23] Between the thought of the Midrash and that of 1. Cor. 15, 44–9 there are two differences. The Midrash speaks only of the "spirit of Adam" and does not absolutely identify the "spirit of Adam" with the "spirit of the Messiah." While these differences are not to be overlooked, it is possible to see how, to a man of Paul's type and training, they might have been negligible. In the first place, Paul speaks of both the Spirit of Christ and the pneumatic Christ, as well as of the Spirit which man receives and the new, spiritual man, using the two designations applied to each almost interchangeably. In the second place all that Paul requires for the identification of concepts and figures of Old Testament tradition is that they be elements of one "row" in other words $\sigma\tau o\iota\chi\epsilon\tilde{\iota}a$.[24]

If the "spiritual man" of 1. Cor. were actually the preëxistent Spirit of Genesis 1, 2, we could understand how he could be identified with the uncreated Christ and how Paul could continue to use the account of creation found in Genesis 1 as the record of the formation of the present world. That he should refer to this "heavenly man" in connection with Genesis 2, 7 would be more natural in this case than in the case of the tradition referred to by Reitzenstein, since this "spiritual Adam" is not referred to explicitly in Genesis 1. His reference to the priority of the earthly man would then serve merely to clarify the matter of the order of their historical appearance.

Whichever view of the origin of Paul's "heavenly man" we adopt, it will be apparent that there is no reason to suppose that Paul was personally influenced by the Anthropos speculation. Only if Paul had been attracted to the "heavenly man" by the existence of cognate speculations in non-Christian circles would

[23] Article *"Adam Kadmon,"* Jewish Encyclopedia, quoting the *Midrash Gen. R.*, viii, 1 and *Midrash Teh.* to *Ps.* 139, 5.
[24] Cf. *Galatians* 4, 21–31.

that be the case. This is of course possible but neither demonstrable nor necessary. Ultimately, it is true, the Jewish tradition which Paul in either case employed, has its origin in the Adam speculation and in so far as this may have been encouraged by the Anthropos tradition we have in the "heavenly man" an echo of the Anthropos. This connection would suffice to explain the correspondence of the figures. A closer relationship, however, cannot be established definitely.

Leaving Paul's "heavenly man," we come now to the "inner man" and the attempts that have made to connect him with the Anthropos. The "inner man" for Paul is that portion of man's natural endowment otherwise referred to by the words "reason" or "I."[25] It is that portion which the divine Spirit vitalizes. Doubtless the "inner man" is an element of the Hellenistic and not of the Jewish heritage of Paul. In seeking an analogy in the Hellenistic sphere it was formerly customary to point to the expression "the man within" found in Plato.[26] Reitzenstein is perfectly correct in maintaining that this analogy is not only too remote but also imperfect.[27] The "inner man" of the Naasene Document and the Mandean Adakas, "the hidden Adam" are much closer in every way. That Paul in his use of the expression is dependent upon the thought of circles such as these, Reitzenstein has made highly probable. The analysis of the context in which the "inner man" appears in II Cor. 4, 16, shows intimate acquaintance with the concepts and metaphors indigenous to the "Erlösungsmysterium" of the Gnostic texts.[28] The question of the relation between Anthropos and "inner man" is therefore identical with that concerning the relation between "Erlösungsmysterium" or Soul Drama and the Anthropos tradition. We have previously found it necessary to question the permanence and originality of the relation in which the last mentioned elements stand to one another in the Anthropos Theology. That

[25] Reference to the "inner man" is made, in *Rom.* 7, 22; 2. *Cor.* 4, 16; *Eph.* 3, 16.
[26] *Republic*, 9, 589A, et al.
[27] HM, p. 205.
[28] Ibid., pp. 205–12.

means that there can be no decisive answer regarding the connection of "inner man" and Anthropos. We must again deal with matters of possibility and necessity. The possibility exists if Soul Drama and Anthropos tradition met prior to the days of Paul. The necessity exists if the genesis of the term "inner man" requires the presence and existence of a "Man" from whom the "inner man" has fallen into the sphere of material creation. The necessity we must deny, however captivating the explanation of the term involved, because, as Plato shows, similar expressions could and did arise wherever mysticism and the idea of divided personality common to mystical thought played a part. The possibility cannot be gainsaid.

3. Leaving Paul with the feeling that even if he was personally acquainted with the person of the Anthropos, it was of little importance to the development of his thought, we come finally to the Synoptic Gospels.

According to the documents in question, Jesus applied to himself, as his favorite self-designation the name Son of Man. He employed it with a threefold connotation, characterizing himself thereby as a man among other men, as one who must suffer, die and rise again, and as the one who is to appear at the consummation with the clouds of heaven in the capacity of judge. Those passages where the name is used with the last of these connotations are directly reminiscent of Daniel 7, 13 messianically interpreted as in the later Jewish apocalypses. To this extent the Synoptic view of Jesus as Son of Man is rooted in Jewish tradition. The question with which we are, therefore, concerned is whether the origin of the non-apocalyptic connotations and the adoption of the name as such have their origin in Jesus' or the early Christians' acquaintance with the Anthropos tradition.

It has become increasingly evident to scholars that we see Jesus to-day not directly but through the medium of the tradition current in the early Christian communities, as that tradition was recorded by unknown writers and by evangelists. To some this signifies that the use of the name Son of Man as applied to Jesus must be credited entirely to the pious reflection of the early believers and the editorial activity of the evangelists. The claims registered by the name Son of Man are considered too brusque to have been advanced by one as reticent as Jesus. Only those who believed that God had elevated him to the position of Messiah and who expected his return in glory could have spoken of him in this sense.

Those who accept this position, and they are many, will in all probability deny the connection of Anthropos and the Synoptic Son of Man. It is much more reasonable that the non-apocalyptic usage, upon which the contact with the Anthropos tradition depends, resulted from the fact that he to whom the name was applied had lived among men, suffered, died and risen again, than that it should be attributed to the Christians' knowledge of the Anthropos.

There are many, however, who feel that to deny that Jesus ever used the name Son of Man is to draw an erroneous conclusion from the observation that we see him through the eyes of the early Christians. They contend that since the name is found independently in all strata of our sources, from the Logia and Mark through Matthew and Luke, the denial of its use by Jesus would place upon all our sources the stamp of complete untrustworthiness, a thing which, evidently, they do not deserve. Reitzenstein, in holding that Jesus' adoption of the appellative was inspired by the existence of speculation concerning the messenger Anosh, of course presupposes the acceptance of this position.[29] That is therefore the basis upon which we must consider the validity of his hypothesis.

To assert that Jesus employed the name Son of Man in speaking of himself, does not mean to affirm that all of the passages where the name occurs represent the *ipsissima verba* of the Master. Literary criticism and the comparison of the Synoptic Gospels have shown a number of instances in which the name has been arbitrarily introduced into the tradition. By examining these first we will gain an idea of whether the early Christians of Palestine were acquainted with a relation between Anthropos and Son of Man.

Secondary introduction of the name Son of Man is probable

[29] MB, p. 72; IE, pp. 115–31.

in the Synoptic Gospels in the following instances. In the Logion concerning blasphemy the Q form represented by Mt. 12, 23 and Lc. 12, 10 "whosoever speaketh a word against the Son of Man" is probably secondary to the form of Mc. 3, 28–9 "all sins shall be forgiven unto the sons of men and all blasphemies." Vice versa, Mc. 8, 38 "whosoever therefore shall be ashamed of me and of my words . . . of him also shall the Son of Man be ashamed" is secondary to the Logion of Q and within the report of this Logion Lc. 12, 8 "whosoever shall confess me before men, him shall the Son of Man confess" is secondary to Mt, 10, 32–3. "Whosoever therefore shall confess me before men, him will I also confess . . . but whosoever shall deny me before men him will I also deny." Similarly Mt. 16, 13 "Who do men say that the Son of Man is" represents an arbitrary change of Mc. 8, 29 "who do men say that I am." Again Mt. 16, 28 "till they see the Son of Man coming in his kingdom" is an alteration of Mc. 9, 1 "till they have seen the kingdom of God come with power." In the Beatitudes, Matthew's words (5, 11) "Blessed are ye when men shall . . . say all manner of evil things against you falsely for my sake" make it probably that neither "for my sake" nor Lc. 6, 22 "for the sake of the Son of Man" are rooted in the common source Q. In the story of the Passion the use of Son of Man in Mt. 26, 2 and Lc. 22, 48; 24, 7 is not grounded either in Mc. or in an independent tradition. In Mt. 19, 28 the words "when the Son of Man shall sit in the throne of his glory" are probably not indigenous to the source Q which the passage reflects.

In compiling this list we have limited ourselves to the enumeration of instances where matters are reasonably clear by virtue of the existence of a definite counter-tradition. None the less we have here ten passages out of a possible 39 into which the name Son of Man has been arbitrarily introduced. Of the ten passages four show that the name was introduced in place of the pronoun "I." The others show that the early Christians employed the designation with no more than the three connotations found in the primary strata of the tradition.

If the ideas associated by Jesus and the early Christians with the name Son of Man were completely coextensive with the ideas associated by the Mandeans with Anosh, the secondary passages of the Synoptic Gospels listed above would have no message to convey. But Anosh has a wider field of associations than the Synoptic Son of Man. To assume that Jesus and his earliest disciples were acquainted with the Anosh speculation of the Mandean type and influenced by it, is out of harmony with the mixed conservatism and carelessness to which the secondary passages testify. Had the earliest disciples known the Mandean Anosh speculation, the probability is that they would have proceeded to embody more and more of its elements in the Synoptic tradition.

To this conclusion there will be one objection. The Mandean Anosh tradition is said to have found an historical focus in the Baptist. Between the followers of John and the disciples of Jesus relations are said to have been somewhat strained. This tension might be thought to account for the failure of the Christians to appropriate the rest of the Anosh tradition. We believe the contrary to be the case. Such a relationship would have served to quicken the assimilation.[30]

That the early disciples at least were not acquainted with the Anthropos tradition may also be inferred from the way in which the unguarded Christian tradition preserved in the apocryphal gospels employs the name Son of Man. The three additional evangels in which the name is found, namely, the Gospel according to the Hebrews,[31] the Traditions of Matthew[32] and the Gospel of Mary[33] use the designation merely as a traditional bit of machinery. The Synoptic coloring has begun to fade but no new elements are added from without. If cognate traditions had existed in cultural and geographical proximity these strands of unguarded tradition would not have resisted entanglement as they seem to have done.

[30] Our position in the matter of the early Christians' knowledge of the Anthropos tradition furnishes an added argument against the contention that the source Q is dependent upon the Mandean Apocalypse (cf. Reitzenstein, MB, particularly, p. 62.)

[31] Jerome, *de Viris Illust.*, 2.

[32] Clem. Alex., *Strom.*, IV, 6, 35.

[33] Hennecke, *Ntliche Apokryphen*, vol. 1 (1904), p. 42.

Did Jesus himself, then, know and make use of the Anthropos tradition? The affirmative answer which Reitzenstein accords this question is supported not by any one specific argument with which it stands or falls, but by his view of the development of Oriental syncretism as a whole and the place of the Anthropos within that development. The religious life of the Orient he contends, expressed itself in two distinct views of existence. The one distinguished sharply between man and God. It is the expression of the old Semitic point of view. The other, a product of the reflection of Aryan peoples in the Inner Orient, brought the nature and destiny of man into direct relation with deity, as personified in a heavenly Man from whom the divine element indwelling in humanity was derived and by whom, as he appeared in the capacity of divine messenger, it was redeemed. Of these two views of existence, the latter became the dominant force in virtually all of the movements characterizing the religious life of the Hellenistic Orient. Not even Judaism in its popular Palestinian, sectarian and Hellenistic phases escaped the influence of this great concept in which is to be found the root of the religion of salvation. By styling himself Son of Man (literally "the man") Jesus gave expression to the conviction that he was the human messenger in whom the heavenly Man manifested himself to save that which was lost. He associated himself thereby, with the expectations of his people and with the great religious hope of the Oriental world. As the messenger of God the Orient accepted him for its savior.[34]

Over against this remarkable construction we must aline in the first place, our inquiry into the Anthropos tradition. We think we have shown that in his earlier forms the Anthropos is not a figure of universal and determinative importance, but merely a type of primordial champion and the father-creator of the human race. It would appear to us, moreover, that those elements of the tradition which connect him with human nature and its redemp-

[34] Reitzenstein's view of the development of religious thought in the Hellenistic Orient finds its clearest expression in the third edition of his "*Hellenistische Mysterienreligionen*" (1927). We regret that we have not been able to make use of it except in connection with the last pages of MS.

tion represent accretions added in the course of its syncretistic adaptation. We have seen fit to suppose that, while he had at one time affected Jewish thought, the capacity in which he appeared in this sphere was that of primordial champion and the influence exerted one of brief duration. Those phases of Hellenistic and sectarian Judaism which seemed to reflect Anthropos Theology, appeared to represent the product of Jewish speculation ultimately stimulated by, but not directly related to the figure of the Anthropos. The similarity between the names Son of Man (literally "the man") and Anthropos, so striking at first glance, is explained, therefore, as the result of the action of parallel processes tending to produce denominations for nameless figures, figures which, while they ultimately revert to the same parent stock, were no longer related to one another when the nomenclature was finally established.

Anyone accepting these conclusions regarding the importance and growth of the Anthropos tradition will find little verisimilitude in the hypothesis connecting the Anthropos and Jesus' use of the name Son of Man. It must be admitted however, that this does not entirely dispose of the matter. The problem of Anthropos and Son of Man, as Reitzenstein has stated it, involves no less than a formula to express the religious genius of what Spengler called "Arabic Culture." Before it will be possible to set aside Reitzenstein's conclusions entirely, it will be necessary to discover a better formula for the analysis of the religious development of the Hellenistic Orient. This is something the scope of which transcends our abilities.

Reitzenstein's hypothesis, though it may not contain the solution of the Son of Man problem, cannot fail to stimulate new lines of thought in connection with the mooted question. Particularly the attention directed by him to the Mandean messengers should prove helpful in future discussions of the subject. They bring to the fore the importance of the role played by lesser personages such as messengers, prophets and forerunners in Jewish religious expectations. Inevitably they will raise the question whether Jesus, in referring to himself as "the man," did not at first employ this expression to designate himself as "the expected man" in the sense of messenger or forerunner, quite apart from the traditions connected with Anthropos and with "the man-like one," and whether the messianic use of the designation was not, as Reitzenstein contends, the result of its being able to convey a higher and more particular meaning. In this respect the hypothesis of Reitzenstein may yet contribute to the solution of the Son of Man problem.

SUMMARY AND CONCLUSION

LET us endeavor to summarize the results of the inquiry embodied in the preceding pages.

1. The Anthropos, it appears, represents in all probability the Hellenistic and Syncretistic form of the ancient Iranian *gayamaretan*, "mortal life," a mythical person originally devoid of a proper name and not removed from ideas of bisexuality, and one of whom story told that that he had formed a part of the preëxistent spiritual creation of Ahura Mazda in the capacity of prototype of humanity, had been embodied in the ensuing material creation, had occupied a role of great importance in the fatal primordial battle with the evil forces of Ahriman, had at the moment of death become the progenitor of humanity, had contributed elements to the formation of material cosmos and would in the future life occupy a prominent place among the blessed.

2. Gayomart became known to the people of Mesopotamia probably in pre-Parthian days. By reason of his place in the primordial conflict he was identified with Marduk and thus transformed into a man-like deity and a primordial champion. Subsequent stages in the development of the tradition demand that he was regarded both as victorious and as defeated champion in the early period of his evolution, all depending upon whether Babylonian or Iranian elements were accorded a position of predominance in the narratives. Simultaneously, in lieu of his original bisexuality, he was associated with a female *paredros*, perhaps the goddess Ishtar.

3. In the capacity of victorious primordial champion and man-like deity he was received into Judaism in the second pre-Christian century, and furnished the inspiration for the properly nameless "man-like one" of Daniel, and for the messianic interpretation

which the figure received in the Book of Enoch. At the same time his humanity abetted the transformation of the Hebrew conception of the protoplast, the common origin of Bar Nasha and celestial Adam giving rise to the coördination of Adam and Christ.

4. The years between the Book of Enoch and Saturninus produced two additional changes in the Anthropos. Mesopotamian teachers made his relation to the human race, his downfall and the fact that this downfall was connected with the birth of the human race intelligible to people of their sphere by introducing the Anthropos into the Hebrew account of the creation of man. In the resultant story, the Chaldean Tale, the Anthropos is brought low because his offspring and image, man, was animated and thus made subject to the inferior powers. Perhaps it was his introduction into the Biblical account of creation and the fact that Genesis derives both the image and the soul from the one God that produced the next step in the development, namely the correlation of Anthropos and a divine element of human nature. This element was originally, no doubt, the Soul of the Soul Drama, though it later appears as Spirit and Reason as well. That the Anthropos was first related to the Soul in Mesopotamia is probable since the relation is presupposed in even the earliest reaches of Syrian and Egyptian Anthropos tradition, and since a knowledge of the Soul Drama is presupposed in the Chaldean Tale.

5. At the end of the first Christian century the knowledge of the Anthropos had spread to the Syrian and Egyptian portions of the Mediterranean littoral. Here the descriptive nomenclature originally applied to the figure gives way to proper names like Anthropos. As a deity of the rank of Marduk, he aspires to various positions (particularly first and third) in the upper strata of the Gnostic pleromata. Where Greek thought is known and catered to, he is identified with metaphysical postulates correspondingly placed in the line of ultimates and thus appears as Nous, Logos and All. Whether the macrocosmic significance accruing to him in this connection is a reminiscence of Iranian tradition it is difficult to say. In Syria, it would seem, he was identified with the Jewish celestial Adam, an identification that produced the Mandean Adam Raba and the designations Adamas and Adakas. In both

SUMMARY AND CONCLUSION

Syria and Egypt two strands of tradition convey the thought of the relation between Anthropos and man. The first relates that he furnished the image for the construction of the human form. The second tells of his contributing an element to human nature. Of these the latter usually presents no motive for or description of the introduction of the element. Both have a common origin. The first represents the Chaldean Tale in a relatively pure form. The second is the final product of the tendency to interpret the Chaldean Tale in the light of the Soul Drama and finally to disregard its Biblical frame-work under pressure of the interest for the fact conveyed. The Poimandres is an elaborated example of the transition going on in this direction.

6. The necessity of bringing Anthropos and Soul together and the occasion afforded either by the Mandean conception of the Adamites as messengers or perhaps by the views connected in Syria with Sophia, resulted in the idea that the Anthropos reappeared for the salvation of the soul in the guise of a divine savior. Among the saviors connected with the Anthropos are first the Adamites then Christ, and finally Buddha, Zarathushtra and Mani. In the earlier phases of the tradition the saviors appear as the sons of the Anthropos. Here we have to reckon with either Christian or Mandean influence, or both. Under pressure of Greek metaphysics the savior becomes the immanent counterpart of the Anthropos. Finally, in the days of christological niceties the saviors are the hypostases or modes of the Anthropos.

7. In Manicheism the Anthropos Theology finds its most complete and coördinated expression. All the steps of the preceding development find an echo here. The Manichean Primal Man is defeated and victorious champion, father-creator of man and the origin of an element of man's constitution, and one who is manifested in seven saviors from Adam to Mani. The intimacy of Mani's contact with Iran resulted in the introduction of new Iranian elements into the tradition. The Anthropos is identified with Ormuzd on the one hand and Mithras on the other. Representing the latter he takes his abode in the sun. The relation of Anthropos and soul is stated in terms of person and self. Eschatological importance attaches to the primordial champion.

8. The last step in the process is identification of Anthropos and *daena* presupposed in the later Mandean texts.

From our study of the Anthropos tradition we gain a limited insight, at least, into the religious development of the later Orient as a whole. We see, in the first place, that Gnostic theology embodies many elements of remarkable antiquity native to the East and possessive of continued importance in this sphere. We perceive that the tradition connected with any one figure may represent a great number of strata deposited one atop the other as the result of the action of shifting winds of influence. We gain the impression, moreover, that the syncretistic movement which took such violent strides forward in the second century, has a history dating back to the second pre-Christian century and finds its origin in a proto-Gnostic sphere of thought. With one phase of the proto-Gnostic circle of ideas, the Mesopotamian, we have become partly acquainted. It contains Iranian, Babylonian and Jewish elements as well as the unlocalized Soul Drama. Influence was apparently exerted upon the littoral Orient from Mesopotamia at two distinct junctures, in the second century B.C., and toward the end of the first century A.D. This phenomenon finds its explanation, no doubt, in the disturbance created in the Orient by the period of Parthian domination. The elements included in the Mesopotamian phase of proto-Gnostic thought, were, so far as we have analyzed them, of no direct importance for the growth of Christian convictions. Indeed, we should be inclined to search for the key to the forces which influenced nascent Christianity in that form of religious life which, since pre-Parthian days, had been moulding itself in Syria.

ABBREVIATIONS

ABA	Abhandlungen der Berliner Akademie der Wissenschaften.
ERE	Encyclopedia of Religion and Ethics.
HAOG	Handbuch der altorientalischen Geisteskultur.
HM	Die Hellenistischen Mysterienreligionen.
IE	Das Iranische Erlösungsmysterium.
JB	Das Johannesbuch der Mandäer.
JAOS	Journal of the American Oriental Society.
LG	Left Ginza.
MB	Das Mandäische Buch des Herrn der Grösse und die Evangelienüberlieferung.
ML	Mandäische Liturgien.
MR	Die Mandäische Religion.
MS	Mandäische Schriften.
PL	Patrologia Latina.
PRE	Protestantische Realenzyklopedie.
RG	Right Ginza.
SBA	Sitzungsberichte der Berliner Akademie der Wissenschaften.
SBE	Sacred Books of the East.
TU	Texte und Untersuchungen.
ZDMG	Zeitschrift der deutschen morgenländischen Gesellschaft.
ZKG	Zeitschrift für Kirchengeschichte.